United Front

APARC
STANFORD
IIS

ASIA-PACIFIC RESEARCH CENTER

Studies of the Walter H. Shorenstein Asia-Pacific Research Center

Andrew G. Walder, General Editor

The Walter H. Shorenstein Asia-Pacific Research Center in the Freeman Spogli Institute for International Studies at Stanford University sponsors interdisciplinary research on the politics, economies, and societies of contemporary Asia. This monograph series features academic and policy-oriented research by Stanford faculty and other scholars associated with the Center.

United Front

PROJECTING SOLIDARITY THROUGH
DELIBERATION IN VIETNAM'S
SINGLE-PARTY LEGISLATURE

Paul Schuler

Stanford University Press

Stanford, California

Stanford University Press
Stanford, California

Printed in the United States of America on acid-free, archival-quality paper

Library of Congress Cataloging-in-Publication Data

Names: Schuler, Paul, 1979– author.
Title: United front : projecting solidarity through deliberation in Vietnam's
    single-party legislature / Paul Schuler.
Other titles: Studies of the Walter H. Shorenstein Asia-Pacific Research Center.
Description: Stanford : Stanford University Press, 2021. | Series: Studies of the
    Walter H. Shorenstein Asia-Pacific Research Center | Includes bibliographical
    references and index.
Identifiers: LCCN 2020025604 (print) | LCCN 2020025605 (ebook) |
    ISBN 9781503614628 (cloth) | ISBN 9781503614741 (paperback) |
    ISBN 9781503614758 (epub)
Subjects: LCSH: Vietnam. Quốc hội. | Legislative bodies—Vietnam. |
    One-party systems—Vietnam. | Authoritarianism—Vietnam. | Vietnam—
    Politics and government—1975–
Classification: LCC JQ854 .S45 2021 (print) | LCC JQ854 (ebook) |
    DDC 328.597—dc23
LC record available at https://lccn.loc.gov/2020025604
LC ebook record available at https://lccn.loc.gov/2020025605

Cover design: Kevin Barrett Kane
Typeset by BookComp, Inc. in 11/14 Adobe Garamond Pro

To Mary

Contents

List of Illustrations ix

Acknowledgments xiii

Introduction 1

1 The Signaling Trap: Why Single-Party Legislatures
Must Be Controlled 17

2 How Elections Work in Vietnam 49

3 "Unconditional Party Government":
Legislative Organization in the VNA 67

4 Explaining the Evolution of the VNA 87

5 Mobilized or Motivated? Voting Behavior
in Vietnamese Elections 124

6 Explaining Oversight Behavior: Position Taking
or Position Ducking? 143

7 Intimidation or Legitimation? The Signaling Value
of the VNA 170

Conclusion: Curbing Our Expectations for the VNA,
Single-Party Legislatures   189

Notes   203

References   221

Index   241

Illustrations

Figures

2.1.	Malapportionment in the VNA	51
2.2.	Candidates per seat in the VNA	52
3.1.	Structure of the VNA, 2016.	69
4.1.	Days per session of the VNA, 1964–2015	103
4.2.	Percentage of delegates in the legislature full time, 1976–2016	105
4.3.	VNA laws and VNASC decisions passed per year, 1975–2016	106
4.4.	Days in VNA session and laws per session, 1975–2016	107
4.5.	Relationship between candidates per seat and non-party members, 1976–2020	115
5.1.	SF ratio in Vietnam and Thailand	130
5.2.	Hypothetical distribution of SF ratio, FL ratio, and implications for behavior	131
5.3.	SF ratio and FL ratio in electoral districts, Thailand (1995 and 1996) and Vietnam (2016)	132
5.4.	Education and general political knowledge among voters	140
5.5.	Education and knowledge of candidates among voters	141
6.1.	How the panel dataset was constructed	150
6.2.	Change in VNA oversight attention/Internet interest on selected issues	151
6.3.	Google searches for the South China Sea.	155
6.4.	Google searches for Cu Huy Ha Vu and Le Cong Dinh	158

6.5.   Google searches for Tien Lang, Van Giang land seizure cases   161
6.6.   Google searches for Vinashin in Vietnam   166
7.1.   Possible effects of exposure to the VNA   172
7.2.   Respondents' estimates of average percentage vote share
        for VNA laws   178
7.3.   Respondents' estimates of average percentage seat share
        for VCP members   178
7.4.   Respondents views of competitiveness of VNA elections   179
7.5.   Respondents' views of VNA debates as formal or meaningful   180
7.6.   Respondents' assessment of VNA's influence over policy   180
7.7.   Impact of treatment on perceptions of VNA   182
7.8.   Impact of treatment dosage on perceptions of VNA   183
7.9.   Impact of treatment on general support, support for regime,
        and willingness to protest   184
7.10.   Impact of treatment dosage on general support, support for
        regime, and willingness to protest   185
7.11.   Sensitivity analysis of mediated effects of treatment through
        feelings toward VNA   187
C.1.   Autocracies, legislative closures, and regime age, 1945–2010   195
C.2.   Impact of regime age on legislative closures by regime type   196

Tables

1.1.   Differences between elections, legislatures, and other
        feedback channels   33
2.1.   Overall attendance at candidate meetings with
        neighborhood voters   57
2.2.   Determinants of attendance at candidate meetings
        with neighborhood voters   57
2.3.   Self-nominated candidates in the VNA   58
2.4.   Well-known self-nominated candidates for the VNA   59
2.5.   Impact of candidate quality on electioneering,
        election results   64
3.1.   Powers of the VNA Standing Committee   70
3.2.   Composition of the VNA, 2007–2021   71
3.3.   Composition of the VNASC, 2007–2016   72
3.4.   Selection to full-time positions in the VNA, 2007–2016   74
3.5.   Timeline of passage of the Special Economic Zone Law   81

4.1.	Factors that should lead to a binding or informative legislature: logic	90
4.2.	Factors that should lead to a binding or informative legislature: Vietnam, 1986–1989	97
5.1.	Observable implications of information and signaling theories for voting behavior	128
5.2.	Sacrificial lamb candidates, descriptive statistics (2007, 2011, 2016)	133
5.3.	Model of candidate election, voting percentage	133
5.4.	Impact of electioneering on district competitiveness	134
5.5.	Probit model of turnout in Vietnam's 2016 election	136
6.1.	Party control over ministries	146
6.2.	Impact of interest in topics on oversight hearings	153
7.1.	Research design of an Internet survey experiment on signaling effect of VNA	175
7.2.	Primes used in an Internet survey experiment on signaling effect of VNA	175
7.3.	Assessment of balance between groups in survey	177
7.4.	Impact of treatment on perceptions of VNA efficacy and competitiveness	181
7.5.	Impact of treatment dosage on perceptions of VNA	182
7.6.	Impact of treatment on general support, support for regime, and willingness to protest	183
7.7.	Impact of treatment dosage on general support, support for regime, and willingness to protest	184
7.8.	Mediated effects of treatment through feelings toward VNA	186

Acknowledgments

This book has been roughly ten years in the making. Throughout this process, I have incurred more debts than I can possibly recount. While the pressure of ensuring that I don't forget anyone is stressful, it is a pleasure to think back to all those who have helped me through the years.

This project grew with the guidance of Eddy Malesky, Philip Roeder, Susan Shirk, Stephan Haggard, and Krislert Samphatharak, who provided excellent advice during the early stages and served as a guide for how I advise students today. To them, I owe great thanks. Eddy in particular is a fantastic mentor, adviser, and coauthor who has helped this project along each step of the way. His unique mixture of enthusiasm and intellectual rigor ensures both that his collaborators finish projects and that they are worth completing. His capacity for constructive feedback for myself and others is unparalleled. For that reason, he remains a role model for me in how I mentor students.

I also want to single out the generosity of those attending my book conference on the sidelines of the 2018 SEAREG East Conference at Yale-NUS. Thanks to Allen Hicken, Amy Liu, Steve Oliver, Tom Pepinsky, Dan Slater, Iza Ding, and Risa Toha for your generosity and comments, which greatly improved the project's clarity and theoretical contribution. I also wanted to credit SEAREG more generally for providing such an important springboard for others interested in Southeast Asia to pursue their research. As an inaugural fellow in 2014, I greatly benefited from the feedback provided at the conference as well as the community the organization built. A great credit should go to Eddy Malesky, Tom Pepinsky, Dan Slater, and Allen Hicken for creating this valuable institution.

This book profited from generous assistance from the National Science Foundation. It also greatly benefited from the Stanford Shorenstein Asia-Pacific Research Center (APARC) Fellowship on Contemporary Southeast Asia as well as the Lee Kong Chian Stanford-National University of Singapore Fellowship. Under both programs, I was honored to receive incisive feedback from preeminent Southeast Asia scholar Don Emmerson. He was generous with his time and comments and ensured that my twin sojourns at Stanford were productive and enjoyable. Thanks also to Takeo Hoshi, Andy Walder, Jean Oi, Xueguang Zhou, and Scott Rozelle for providing helpful advice during these periods. I want to thank Justin Grimmer for allowing me to audit his Text-as-Data course and Frances Zlotnick for helping me with coding issues regarding the text analysis portion of this book.

In Singapore, thanks especially to Soo Yeon Kim for providing me with office space and making me feel like part of the community. Also thanks to Terence Lee, Jamie Davidson, Deepak Nair, Gerard Sasges, Jamie Gillen, Jason Morris-Jung, and Simon Creak for your wonderful feedback and companionship. It was a fantastic and unique experience to be immersed in a setting with such great knowledge of Southeast Asia.

Portions of the book also benefited from other workshops. Thanks to Ben Noble for arranging the New Politics of Authoritarianism conference at Oxford, including great feedback from Jennifer Gandhi, Milan Svolik, Xiaobo Lu, Rory Truex, Yue Hou, Henry Thomson, and Ben Ansell. Also deep thanks to Kai-Ping Huang, Jason Kuo, and Yu-Tzung Chang for inviting me to National Taiwan University for your comments. I also want to acknowledge great feedback along the way from Kevin O'Brien, Dan Mattingly, Tuong Vu, Christopher Heurlin, Ashley Esarey, Jennifer Pan, and Meredith Shaw.

This project also would not have been possible without my former graduate school colleagues. They include Rupal Mehta, Lindsey Nielson, Micah Gell-Redman, Justin Reeves, Mike Rivera, Neil Visalvanich, Don Lee, Jonathan Markowitz, Rob Bond, Brigitte Zimmerman, Daniel Smith, Cesi Cruz, Benjamin Graham, and Jeremy D. Horowitz. I wanted particularly to single out Michael Davidson and Chris Fariss for providing me with tremendous assistance in processing the data for chapter 6.

I especially want to acknowledge Dimitar Gueorguiev and Kai Ostwald, my former officemates. They not only provided countless hours of constructive criticism, but their friendship both during and after our time together is one of the most rewarding aspects of having embarked on this academic path. It was a great honor to share an office with them for six years of my life! Hopefully the collaborations and friendship will continue into the future.

In writing this book, I am also deeply indebted to Vietnamese scholars of political institutions that go unrecognized outside of Vietnam. I have greatly benefited from the works of Huy Duc, Nguyen Sy Dung, and Nguyen Duc Lam, whose pathbreaking work informs much of what follows. Former chair of the Office of the VNA Vu Mao is also a fount of wisdom on the Vietnam National Assembly. In terms of fieldwork, this project could not have been completed without help from Do Thanh Huyen, Dau Anh Tuan, Nguyen Thi Kim Chung, La Khanh Tung, and Nguyen Tri Dung. I am also deeply indebted to the others who agreed to provide me with their insights. Hopefully this book does justice to their profound efforts to help me at various stages of the project.

I want to finish by thanking my family for encouraging me along this process. To my parents, Reece and Elizabeth Schuler, your encouragement to travel and try to understand the world inspired me to take this path. I am deeply grateful for your love and encouragement, without which this project would not exist. I also want to thank my brothers Reece, Phil, and Jon as well as my sisters-in-law Melissa and Rachael, my Aunt Mary, and old friend Nate for being part of the process! My grandmothers Mildred and Edna also provided inspiration at early stages of the project.

Thanks also to Martin and Emily. Since Martin and Emily were born, I've had to go to Vietnam three or four times a year. I know it's probably not worth the toys I pick up from Japan on the way back, so thanks for allowing my frequent absences halfway across the world. Finally, a special thanks to Mary. You have made the greatest sacrifices to see this project through, and you have provided the support to ensure that I complete it. This is our book, as it would not have been possible without your support. For that reason, with love I dedicate this book to you.

United Front

Introduction

As a communist country, Vietnam's legislative debates are not supposed to be must-see-TV. That is why what occurred on November 2, 2010, was so surprising. Leading up to that event, the state-run media had leaked stories that a major state-owned enterprise was more than US$4 billion in debt. The size of the debt was such that it nearly single-handedly caused Moody's to downgrade Vietnam's credit rating.[1] In this context, a largely unknown legislator stood on the floor of the Vietnam National Assembly (VNA) and proposed a vote of no confidence in the prime minister: "[T]here is evidence of an effort to cover up wrongdoings and crimes that have caused massive losses of state money and resources. . . . On this basis. . . . I request a vote of confidence in the prime minister and some members of the government."[2]

According to conventional wisdom, communist legislatures are supposed to be rubber stamps. Yet proposing a vote of no confidence in the second highest ranking member of the Vietnam Communist Party (VCP) is anything but rubber stamp behavior. For this reason, Nguyen Minh Thuyet's speech immediately attracted domestic and international media attention.[3] Perhaps even more noteworthy is that Thuyet was never punished.

For scholars of other single-party legislatures, such as in China or the Eastern Bloc, such a public challenge of a party leader by a low-ranking official is a rarity. Furthermore, in those cases where delegates do dissent, they are often punished (Allmark 2012). For example, some members of Eritrea's unelected legislature challenged the president's consolidation of power and demanded major political reforms (Hedru 2003). Similarly, in Syria, during the "Damascus Spring" a delegate called for multiparty politics on the floor of the legislature. What is notable is that in both these cases the regime leaders clearly did not welcome the comments, and the speakers were jailed or killed (Hedru 2003).[4] These were clearly cases in which legislators acted in ways *not intended* by the regime.

In Vietnam, the fact that Thuyet made the speech, had the opportunity to make the speech, and was not punished for making the speech raises several questions about our understanding of Vietnam's legislature and single-party legislatures more broadly. How did the VNA evolve so that Thuyet had the opportunity to make a speech on live television? Given the opportunity, why did he make such a provocative speech when so many others in the legislature remained silent? Finally, who within the regime could possibly gain from his speech?

This book addresses these questions by examining legislative behavior, legislative institutionalization, and legislative elections under single-party rule. By single-party rule, I mean regimes sometimes also referred to as "closed" (Diamond 2002), in which all opposition parties are banned. Although the number is lower than during the Cold War era, thanks to China, more than one-sixth of the world's population still lives under single-party rule. Given that two of the remaining single-party regimes, Vietnam and China, have been among the fastest-growing countries in the world for the past two decades, understanding governance in these systems is of profound interest. Furthermore, a growing literature on authoritarian regimes suggests that legislatures can facilitate economic growth. This raises the question: Have Vietnam and China managed to design legislatures that provide the supposed benefits of a democratic assembly without allowing even nominal opposition parties to run?

The Role of Single-Party Legislatures

Our current understanding of legislative behavior and institutionalization under single-party rule comes from two sources. The first is work on hybrid regimes, which combine elements of autocracy with multiparty elections. Research in this vein challenges classic studies of the Eastern Bloc contending that legislatures play peripheral roles (White and Nelson 1982; Fainsod 1963). Revisionist views from research on hybrid regimes suggest that such legislatures may do far more. In particular, legislatures may co-opt and placate potential opponents (Gandhi 2008; Gandhi and Przeworski 2006;

Bonvecchi and Simison 2017).[5] The general argument from the hybrid literature is that authoritarian legislatures assist the regimes in improving performance by providing some level of constraint on the autocrat (Gandhi 2008; Gehlbach and Keefer 2012; Warshaw 2012; Wright 2008).

Responding to the preceding work, a second cluster of publications has emerged from research on China that is potentially more relevant for single-party Vietnam. These scholars argue that co-optation is not possible when opposition parties are banned (Truex 2016; Lu, Liu, and Li 2019). They suggest that single-party legislatures instead provide information about citizens' preferences to autocrats so that they can make more informed policy decisions (Truex 2016; Manion 2016). This argument fits with a more general observation that China increasingly relies on consultation mechanisms to improve governance (Bell 2015; Teets 2013; Tsang 2009; He and Thogersen 2010; Gueorguiev 2014). Indeed, Xi Jinping has made "socialist consultative democracy" a cornerstone of his rule in China (He and Warren 2017). This view fits within a growing number of theories suggesting that quasi-democratic institutions are designed to provide information (Lorentzen 2014, 2013; Egorov, Guriev, and Sonin 2009; Little, Tucker, and LaGatta 2015).

At first blush, the information argument offers some compelling answers to the questions raised in this book. First, it may help explain why the ruling VCP reformed the VNA starting in the 1980s so that delegates like Thuyet could raise their voices. Given that the VCP also instituted a number of economic reforms at the same time, it seems plausible that the party liberalized the legislature in order to gain more information from society to improve economic governance and the overall investment environment. As this book discusses, the fact that the economy improved following these reforms and that the VCP has maintained power suggests that these efforts were successful. If this is true, a plausible explanation is that Thuyet was allowed to make the speech because he was providing the type of information the party wanted. By highlighting governance failures perpetrated by the government, he alerted the party to grave transgressions that negatively impacted citizens.

Puzzles with the Revisionist Account

While both theories are plausible, a number of puzzles arise when we apply either theory to Vietnam. First, despite the correlation between legislative reform in Vietnam and its dramatic economic growth, it is not clear that active legislatures in democracies or autocracies cause economic growth or improvements in public goods outcomes. Indeed, research on democracies suggests that although strong legislatures may constrain confiscation by executives irrespective of the size of the deficit, budget deficits may actually increase when legislatures have strong budgetary authority (Wehner 2009). Consistent with this finding, studies on local legislatures in Vietnam actually show that *governance improved* when they were eliminated (Malesky, Nguyen, and Tran 2014).

A second concern is how or why the VNA would actually represent citizen interests. As this book emphasizes, even in Vietnam, which features a more robust electoral connection between citizens and national-level legislators than nearly all other past or present single-party legislatures, the electoral connection remains weak. All candidates, whether party or non-party members, are vetted by the party. Candidates for office are not allowed to campaign or to advertise their policy positions. There are also limits on how many incumbents may run. Given the hurdles that even democracies face in generating informed participation by their citizenry, why should we believe that citizens in Vietnam take their votes seriously? Following from this, if citizens do not take their votes seriously, what incentives do legislators have to represent the wishes of their citizens?

On this point, existing work suggests that nonelectoral incentives such as solidary group membership (Tsai 2007) or the threat of revolution (Dickson 2016; Tang 2016) could drive responsiveness. It is thus possible that legislators could be influenced by nonelectoral incentives. However, if this is the case, what is the purpose of a legislature? Bureaucrats, local officials, and party members should also be susceptible to these pressures without needing legislators to push them.

Alternatively, top-down incentives could drive responsiveness from legislators in the same way that cadre evaluations structure bureaucratic behavior (Truex 2016). Theoretically, the regime could reward those lawmakers who accurately reflect the wishes of citizens. However, if the purpose of legislators is to provide information, how can the regime know when to sanction a lawmaker unless there is a credible electoral signal suggesting that person is not performing his or her duties? Put another way, if the regime has enough information to punish the legislator for not performing those duties, why have the lawmaker in the first place?

An additional puzzle pertains to the utility of using a legislature as a way of generating information. Authoritarian regimes have a variety of other means of gaining information, such as petitions (Heurlin 2016), online notice and comment (Stromseth, Malesky, and Gueorguiev 2017), the media (Egorov, Guriev, and Sonin 2009; Lorentzen 2014), and even protests (Lorentzen 2013). As chapter 1 of this book discusses, some of these institutions possess significant advantages in their ability to provide information compared to legislatures. Unlike legislative input, information provided through online comments or petitions will be private and therefore less likely to spark antiregime collective action. Given these options, single-party regimes like the VCP should resort to those less public channels rather than the legislature to gather information.[6]

A final puzzle relates to the informational utility of legislatures in general. Even in democratic contexts, scholars are skeptical that speeches and legislative hearings are actually intended to inform policy makers (Proksch and Slapin 2015, 2012). Furthermore, the informational models of legislative institutions are largely meant to explain how legislatures cope with their *informational deficiencies*. These arguments do not suggest that legislatures are optimal information provision devices (Krehbiel 1991). Committees and legislative staff do not constitute evidence that legislatures are useful information providers. Instead, they are mechanisms designed to mitigate the fact that executive agencies are better placed to have access to good information than is the legislature.

With these concerns in mind, there is much at stake in correctly understanding the role of the VNA and single-party legislatures more generally. It is certainly the case that some single-party regimes have succeeded, at least based on the twin metrics of economic growth and longevity. Furthermore, it is also the case that some of these successful countries, like Vietnam, have partially reformed their legislative institutions. However, attributing that success to the partial reform of these institutions runs the risk of incorrectly validating a key plank of the "China model": the notion that legislatures with debate but without contestation provide tangible benefits for both the regime and citizens. Before reaching such a conclusion, it is worth assessing how well this argument stands up to scrutiny even in a most likely case such as Vietnam.

Theory: Signaling and Deflecting

This book challenges the revisionist view that single-party legislatures improve policy performance by constraining the autocrat or by providing information. The central argument of this book is that the purpose of legislatures in single-party regimes is first and foremost to *signal authoritarian dominance and legitimacy.* Similar to arguments made about the role of propaganda (Huang 2015, 2018), I argue that overwhelming regime victories, nearly universal turnout, and nearly unanimous support for even controversial laws *signal dominance* and *provide legitimacy.* Because of this support, these institutions are ultimately unable to fulfill the roles revisionist theories ascribe to them. This is because providing unwelcome information, even on nonsensitive issues, or checking the autocrat would undermine the signal the regime is attempting to send.[7]

The fundamental problem is that to perform their signaling function, representative institutions must be *public.* If they are not, legislatures are simply inferior duplications of other tools the regime has at its disposal. For this reason, single-party legislatures and elections are unsuitable for the other functions previously mentioned. To stabilize power sharing or provide information, the legislature must act as a check on the regime or at least have an independent voice. To stabilize power-sharing arrangements or co-opt opponents, either elites or outsiders must be willing to challenge the prerogatives of the autocrat. For information provision, they must also be willing to bring unpleasant facts before the regime (Wintrobe 1998). Performing any of these roles would ultimately undermine the public signal the legislature is intended to send.

This is why although single-party leaders often express the desire for greater activity from legislators, these same leaders ultimately refrain from using their power to make the necessary reforms to encourage such behavior. Julius Nyerere, ruler of single-party Tanzania in the 1960s, lamented that legislators demonstrated a "failure to make more than minimal use of their prerogative to criticize in the Assembly" (Hopkins 1970, 763). In Vietnam, General Secretary Do Muoi also chastised the VNA for its docility (Turley 1993, 264). I argue that such failures are structural, not the fault of nervous legislators. If these leaders had really wanted more independent legislatures, they could have made structural changes to the electoral and legislative system to generate them. This book explains why they did not.

So far, my argument is simple. Although I provide new evidence to support my view, it has similarities to classic work on single-party representative institutions from the Soviet Union and the Eastern Bloc. However, like this classic literature, my argument faces important challenges. A first question is: If such legislatures are used for signaling purposes, why do some regimes nonetheless enact reforms that increase the apparent activity of legislators? Vietnam, as this book shows, did reform its legislature to be more *visible* and *active*. Why?

I argue that the reason lies in the structure of executive authority and the impact this has had on the incentive for the autocratic leaders within the party to use the legislature to *damage rivals* and *deflect blame* for policy failures. Although some research acknowledges the possibility of "fragmented authoritarianism," in which the ruling party is not united, much of scholarship focuses on either unintended fragmentation due to factionalism or bureaucratic infighting (Lieberthal and Lampton 1992; Truex 2018; Lu, Liu, and Li 2019), and it does not consider contexts wherein autocrats may *formally* delegate authority to the government over some issue portfolios. In communist regimes, such as China, the debate over delegation takes place within the context of discussions of the separation between the party and the state. In the 1980s, the ruling parties in both Vietnam and China considered a greater separation of the party and the state as a way of improving bureaucratic efficiency. In China from 1980 to 1989, Deng Xiaoping and Zhao Ziyang worked to separate the party from direct management of economic reforms (Shirk, 1993, 62–68). However, this drive for separation stopped after the Tiananmen crisis (Shirk 1993, 67–68).

While the attempt at separation stalled in China, in Vietnam, much like in Iran, the "autocrat," which in Vietnam's case refers to the party leadership, delegates significant independent authority to the government. Therefore, some within *the party* find it advantageous to embolden the legislature to deflect blame for poor performance onto the government without attacking the party. By doing so, the legitimacy of the party and the legislature is bolstered by redirecting criticism for poor performance onto the government. In other single-party regimes, however, where delegation is more superficial, the party has no incentive to empower a third body to publicly hold the government to account. This is because the government and the party are ultimately united.[8]

A second question for my theory is: Why are single-party legislatures associated with economic growth and political stability if they are so ineffectual? As I discuss in the conclusion, one possible reason is that nearly all single-party systems have legislatures. Therefore, it is just as likely that the effect of legislatures on outcomes is a result of the peculiar conditions in countries without legislatures. As I also discuss in the conclusion, most countries without legislatures are simultaneously undergoing regime consolidation, which occurs alongside violence and instability that could cause poor economic performance. Therefore, legislatures themselves may bring few benefits. It is the instability associated with the lack of a legislature that cannot be controlled for with standard control variables that leads to the supposed benefits of an authoritarian legislature.[9]

IMPLICATIONS

My argument speaks to the ambiguous effects a more active legislature may have on performance. If the purpose of the legislature is not to provide information but rather to burnish the image of the party and throw blame on the government, it is not clear that legislatures necessarily improve performance. If we assume legislatures represent *party* interests rather than *citizen* interests, whether or not legislatures improve outcomes ultimately depends on the capabilities and intentions of actors within party, legislative, and government institutions. If government institutions are the locus of the main policy experts, empowering legislative activity may actually undermine performance.

I also suggest that using the legislature and elections to signal party dominance limits the ability of the legislature to generate meaningful, credible information. Critically, this does not mean that some inside or outside the party do not *believe* that the legislature actually provides meaningful information. Indeed, scholars suggest that Mikhail Gorbachev may have believed previous docile debates in the Supreme Soviet were evidence of a supportive public. The Communist Party's routine victories and the ability to control behavior in the Supreme Soviet may have led the "Leninist romantic" Gorbachev to believe that repression was not necessary to control the Supreme Soviet, perhaps factoring into his reforms, which ultimately contributed to the demise of the regime (McCormick 1996, 46). To the extent that such docile debates dupe the leadership, this speaks to the possibility that legislative debate actually *distorts information* for both citizens and regime leaders.

My theory also has implications for our broader understanding of authoritarian politics. In some quarters, in the literature on both Vietnam and authoritarianism more broadly, there is a growing skepticism of the role of such representative institutions (Pepinsky 2014). Alongside this critique is the suggestion that the study of such institutions has come at the expense of more important, repressive institutions (Art 2012; Greitens 2016). However, as my study shows, quasi-democratic institutions need not always be considered the *velvet glove* of the state, but instead, as Slater (2003) calls it, the "*iron cage in an iron fist*" (emphasis added). Rather than seeing such representative institutions as deliberative or consultative, this book ultimately casts them as signaling tools to demonstrate unity and strength (Schedler and Hoffman 2016; Simpser 2013). Furthermore, much like propaganda, the ultimate purpose is not to represent but to shape public opinion (Huang 2018, 2015; Wedeen 2015).

The Case: The Vietnam National Assembly

The signaling theory previously described is meant to apply specifically to single-party regimes. Some elements of the argument may also apply to hybrid regimes, and where they do, I highlight this. My concluding chapter in particular deals with the issue of generalizability. However, it is important to note that single-party regimes differ from hybrid regimes in important ways that impact how the legislature will behave. Most important, as Truex (2016) notes, the lack of opposition parties means that co-opting meaningful opposition through a legislature will not be possible; instead, opposition will be co-opted through party institutions. However, the lack of opposition parties also generates other differences from hybrid regimes. Most notably, the lack of opposition parties means that it will be difficult for legislative actors to provide information or check the autocrat and simultaneously signal regime strength. This is because when all the legislators are either party members or vetted by the party, criticism directed at the party could be seen as a potential cleavage within the party.

Because my argument is tailored to single-party regimes, a natural question is why we should care, given the collapse of the Soviet Union and the concomitant evaporation of a large number of single-party regimes. Indeed, the number of single-party regimes has dwindled to a handful (Diamond 2002; Magaloni and Kricheli 2010).[10] Yet despite their endangered status, the inner workings of these regimes remain important for a number of reasons. First, single-party regimes remain the most resilient, stable form of authoritarianism in terms of duration since the end of World War II (Brownlee 2009; Smith 2005). While the Soviet Union collapsed, it still lasted more than seventy years, a remarkable period of time for an authoritarian regime.

The remaining single-party regimes in existence today show similar signs of durability, despite widely varying degrees of economic performance. What explains the endurance of these regimes? Existing literature suggests that legislatures, which they all have, figure importantly into their longevity (Svolik 2012; Gandhi 2008).

A second reason that understanding the interaction between legislatures and single-party rule is important is the implications it has for the collapse of the Soviet Union and the Eastern Bloc. While a number of theories have emerged to explain the collapse of the Soviet Union (Kalyvas 1999; Kuran 1991; Lohmann 1994; Roeder 1995; Beissinger 2002), the reasons remain contested. More important, some research suggests that the Soviet Union's and Poland's attempts to reform their legislative electoral systems played a role in the unraveling of communism in both of those countries (Kaminsky 1999; Marples 2015). Indeed, in the Soviet Union, the decision in 1989 to allow for the first time competitive elections for the Congress of People's Deputies and the televising of legislative sessions transfixed the nation but also challenged Gorbachev's control of the reform process (Marples 2015, 66). If China and Vietnam truly have reformed their legislatures, even if only to a limited degree, how have they succeeded where the Soviet Union and Poland failed?

Finally, despite the few remaining single-party regimes, two of them—China and Vietnam—present seemingly attractive models for the developing world. While China has been historically reticent to promote itself as a model for the developing world, in recent years it has more confidently owned the "China model" label. Indeed, He Yafei, a former vice minister of foreign affairs in China, recently wrote that the "success of the 'Chinese model'. . . offers other developing countries an option different from the 'American model' for economic development."[11] A key component of the Chinese model is the marriage of capitalist economics with sharp restrictions on political contestation. If China and Vietnam continue to grow at their present rapid rates, other countries may increasingly look to their single-party systems as an advantage rather than a hindrance.

THE VIETNAM NATIONAL ASSEMBLY

I examine my theory in the context of Vietnam. Vietnam is an important case for two primary reasons. First, within scholarship on Vietnam, debate exists about the role the VNA plays in governance. At the risk of oversimplifying, there are two poles in research on Vietnamese politics. At one extreme are those who dismiss the importance of any state institutions whatsoever for political outcomes. This view downplays the importance of party congresses (Gainsborough 2007; Fforde and de Vylder 1996) and the state (Fforde and de Vylder 1996; Fforde 2009; Gainsborough 2010) in driving policy making. This fits in with a wider segment of the literature that focuses more on societal or grassroots factors than on institutions in explaining political outcomes. This literature emphasizes "everyday resistance" as the primary driver of politics (Kerkvliet 2005; Scott 1990; Kerkvliet 1995).

Logically, this perspective suggests that the role of the VNA is minimal and therefore ignores it when analyzing Vietnamese political and economic reforms. Some take this argument further and challenge the notion that the VNA should even be studied at all. Gainsborough is the clearest proponent of this view: "[We should] ask ourselves whether it is meaningful and/or helpful to debate whether Vietnam's National Assembly is becoming a more effective law-making body or whether we think this is a distraction from politics as it really is" (2018, 19). From this perspective, not only does the VNA not matter, but the mere study of the institution distracts from "real" politics, which lies elsewhere.

At another pole, perhaps reflecting the maligned "old institutionalism" in political science (March and Olsen 1984), much of the Vietnamese-language literature describes Vietnam's formal political institutions in great detail. This literature discusses the intricacies of the Election Law and the Law on the Organization of the National Assembly (D. D. Nguyen 1992, 2007; Bui 2007).[12] Although this work sometimes presents stinging criticisms of the actual functioning of such institutions, ultimately it ignores the politics of institutional design. In advocating reforms to strengthen the actual functioning of the legislature, these authors are largely silent as to the coalitions within the regime that have blocked such reforms in the past.[13]

Between these poles, other work on Vietnamese political institutions does note generally that the legislature has become more active, while cautioning that the party remains dominant (Turley 1993; London 2014; Womack 1997; Porter 1993; Dang and Beresford 1998; Bui 2007; D. S. Nguyen 2017). This work tends to highlight evidence of increased activity since the economic reform era, suggesting a teleological "increasing assertiveness" (Malesky 2014). This formulation implies that eventually the legislature will become genuinely assertive. Typical of this approach, one scholar suggests: "Although it meets only twice a year, for about three weeks, the 395-member National Assembly has become increasingly vocal under *doi moi* [Vietnam's economic reforms in 1986], enhancing the possibility that it will vie with the VCP for political power" (Rose 1998, 100). Another notes: "Even though [the VNA] continues to fall short of the constitutional ideal, we should expect more from this body in the future; it holds the key to political reform in Vietnam" (Abuza 2001, 103).

Taken together, these accounts leave scholars with several puzzles that merit a closer examination of the VNA. First, should the VNA or political institutions in Vietnam be taken seriously, or even be studied at all? Second, how should we interpret the activity of the legislature more specifically? Finally, what factors should inhibit or promote change to the VNA? The fact that the VCP remains in power and that the number of non-party members in the legislature has declined more than twenty years after the cited observers predicted "more to come" from the VNA suggests a need for a closer look at the logic of institutionalization.

A CRUCIAL CASE

The second reason to study the VNA pertains to research design. I argue that the VNA constitutes a *most likely case* for some of the theories this book challenges and a difficult case for my signaling argument. Among single-party legislatures, Vietnam's is one of the most active and most visible in a single-party regime since World War II. Furthermore, its increase in activity coincides with Vietnam's remarkable economic development, seeming to support revisionist arguments that single-party legislatures can improve governance. Consistent with the logic of a "crucial" or "most likely" case, if any legislature in a single-party regime could be construed as a meaningful political player, it should be Vietnam's. By contrast, if we do not see the theorized dynamics at play in Vietnam, this suggests that we need to revise the theories and empirical relationships used to support such theories (Gerring 2007; Eckstein 1975).

Data

This book relies on several different sources of data collected over more than ten years. First, it takes advantage of survey data collected from the

Vietnam Provincial Governance and Public Administrative Performance Index (UNDP 2017). These data provide information on participation in elections, participation in meetings with VNA delegates, and knowledge of VNA candidates. They are used primarily to examine voting behavior. In addition, the book contains original observational data on delegate speeches and biographical characteristics, which are used to examine institutional design and delegate behavior. Chapter 7 uses an original, Internet-based survey to examine the signaling role of the legislature on public opinion.

Throughout each chapter, I also bolster my arguments with qualitative information collected through thirty-two interviews conducted intermittently between 2007 and 2018. With the exception of one interview done in La Jolla, California, all of these interviews took place in Vietnam. The interviewees include former VNA delegates. Others are members of the Office of the VNA or VNA committees, journalists who cover the VNA, or government officials who have worked closely with the VNA. Because the interviews were conducted on background only, I do not include the interviewees' names in the book.

Plan for the Book

This book has been written with three audiences in mind. First, I hope it will appeal to those interested in the role of representative institutions in authoritarian regimes broadly. Second, I hope to engage scholars of Vietnamese politics and society. Third, given the profound interest inside and outside Vietnam on China, where possible I engage scholarship on Chinese political institutions. I am mindful that certain topics will be of greater interest to some audiences than others. While I believe that scholars of Vietnam will find some of the theoretical discussion of authoritarian representative institutions compelling, and that political science and China scholars may find the details of the Vietnamese case illuminating, I am also cognizant that some may wish to focus on the portions of the book of greatest interest to them.

Therefore, I have attempted to organize the book in such a way that while it can be read in order, those who are interested in certain portions can skip to chapters that most interest them. In that vein, Chapter 1 starts with a general discussion on authoritarian legislatures, in which I provide a general theory of single-party representative institutions, which I contrast with existing literature on the subject. This chapter will have greatest relevance for those interested in the general theoretical implications of the book and how I differentiate my analysis of single-party legislatures from existing revisionist accounts. While some conversant in Vietnamese politics may find the theory presented intuitive and perhaps not particularly controversial, it may be more relevant to scholars of authoritarian and Chinese political institutions.

The book then moves to a description of the case and an empirical analysis. Chapters 2 and 3 provide an explanation of the current electoral and legislative institutions that are fundamental for understanding the degree of party control over the VNA. These chapters may be of interest to Vietnam specialists. Those interested in the general argument may focus on these chapters as reference material.

Moving on to my argument and responding to concerns about functionalist explanations of authoritarian institutions, chapter 4 then shows how the VNA acquired these roles. Using existing theory about when and why legislatures are supposed to acquire additional powers under single-party rule, the chapter shows that information provision and providing a constraint on the party were not the goals of the legislative reformers. Rather, the increased institutional powers were initially designed so that opponents of economic reforms in party institutions could challenge proponents of economic reforms in the government. Later, party leaders used the VNA to throw blame on the government for governance failures. While this chapter should appeal to generalists interested in institutional change, it provides an alternative argument for the evolution of the VNA that should interest Vietnam specialists as well.

With the institutional features of the VNA and the historical background laid out, the following three chapters examine the degree to which the current functioning of the VNA corresponds with the logic of the institutional designers. Chapter 5 matches unique survey data on participation in elections in Vietnam to actual election returns to show that candidate knowledge plays little role in participation in legislative elections. Rather, consistent with the theory, electoral behavior is driven by party mobilization. This suggests that elections, even in Vietnam, do not generate significant citizen interest but rather serve to demonstrate the ability of the party to mobilize the vote. Chapter 6 turns to legislative behavior. Using a combination of automated text analysis and cases of specific debates, this chapter shows that debates on hot button issues in the VNA, such as the Vinashin case, do not result from bottom-up citizen frustration but rather because party leaders mobilize proxies in the legislature to challenge government officials.

Chapter 7 tests the argument that elections and legislative behavior do in fact signal strength or legitimacy to the population. Using an online survey of Vietnamese citizens, this chapter shows that information about VNA activities increases the perception that the legislature is a competitively elected, meaningful institution. This in turn leads to an improved assessment from citizens. This suggests that the signaling role of the legislature does shift public opinion in a direction that favors the regime. However, in combination with the findings from Chapter 5, this shift in public opinion is not sufficient to generate meaningful participation in the elections themselves. In short, elections signal that the regime is legitimate but do not encourage citizens to engage with it meaningfully.

Finally, in the conclusion I examine the generalizability of my argument and its implications for Vietnam. I discuss how single-party regimes like Vietnam's differ from the more numerous hybrid regimes, which allow nominal opposition parties to compete. While this difference is important for the consequences of elections, I suggest that some theories developed in this book also apply to behavior in hybrid legislatures. Through the ability to control the agenda, legislative leaders in single-party and hybrid regimes alike can effectively shut out the opposition. In the conclusion I suggest that contrary to existing theory, the only truly constraining or binding legislatures that may exist in the authoritarian world occur in monarchies, military regimes, or unconsolidated personalist regimes, where the executive may not fully control the legislature. This suggests that the theories contained in this book about the relative inability of the legislature to check the autocrat should apply outside the case of Vietnam.

Also in the conclusion, I offer some thoughts about what insights the theory and findings generate for our understanding of Vietnam's recent political past and its future. Contrary to many accounts of Vietnamese political reform, I argue that the liberalization of the VNA did not result from the efforts of those commonly associated with Vietnam's economic reforms. Rather, opponents of economic reforms pushed to increase the visibility of the VNA. Furthermore, the goal was not to advance greater debate but rather to manage an increasingly independent government apparatus. Given recent efforts by the VCP to exert direct control over the state, such as by consolidating the position of the presidency and the general secretary, the role of the VNA may diminish in coming years (Schuler and Truong 2019).

ONE

The Signaling Trap
Why Single-Party Legislatures Must Be Controlled

This chapter lays out the basic theory of authoritarian legislative and electoral behavior assessed in the chapters that follow. In this chapter I address the possible functions a legislature in a single-party regime might perform, paying close attention to the mechanisms linking institutional design to outcomes. I then discuss the possible complementarities as well as contradictions in these specific functions. This section shows how different forms of information may be compromised by trade-offs in electoral procedures and legislative institutions (Malesky and Schuler 2011). In particular, I show how using elections and legislatures for mobilization and signaling is fundamentally incompatible with more substantive roles that recent theories suggest.

I pay particular attention to the institutional requirements necessitated by the competing theoretical arguments. Exploring micro-level institutions is imperative (Schuler and Malesky 2015; Art 2012). My basic argument is that micro-level institutions designed to signal strength will preclude co-optation, power sharing, and information provision. While this is not an entirely novel observation in comparative literature on electoral fraud (Simpser 2013; Gehlbach and Simpser 2015; Rozenas 2016) and propaganda (Huang 2018, 2015; Wedeen 2015), literature on single-party electoral and legislative institutions is less clear on these trade-offs. This chapter discusses why certain goals are mutually incompatible and why single-party regimes will not sacrifice the projection of dominance for genuine information provision or constraints in their management of these institutions.

Existing Explanations for Authoritarian Representative Institutions

This section details the existing explanations for the role legislatures play in single-party settings and the empirical data used to support those arguments.

CO-OPTATION

One prominent theory of how authoritarian legislatures assist autocrats is that they neutralize opponents outside of the regime (Gandhi 2008; Gandhi and Przeworski 2007; Reuter and Robertson 2015; Malesky and Schuler 2010; Lust-Okar 2006). Rather than rely on force to neutralize outside threats, which can be costly and potentially counterproductive, the regime instead opens space for them in a legislature. In this space, their demands can be heard and met without the opposing sides having to resort to open conflict. This theory is compelling for a number of reasons. First, evidence suggests that regimes with legislatures experience greater economic growth (Gandhi 2008; Wright 2008) and fewer protests (Reuter and Robertson 2015), indicating that such institutions do generate cooperation. In addition, consistent with the theory's predictions, the regimes most likely to set up multiparty legislatures are those that are in greatest need of cooperation from regime outsiders. In particular, countries with fewer natural resources are more likely to depend on legislative institutions (Gandhi 2008).

Despite these relationships, the underlying behavioral and micro-level mechanisms linking legislatures to such outcomes are rarely explicated (Art 2012; Schuler and Malesky 2015). In previous work with Malesky (2010), we outline at least one behavioral implication, which is that a legislature serving this purpose should on occasion exhibit critical behavior. However, this study shows only that it is possible that the legislature is engaging in behavior consistent with co-optation. It is also possible that the criticisms from the legislature are in fact leveled for different purposes, such as attacking rivals.

What institutional and behavioral mechanisms should we observe if the legislature is intended to play such a policy co-optation or power-sharing role? Mechanisms should exist in electoral institutions to allow regime outsiders whose cooperation the regime wants to secure to win seats. These institutions should include a nomination process that permits genuine outsiders or important elites to win seats, with elections allowing citizens to provide input on the identities of the genuine elites (Lust-Okar 2006).

Next I consider the behavioral and institutional implications of co-optation theory once the legislature is elected. The mechanism linking co-optation to outcomes is that co-opted outsiders gain some influence over policymaking. Accomplishing this requires two things. First, those regime outsiders must be given a position of policy-making influence. Given that all democratic and nondemocratic legislatures have hierarchies in order to perform efficiently (Cox 2006), these hierarchies grant certain legislators greater control over the agenda, which can play a major role in shaping outcomes (Cox and McCubbins 1993; Gailmard and Jenkins 2007).

If co-optation is to achieve its desired ends, regime outsiders must have some mechanism through which to challenge the regime. Given our understanding of democratic legislatures with high party cohesion, this would require the opposition to have some control over key leadership positions in the legislature or control of the legislature itself. Indeed, this seems to be the case in a number of legislatures in monarchies. The strongest examples of co-optation in contemporary regimes come from Morocco and Kuwait, where the legislative leaders were institutionally separate from the monarchy (Herb 2014; Gandhi 2008). North and Weingast's (1989) seminal analysis of parliamentary institutions under the Stuart monarchy in England, where the aristocratic leaders of the parliament were institutionally distinct from the monarchy itself, provides another example. Outside of monarchies, it is also possible that regime outsiders may wrest control of local legislatures despite their permanent minority status at the national level, as appears to be the case in some regional legislatures in Russia (Reuter and Robertson 2015).

This highlights an important puzzle when exporting this theory to single-party regimes where there is high party cohesion. Even in democracies, when a single party wins a majority in the legislature, outside of appealing to the public, the opposition has very little influence over policy. In fact, in parliamentary systems with ruling majorities, it is rare that backbenchers within the party, much less opposition party members, have the ability to influence policy (King and Crewe 2014; Hasson 2010). For this reason, as others have suggested, the co-optation theory likely does not apply to legislatures in single-party regimes (Truex 2016; Lu, Liu, and Li 2019).

POWER SHARING

An alternative to the co-optation model is one in which legislatures stabilize power-sharing arrangements (Svolik 2012; Gehlbach and Keefer 2011, 2012).

The logic is that legislatures grant important intraregime elites preferential access to information on the policy of the dictator. This privileged information mitigates elite collective action problems, thus enabling regime elites to defend their economic and political interests without having to resort to a costly revolt.

Related to this theory is a more recent wave of literature suggesting that legislatures may be venues for intra-elite bargaining (Noble 2014; Truex 2018; Bonvecchi and Simison 2017; Lu, Liu, and Li 2019). Building on the "fragmented authoritarianism" model (Lieberthal and Lampton 1992), this literature shows how legislatures can challenge and amend legislation as different actors within the party continue the fight for policy. This aligns with Tanner's (1999) observation that the National People's Congress (NPC) can act as a last-ditch forum for losers of intraparty struggles. While this view aligns with the power-sharing argument, it is less clear from the work of this last set of scholars whether this is the *purpose* of the legislature or an unintended side effect. While the power-sharing theorists suggest that legislatures are *designed* to engender such infighting, the latter empirical pieces are more agnostic as to whether such bargaining ultimately serves the regimes' goals.

RENT DISTRIBUTION

Authoritarian legislatures may also be a mechanism for rent distribution (Blaydes 2011; Magaloni 2006; Morgenbesser 2016; Lust-Okar 2006). This argument has similarities to the co-optation and power-sharing theories in that the purpose is to placate elites either within or outside the regime. However, in contrast to the co-optation or power-sharing theories, in this model elites do not fight for policy. Rather, their goal is simply to secure rents, which serve to neutralize any potential antiregime activity. Some support for this theory from China suggests that elected delegates with businesses do enjoy benefits relative to businesses without elected leaders (Truex 2014).

INFORMATION

In recent years the most dominant explanation for the development and evolution of elections, legislatures, and a host of other institutions under single-party rule is information acquisition. At a general level, these theories suggest that allowing citizens to voice their opinions at all can be helpful because it will reveal dissatisfaction with the government and allow autocrats to moderate their policies accordingly (Miller 2013; Truex 2016; Little 2017;

Geddes 2006; Myagkov, Ordeshook, and Shakin 2009; Pop-Eleches and Robertson 2015). Importantly, these information channels help the regime overcome known concerns with *preference falsification* (the idea that citizens are too fearful to reveal their true opinions to the regime), under the important assumption that the votes and the elected delegates actually contain information on genuine voter preferences (Kuran 1991; Wintrobe 1998).

In considering the information argument, it is important to note that not all authors mean the same thing when discussing information.[1] For many of the theories, the information provided by elections refers to information on satisfaction with the regime—a theory I call the *regime strength information theory* (Chen and Xu 2017; Little 2017, 2012; Miller 2013; Little, Tucker, and LaGatta 2015). Regime strength information is useful, because the regime can then assess its performance and provide more public spending or perhaps greater liberalization to nip any incipient protests in the bud (Miller 2013; Pop-Eleches and Robertson 2015). Little (2017) argues that citizens will benefit from this information even when the election shows high levels of regime support because the results will convince them to avoid participating in futile protests.[2] By contrast, when no elections occur, citizens will have no information and will be less sure about whether participating in a protest will be successful. These studies also note that information may be provided even when victory is guaranteed. The key source of information in these cases is simply the performance relative to the previous election. The logic is that if the regime or the president won an average of 95 percent for the previous elections, a victory of 90 percent would signal weakness (Little 2017).

Related to but also distinct from this view is the argument that elections and legislatures can be used to provide information about *citizen preferences*. The *citizen preference theory* is related because for some regime strength theorists, the information derived from elections can directly lead to information about what policies voters prefer. Miller (2015), for instance, shows that when regimes perform more poorly than expected, they increase public spending and decrease military spending, under the plausible assumption that citizens prefer public spending to military spending.

A different take on the citizen preference theory draws on citizen-representative congruence theories and related theories of representative responsiveness from democracies (Golder and Stramski 2010; Eulau and Karps 1977), suggesting that elections for delegates from geographically defined areas provide information on local citizen preferences (Truex 2016;

Manion 2016). Under this theory, citizens in a given election district have preferences about policies or policy agendas, which they transmit to the center through their elected representatives. Two key pieces of evidence support this theory. First, at the electoral level, voters are shown to nominate and elect legislators with stronger local ties than those nominated by the party (Manion 2016). Second, once elected, the issues these delegates discuss tend to cohere with the economic profile of the geographical areas they represent (Truex 2016). The key mechanisms for this literature are that citizens know the preferences of the representatives and/or the representatives know the preferences of the citizens. Then, knowing the preferences, the representatives transmit this information to the center, which otherwise would not have such information.

A final, and potentially less auspicious, form of information that elections provide is on the degree of control over local agents. Under this view, elections and the management of elections reveal information about the quality of local agents (Geddes 2006; Myagkov, Ordeshook, and Shakin 2009). I call this the *cadre control information theory* of elections. This theory is potentially inauspicious depending on how the regime interprets "good performance." One interpretation is that elections pit candidates against each other who have an equal chance of victory. Citizens, seeing this, will punish the candidate if she has performed poorly and reward her if she has not. This interpretation is beneficial in the short run for citizens and regime performance.

Another interpretation, proposed by Myagkov, Ordeshook, and Shakin (2009), is that elections provide the regime with information on the ability of local agents to "deliver the vote" (Rundlett and Svolik 2016). Under this theory, if vote returns in a given precinct do not meet the regime's expectations, this acts as a signal that the offending official needs replacing. While this form of information may be useful for the regime, ultimately it is less useful for citizens, as it helps fine tune the regime's repressive capabilities.

RATIONALIZATION AND BUREAUCRATIC BARGAINING

An alternative theory of legislative institutionalization is the "rationalization" of lawmaking (O'Brien 1990; Tanner 1999; Dowdle 1997; Paler 2005; Gueorguiev 2014). Rationalization focuses heavily on improving the *quality of legislation* and the *process by which it is produced*. The definition of "quality" here is narrow, in the sense that it need not cohere with the preferences of citizens. Indeed, citizen information theory describes the idea that oversight or legislation coheres with the preferences of citizens. Quality legislation relates to the degree to which legislation does not conflict with other directives. Quality legislation also describes the degree to which the legislation can be implemented. As Gueorguiev (2014) shows, when legislation in China undergoes debate, it is less likely to be amended. While this could be interpreted as evidence for congruence with citizen wishes, it may also be that the legislation is simply administratively easier to implement gone through a consultative process.

The information and rationalization theories may sometimes be conflated because some of the observable implications appear similar. Indeed, the models are similar to what are called "informational" models from the US Congress. Under this theory, congressional leaders form committees and appoint committee members in order to use the motivation, experience, and knowledge of certain legislators to provide information on a given policy (Gilligan and Krehbiel 1989, 1990; Krehbiel 1991). However, there are differences. While citizen preference information requires a connection to citizens, rationalization may simply require *technical expertise*. Therefore, a legislator who is well qualified for a rationalizing legislature is not one with a strong connection to voters, but rather one with technical skills. This is a key distinction because it highlights the fact that for technical expertise, one may more profitably rely on a bureaucracy than on a legislature. Indeed, for a legislature to provide technical expertise, it will likely need to bolster its nonelected backroom staff to help it stay informed about legislation.

SIGNALING

A final set of perspectives on the role of authoritarian legislatures and elections is signaling. According to this argument, elections do not transmit information from citizens to the regime. Rather, elections serve to deliver a message of dominance. The intended target of the message can vary from citizens (Wedeen 2015; Przeworski 2009), to potential regime defectors (Magaloni 2006), to the bureaucracy (Simpser 2013; Gehlbach and Simpser 2015). This literature features strong parallels to arguments made regarding hard propaganda. Similar to propaganda, the goal of elections and legislatures is not to be believed or provide information, but rather to cow the population, bureaucrats, and potential opponents by *intimidating* and *distorting information* (Huang 2015, 2018).

A number of specific mechanisms are suggested in the signaling literature. The first is that elections and legislatures signal *regime strength*, which I call the *regime strength signaling theory*. Under this theory, strength is defined by the ability of the regime to repress individuals and potential opposition movements (Simpser 2013; Gehlbach and Simpser 2015). Alternatively, overwhelming victories can signal the futility of defecting to the opposition (Magaloni 2006). There are two variants of this model. In one, the elections and legislatures provide a costly signal of the regime's type. In this case, a potential opponent sees the regime winning by a large margin or observes high turnout in a plebiscitary election and calculates that the regime is strong. Thus, the potential opponent reluctantly cooperates with the regime. This is in fact quite similar to the regime strength information theory, except that the goal is not for the regime to use the information to modulate policy but rather to distort information in order to affect behavior among citizens.

In a second variant, the level of fraud provides little information on the regime's type because even weak regimes can commit fraud ("bluffing" regimes) (Simpser 2013, 107). However, the weak regime still manipulates, because not manipulating would be a dead giveaway that the regime is weak. This subtle distinction is nonetheless important because of its welfare implications. As Simpser notes: "In the former, electoral manipulation reveals new information about type; in the latter, it potentially distorts or obscures such information: specifically, it preserves pre-existing beliefs about type even when they do not correspond to actual type" (2013, 107). A number of cases are consistent with this theory, such as the Hosni Mubarak regime in Egypt; the Suharto regime in Indonesia; and Tunisia, where regimes won elections by large margins only to fall within a few years.

Applying Little's (2017) theory about the welfare benefits of elections, if elections provide citizens with *misleading* information, the citizens are *worse off* than if no election had been held. This is because they are now less informed about the true strength of the regime and will be less likely to protest than they otherwise should be. In short, misleading information allows a weak and feckless regime to persist past the point where it would be possible for citizens to actually topple it. Therefore, in considering the *strength signaling* theory, a key question is whether an election carries information about the strength of the regime or if the regime is bluffing. In the following section I consider how the implications of this theory potentially conflict with the regime strength information theory.

Recent work has added to this literature, specifying exactly what it is that regimes might want to signal. While popularity or strength is one important message, another is the degree of unity within the regime (Schedler and Hoffman 2016). According to this theory, single-party regimes face the constant difficulty of communicating to the population that the regime is unified. This is important because opposition parties, while weak, may exploit any evidence of regime fragmentation to try to induce an elite split. An overwhelming electoral victory replete with effectively implemented mobilization may signal that the regime is unified, and thus that efforts to split the regime will likely be futile.

Another variant is that elections and legislatures force citizens or regime officials into a "complicit" relationship with the regime (Mertha 2017; Wedeen 2015). Therefore, even if citizens or officials privately oppose the regime's policies, by participating in regime-backed rituals, citizens express support for the regime in their actions to avoid cognitive dissonance with their actions.

Finally, it is important to consider a basic but potentially overlooked signal sent by elections: persuading the public to support the regime's views. That is, the election campaigns and the results of the election convince citizens that the regime is popular or convince citizens to support the ruling party's platform. Consistent with research on propaganda from Nazi Germany, China, and other contexts, some research finds that propaganda may be genuinely convincing for at least some citizens (Adena et al. 2015; Peisakhin and Rozenas 2018; Cantoni et al. 2017). It is possible that debate in legislatures in particular may contribute to changing the attitudes of citizens. Ensuring the effectiveness of this mechanism will require strict management of the "public transcript" to ensure that criticism of the autocrat is not allowed.

Before proceeding, it is worth noting that the signaling argument has similarities to the classic rubber-stamp view that elections and legislatures simply serve to legitimate the regime without having any meaningful impact on policy (Lockhart 1997; Fainsod 1963). Indeed, for both views the legislature does not serve as a forum for "real politics" and decision-making. At the same time, a key difference between the two is that for the rubber stamp view the legislature and elections merely serve to legitimate the regime and its decisions, while for the signaling view the legislature and elections serve an additional purpose in changing the beliefs of citizens about the strength of the regime and the support it has in society.

Theory: Legislatures as Multitask Institutions

In developing a theory of representative institutions under single-party rule, one need not settle on a single answer. These theories are not necessarily mutually exclusive, and institutions such as elections and legislatures are almost certainly "multitask" institutions (Holmstrom and Milgrom 1991). They may simultaneously serve different goals at the same time as different actors take advantage of them to serve different agendas.

With this in mind, in developing a theory of representative institutions, I ask two questions. First, from the perspective of the autocrat, is any one function necessary for a single-party representative institution? Second, does this function conflict with any of the institution's other functions? In taking this approach, my theoretical starting point is similar to work discussing role strain at the level of the delegate in single-party legislatures (O'Brien 1994; Huang and He 2018; Manion 2016). This work shows how delegates attempt to achieve multiple goals, some of which conflict with each other. While similar, my approach considers *institutional role strain*, which occurs when a regime attempts to achieve different goals through a single institution.

I am not the first to consider authoritarian legislatures and elections as potentially multifunctional, with signaling being one function. Several influential works suggest that elections and legislatures may play multiple roles at the same time. This is particularly true in the literature on elections. Magaloni (2006, 8–9) suggests that Mexico's elections helped the Institutional Revolutionary Party (PRI) manage power sharing, signal strength, provide information on regime and opponent strength, and trap the opposition into investing in the regime. Similarly, Morgenbesser's (2016) analysis of elections in Southeast Asia suggests a range of possible uses for elections, including information, legitimation, regime management, and rent distribution. This perspective on elections and legislatures as multitask institutions is undoubtedly true and conforms with similar points made about the roles of legislatures in democratic settings.[3]

In addition, the important work on authoritarian elections highlighting the multiple functions an election might perform rightfully notes that in a given election, these different functions are not necessarily mutually exclusive. At the same time, it also ignores how the institutional framework designed to maximize one function could increase the risk of undermining one of the others. Indeed, in Mexico, while some routine elections did provide a signal of strength while also facilitating power sharing and information provision, less appreciated is how the institutions necessary to achieve these latter outcomes undermined signaling in key elections.

As Magaloni (2006, 17) discusses, one of the important features of government in Mexico is that the power-sharing function of elections has been enhanced by the frequent rotation of the presidency. In addition, acquiring information on the opposition has required the ability for an opposition party to form. However, both of these features of Mexico have ultimately led to important elections that revealed as much weakness as strength. Indeed, the frequent rotation and availability of opposition parties increased the possibility that disgruntled failed candidates for the PRI nomination could run on an opposition ticket, as has occurred several times in Mexico (Magaloni 2006, 17). The same occurred in Malaysia in 1990 with the creation of a splinter party, Semangat '46, and ultimately undid the regime in 2018. In short, using elections for power sharing and information requires certain conditions that place an upper limit on the degree of signaling one can guarantee through an election.

Some formal work also takes up the possibility of trade-offs, For instance, several publications make the point that increased electoral fraud may impact the ability to collect information on citizen preferences (Little 2017; Miller 2013). However, this work considers only a specific type of information, on the policy preferences of citizens. Crucially, the *strength of the regime*, which is an important type of information elections are supposed to generate, is assumed in these models. That is, leaders know their level of strength ahead of the election and manipulate elections accordingly. If they observe a "shocking" result, they use this information to adjust policy preferences. But they will only allow elections to be competitive enough to generate such information if they are strong. Less considered in these models is the possibility that a "shocking result" could also undermine strength by signaling weakness. The endogeneity of the strength of the regime to electoral results is not modeled in these accounts.

Truex (2016) also notes potential trade-offs, suggesting that the Chinese Communist Party needs to maintain control of the NPC while at the same time allowing it to generate information. While the NPC encourages greater activity, he notes: "None of this should be take as evidence that the CCP is losing control of the institutions. . . . In the post-Tiananmen era, the regime has relied heavily on the manipulation of personnel to rein in the parliament, as it has throughout the history of the institution" (Truex 2016, 169). The crucial question is: Even in those areas within bounds, do these delegates represent citizens or someone else? Furthermore, how does even limited information provision impact the signaling function of the legislature?

The "China model" (Bell 2015), "consultative authoritarianism" (Teets 2013), "consultative Leninism" (Tsang 2009), and "authoritarian delibera-tion" (He and Warren 2011; He and Thogersen 2010) also emphasize the possible synergies between these different objectives. Namely, it is possible that the regime can overcome familiar information problems without hav-ing to risk giving up power. In short, the regime can have its cake and eat it, too. Typically what is ignored in these accounts is the degree to which cer-tain institutions are required to serve other potentially contradictory goals, such as signaling power.

THE TRADE-OFF BETWEEN DOMINATION AND PARTICIPATION

I suggest there is a fundamental trade-off in the purposes elections and leg-islatures serve for single-party regimes. In particular, electoral and legislative institutions designed to *signal* fundamentally limit their ability to co-opt opposition, share power, or collect information. What is the source of this trade-off? In this section I discuss the idea of *extreme signaling*, wherein the regime effectively forestalls the possibility of any opposition candidate win-ning a seat or of any elite split emerging from the legislature, which I, along with others, argue is the case in single-party legislative elections (Truex 2016; Malesky and Schuler 2011). In short, for the legislature to provide any meaningful check on the autocrat, even in the form of power sharing, there needs to be at least the *threat* that a member of the legislature will publicly challenge the autocrat or perhaps threaten to resign from the legislature if the autocrat does not consider the member's policy positions.

I argue that this situation is fundamentally at odds with extreme sig-naling. Designing a legislature with the goal of extreme signaling has two effects. First, it has an impact on how the regime is likely to structure elec-tions and selection into the legislature, which will impact the likelihood of elite defection within the legislature. Theoretically, a regime could design institutions that include regime opponents or regime elites while signaling strength. The regime, for example, could secure a limited number of seats for the opposition party either by directly appointing those members, like Singapore's nominated members of parliament (Rodan 2018), or by only allowing competition for a certain number of seats, as is done in Myanmar (Ostwald and Schuler 2015).

While the preceding is possible, if the regime wants to ensure that it sends a signal of dominance, it will prioritize loyalty rather than inclusion in its design of electoral and legislative institutions. The more a regime limits electoral competitiveness in order to reduce the possibility of an elite split, the less that regime has to consider even the possibility of a defection. This in turn reduces the degree to which the leader has to consider the possibility that the legislature will coordinate against the autocrat in the event that the latter attempts to centralize power, which is a key mechanism underlying the constraining role of institutions under the power-sharing model (Svolik 2012).

The tighter alignment between the preferences of the legislature and the autocrat also means there is less chance that diverse demands will be represented in the legislature and that the autocrat will need to consider such demands from the legislature when crafting policy, key mechanisms underlying the *policy* co-optation model (Gandhi 2008). Again, suggesting that highly constrained legislatures will not fulfill policy co-optation or power-sharing functions is not to say that other institutions in single-party settings, such as party institutions, cannot play this role. I simply suggest that the legislature is not likely to play such a role in contexts where it is designed to signal strength. Indeed, case studies from the Soviet Union (Svolik 2012) and China (Gehlbach and Keefer 2012), as well as research on Vietnam (Malesky, Abrami, and Zheng 2011), focus on party institutions such as the central committees and politburos as venues for power sharing and negotiation rather than on the Supreme Soviet, National People's Congress, or VNA.

It is of course possible, in contrast to the policy co-optation model, that the legislature is designed to buy off potential opponents through rent distribution (Blaydes 2011; Lust-Okar 2006). Indeed, research on China shows that business owners, for example, may join legislatures to generate increased profits or protect private property (Truex 2014; Hou 2019). It is possible that this form of co-optation could coexist with extreme signaling. However, this form of co-optation is distinct from *policy* co-optation in that the regime is essentially buying silence and does not intend to risk having the legislature act as a check on its policy prerogatives. Indeed, as Blaydes (2011) notes in the context of Egypt, the parliament under Mubarak was distinctly *not* a venue for checking the autocrat or making policy. Furthermore, with rent-based co-optation, the co-opted are looking out for their own particularistic self-interests rather than the interests of their economic sector.

However, even here I argue that in Vietnam, which has strong party in-stitutions, the purpose of the legislature in distributing rents is redundant with the rent-based co-optation that already occurs within party institu-tions. Where there is a strong party, the regime already has a tool to pro-vide perks to societal and economic elites in exchange for compliance. In Vietnam and China, research shows that both parties attempt to induce educated elites to join the party (Markussen and Ngo 2019; Xie and Zhang 2017), which can be useful in investing these elites in the survival of the party (Svolik 2012). This may explain why despite the potential role of the legislature in distributing rents, as table 3.2 in chapter 3 shows, business-people comprise less than 3 percent of the overall legislature.[4]

In addition to extreme signaling's impact on elite behavior within the legislature, it may also have an impact on the possibility of generating infor-mation from the public. The goal of extreme signaling is to cow those who might potentially oppose the regime into behaving as if they support the re-gime.[5] In effect, extreme signaling *causes* preference falsification. This imme-diately exposes how signaling is fundamentally opposed to *regime strength* information. If, through signaling, the regime induces those who privately oppose it to behave as if they support the regime, this means that the elec-tion will not generate accurate information on the strength of the regime.

It is theoretically possible that heavily manipulated elections that deliver overwhelming support for the regime could still provide *some* information on citizen preferences if at least some voters are still willing to oppose the regime. Indeed, as Little (2017) suggests, even with elections in which 95 percent support the regime, if this represents a drop from 99 percent, the regime may calculate that its support has dropped. Furthermore, it may be possible to observe the location of these opposition voices and thus who needs to be silenced or placated.

However, even if this is true, there is another issue with heavily manip-ulated elections, which is that they may induce citizens to retreat from the political process entirely. Indeed, as Simpser (2013) shows, citizens in more heavily manipulated elections are less likely to vote. Furthermore, even those who do vote for the incumbent may do so not out of genuine support for or even knowledge of the candidate's positions, but instead out of pressure or obligation. If this is the case, the informational content of the vote in terms of policy preferences or regime preferences will be minimal. Furthermore, the change in support from 99 to 95 percent could represent a genuine decline in support or could simply mean that disaffected citizens, who previously did not vote, simply voted in greater numbers. Therefore, the meaning of a small change in overwhelming support or turnout is not clear.

It is also possible that the regime trains the delegates to provide information on the preferences of voters (Truex 2016; Manion 2016). In this case, the regime essentially tasks the legislature in a top-down manner with the responsibility of reflecting citizen views without the pressure of elections. This renders a legislator no different than a government pollster, government bureaucrat (Heurlin 2016), or state-run media reporter (Dimitrov 2017), all of whom also have the responsibility of reporting on citizen views. Without meaningful elections, it is not clear why legislators would be any more likely to accurately reflect the views of citizens than these other information provision channels.

It is important to note that these constraints on bottom-up accountability will be important for both *cadre quality* information and *citizen* information. If the elections cause citizens to vote out of obligation and legislators imperfectly reflect the wishes of citizens, then legislators or legislative elections may not provide meaningful feedback on the quality of local officials. As chapter 6 discusses in greater detail, if citizens even in democracies have minimal incentive to vote in an informed manner, the electoral conditions in single-party settings should reduce the motivation of citizens to inform themselves about their choice of candidate. Therefore, using a legislature to signal strength by manipulating the elections is fundamentally at odds with generating information.

This leads to the first theoretical argument of the book:

Theoretical Argument 1: A regime will limit its ability to inform itself through a legislature or an election if it intends to signal strength through the same institution.

While signaling may contradict information, power sharing, or cooptation, it may nonetheless be consistent with rationalization. That is, a legislature may provide more technocratic advice on legislation without necessarily threatening the signaling role of the legislature. The information should come in the form of expert opinion and advice, which should require two things. First, more experts should be selected into the legislature. Second, those experts should be able to rely on greater institutional capacity to research issues. To ensure that such experts do not threaten the ability of the legislature and elections to project unity, the legislature may ensure that only those with close ties to the regime leaders are selected for high-ranking positions in the legislature. This will help ensure that those selected for their technical expertise do not inadvertently use this expertise to challenge core regime prerogatives.

The Regime's Public Face: Why Authoritarian Electoral and Legislative Institutions Are Unique

If signaling strength through elections and legislatures is ultimately incompatible with other objectives, the question then is: Which of these objectives will a single-party regime seek to maximize through its representative institutions? Answering this question requires understanding what makes elections and legislatures unique compared to other potential channels of information, co-optation, or power sharing, such as party institutions, the media, direct citizen engagement, and protests. I argue that the degree to which a single-party regime is likely to use an institution for signaling purposes depends on two factors: the *visibility* of the institution and whether the institution is *state sanctioned*. I argue that these features are what distinguishes legislative and electoral institutions from other institutions and makes them so useful for signaling as opposed to other purposes in a single-party context.

Visibility is clearly important for signaling purposes. If the regime wants to dominate the opposition through elections and the legislature, the targets of the signaling, who are primarily outside the regime, must observe the signal. This means, most obviously, that the targets must observe the election returns (whether real or falsified). In the legislature, they must also observe the debates and votes, which serve to bolster confidence in both the policies passed by the regime and government performance. In assessing the visibility of the competing information channels, legislatures, elections, the media, and protests tend to be visible to the public. Of the other channels, party institutions and petitions are not.

On this point, it should be noted that legislative institutions *could* be made less visible. The regime can allow the legislature to only debate issues in private. Indeed, in Vietnam and in China, legislators do in fact hold closed-door hearings. However, in these sessions, the function of the legislature would be duplicative of party conclaves, which also discuss policy decisions behind closed doors. To the extent that such meetings provide *additional* insights or information compared to party conclaves depends on the degree to which those delegates are seen as more informed, more representative of citizen interests, and more willing to express an independent voice than those officials meeting in party meetings.

The visibility of the proceedings for these outlets impacts their relative risks. Within the party, greater discussion and deliberation can occur. This is perhaps why Nikita Khrushchev's famous speech criticizing Joseph Stalin occurred behind closed doors. In single-party regimes, most leadership decisions are made within party conclaves and not on the floor of the legislature. In Vietnam and China, for example, it is the politburos and central committees within the parties that provide the challenges to the regime, not the legislatures (Abrami, Malesky, and Zheng 2013; Schuler and Ostwald 2016). It is also perhaps for this reason that the one time the VNA did deviate from the norm and introduce a different candidate for prime minister in 1988 than the one introduced by the Politburo, that fact was not mentioned in the leading party newspaper.[6]

As table 1.1 notes, petitions and denunciations are not visible; they operate differently in that they involve an individual exchange with the regime. Other individuals cannot observe a denunciation made by another person (unless of course they post it to the media). This makes these exchanges, much like the opinions and petitions that NPC delegates in China can put forward, easier for the regime to control. They are much like the citizen feedback the regime can acquire on draft laws from party-controlled meetings. The regime may observe the information, but the information cannot be used to generate collective action from others.

Media reports and protests, however, are public, meaning that they are also potentially dangerous. This leads to a second distinguishing factor for

TABLE 1.1.
Differences between elections, legislatures, and other feedback channels.

	Legislatures/ elections	State media and propaganda	Party institutions	Protests	Petitions/ denunciations
Visible	Yes	Yes	No	Yes	No
State sanctioned	Yes	Yes	Yes	No	Yes

the different channels, which is whether they are state sanctioned. State-sanctioned institutions are important because the regime cannot disavow them. If the regime creates an institution and that institution makes a claim, this sends an immediate signal about shifts in the "public transcript." Crucially, this shift can impact both public opinion and opinion within the regime itself. For instance, if the regime criticizes a person in the party or accuses someone of corruption, this signals to the rest of the regime that it is now acceptable to criticize that person.

For a dramatic example of how a statement from an official organ can have such an effect, consider the blunder on the part of former East German Politburo spokesperson Gunter Schabowski. Facing pressure from increasing protests to open the border, the Politburo attempted to draft a new emigration law that would appear more democratic while still allowing it to maintain control. Schabowski, however, announced the proposal that citizens could freely emigrate without any of the qualifications that the report suggested. Furthermore, he indicated it was effective immediately.[7] As a consequence, thousands of East Germans streamed to the wall to confront border guards, who, just as perplexed, allowed them through.

This episode reveals the importance of the *source* of information in single-party regimes. It is unlikely that if media loosely linked to the regime, a dissident, or a protester had made the claim that the border was open, it would have had such an effect. Even if such information caused citizens to rally and act collectively, it is unlikely that border guards or regime officials would have taken the information as official policy. The source of the information carries the imprimatur of the party and thus sends the signal that others who act in accordance with that information will not be repressed. If a state-sanctioned institution criticizes a person, that person is now fair game. If a state-sanctioned institution criticizes a policy, that policy is fair game.

This is why an institution used for signaling may be unsuitable for genuine information provision or any checking of the autocrat. Because elections and legislatures are sanctioned by the regime, what occurs on the floor signals what is acceptable for the public transcript (Scott 1990). Therefore, the bounds of criticism within the assembly—to the extent that citizens are able to observe them—signal what is acceptable for civil society, individuals, and potential opponents to criticize outside the legislature.

This is what distinguishes the legislature and elections from some media outlets and protests. Because elections and legislatures are sanctioned, they are more difficult to rebuke. Media outlets and protests, however, can be chastised as representing "foreign elements" or "deviating from the party line." In particular, as the media have become more independent and fragmented in both China and Vietnam, it has become easier for the regime to punish outlets that stray from the "public script" (Shirk 2011). Therefore, while these outlets can provide information to the regime (Lorentzen 2014, 2013; Egorov, Guriev, and Sonin 2009), they can ultimately be shut down if they deviate too far from the party line. As such, they are not ideal for signaling strength, because they are not explicitly tied to the regime. However, they are better for generating information due to their independence.

Because of these two factors—visibility and state sanctioning—legislatures and elections are uniquely suited to generate a signal of regime strength. Their visibility enables the message to reach the intended targets. The state sanctioning allows for precisely the signals the regime wants to send—that the state dominates any real or potential opposition. For these two reasons, I argue that single-party regimes, which can design institutions nearly any way they wish, will use legislatures and elections for signaling. This leads to the second theoretical argument of the book:

> *Theoretical Argument 2: Single-party regimes will prioritize the signaling function for legislatures and elections, thus minimizing their constraining or informational role.*

It logically follows, then, that if the first and second theoretical arguments hold, elections and legislatures in single-party regimes are unlikely to provide meaningful information or to check the party leadership.

It should be noted that this argument offers a different theory than work from China stressing the informative role of elections and legislatures (Truex 2016; O'Brien 1990; Manion 2016). The evidence from this book comes solely from Vietnam, so it cannot directly challenge the evidence provided in those studies. While it is entirely possible that the logic of the Chinese NPC operates differently than the system in Vietnam, a reexamination of the evidence from China could also reveal patterns consistent with the argument offered in this study.[8] Unfortunately, due to the focus here on Vietnam, such a reexamination requires further study.

THE SIGNALING TRAP

While the preceding section made a clear theoretical prediction, it does raise an important question. If signaling imperatives dominate other potential benefits and regimes are reluctant to reform their institutions, how and why do single-party regimes voluntarily transition to multiparty regimes (Gandhi 2008; Miller 2013, 2017)? This section considers why single-party regimes are so slow to make such a transition. Indeed, as noted in the introduction, leaders of single-party regimes often express a desire to gain more information through their legislatures. As Miller (2013) shows, the only single-party regimes that have reformed are those that were forced to do so by the collapse of the Soviet Union. Why? Why don't such regimes open up to multiparty politics voluntarily?

Precisely because of the lack of information and the stilted nature of official commentary, single-party regimes become caught in a signaling trap, wherein any move from the heavily controlled public transcript constitutes a greater risk than would exist in a hybrid regime. There are two reasons for this. First, past signaling creates the expectation of future signaling. If the regime uses control of the institutions to signal strength, then any subsequent move to reduce control of those institutions could be interpreted as weakness.

Although this is seemingly similar to the theory of elections as informative of public sentiment, I argue that the shift in the public transcript or the election turnout levels will not generate actual information on the popularity of the regime that the regime can or should use to modify policy. Rather, because a change in the public transcript will require the regime to relax its electoral controls or agenda setting within the legislature, the regime will know that the shift only occurred because of its policy decisions and thus will not interpret the shift as a need to change policy.

However, the change will look significant from the public perspective. In a single-party context, wherein every election features 100 percent turnout and 100 percent of the candidates are regime backed, any move toward a multiparty system will necessarily shift this support downward. Using the inverse of the signaling argument, this could lead to a signal that the regime is weak and therefore increase the odds that citizens and bureaucrats will abandon the party. Therefore, the shift in support from 99 to 95 percent will not provide the regime with new information that it is unpopular but may nonetheless be misinterpreted by the public as a sign that the regime is weak.

The second reason is that single-party regimes are ultimately *less sure of their strength* vis-à-vis an opponent than are multiparty regimes. There are a number of reasons for this. First, there is the simple fact that a single-party regime, by definition, has not faced an opposition party. Therefore, by allowing one to exist, the regime is allowing competition with an opponent with little information about the strength and support of that party.

In addition, the regime may also be unaware of how the public will respond to the new opponent. With liberalization, the regime must now allow citizens to hear an *alternative* message. This means that any support that was previously predicated on the *assumption* that the ruling party is strong could evaporate once a campaign is allowed. Indeed, studies show that in Poland in the 1980s, polls shifted in the direction of Solidarity not when it was allowed to compete, but when Lech Walesa was allowed to debate official union leader Alfred Miodowicz on television (Kaminsky 1999; Nalepa and Pop-Eleches 2014).

Because of these factors, in contrast to electoral regimes, single-party regimes are ultimately unaware of their strength vis-à-vis potential opponents, which means they cannot use this information in their calculations of when to liberalize (Slater and Wong 2013; Miller 2013). It is perhaps for this reason that although Miller (2013) theorizes that single-party regimes may transition to electoral authoritarianism under conditions of inequality, uncertainty about citizen preferences, and international pressure, his empirical analysis shows that only international pressure plays a meaningful role in inducing single-party regimes to allow multiple parties (Miller 2017).

What this suggests is that in contrast to electoral authoritarian regimes, which can modulate their repression and electoral manipulation based on information from previous elections and polls regarding opposition parties, single-party regimes are ultimately flying blind. Furthermore, citizens experiencing only 100 percent turnout for 100 percent of the candidates expect that those figures signal strength, and consequently, any deviation could be perceived as regime weakness.

In short, I argue that the total domination exhibited by single-party regimes places them in a signaling trap, in which past dominance *requires them* to continue such dominance even when, for other reasons, it may be strategically beneficial to open up the process. It is for this reason that only single-party regimes *forced* to open up by exogenous, international pressures have done so, and the two countries that attempted to do so endogenously—Poland and the Soviet Union—collapsed. This is a fundamental insight of research on a regime's "public transcript" or cult of personality (Scott 1990; Wedeen 2015). A regime may use control over the public transcript to enhance its rule. However, the more a regime relies on such signaling, the more it is bound to it, as any deviation from the transcript could signal weakness. This leads to a final theoretical argument:

> *Theoretical Argument 3: Due to regime uncertainty over performance against future opponents, single-party regimes will not respond to the need for more information or improved performance by allowing meaningful competition for seats or debate on party-backed policy.*

WHY ALLOW DEBATE AT ALL?

The previous sections suggested that single-party regimes are trapped in a cycle of signaling due to the signal any change in support would send and their inability to know the strength of a hypothetical opposition candidate. This raises a final question important for the case of Vietnam, which is why Nguyen Minh Thuyet and other delegates have been allowed the opportunity to criticize government officials in the legislature. As noted, Vietnamese legislators can and do sometimes attack government officials on the floor of the legislature. Furthermore, as chapter 5 discusses, regime leaders sanctioned institutional changes to the way the VNA operates to allow them to do so. Why?

The signaling theory suggests that the *party* must project unity and strength. However, I argue that it is possible in theory for the regime to allow criticism while projecting unity if it can credibly signal that the object of the criticism is independent from the party. As Beazer and Reuter (2019) show, in Russia the ruling party was able to deflect blame for poor economic performance at the local level when mayors were elected rather than appointed. The logic is that the more plausibly independent the mayors are from the ruling regime, the less blame for poor performance the public will lay at the regime's feet.

I argue this is also true with regard to the degree of delegation from the autocrat to the government. As chapter 5 discusses in detail, during the economic reform process the VCP delegated greater independence to the government and the prime minister to manage the economy than previously had existed. This degree of delegation varies from regime to regime. In other countries, such as Iran, the autocrat delegates a relatively large degree of autonomy to the government. In others, such as China, the delegation is more restrained. As Beazer and Reuter (2019) and my own previous work (Schuler 2018) show, where delegation is greater the autocrat may surmise that it can allow greater criticism in order to deflect blame from itself onto the government.

Of course, this does present risks. To the degree to which citizens do not see daylight between the regime and the government, such criticism may undermine the projection of unity. However, if the government is seen as plausibly distinct from the autocrat, which controls the regime's repressive apparatus, citizens may well see criticism as punishing poor performance while not undermining the credibility or unity of those in control of the repressive organs of the state. That is, the Ayatollah may allow criticism of the president on the floor of the Iranian Parliament without undermining the perception that he is in control of the Revolutionary Guard.

Critically, however, this form of criticism is distinct from power-sharing, information, or co-optation models. For power sharing, the role of the criticism in the legislature is to allow regime elites the ability to restrain the autocrat. Under my theory, however, the role of criticism is to manage the autocrat's agents. Furthermore, the information and co-optation views suggest that the criticisms expressed in the legislature result from citizen preferences or the preferences of some group outside of the regime. My theory, however, suggests that the criticism expressed in the legislature *emanates from the regime itself.*

Finally, regarding the possibility of shifting blame, this raises the question of whether or not citizens actually perceive any daylight between the party and the state. Indeed, in Vietnam confidence in the party and the central government is remarkably high. Indeed, in the 6th Wave of the Asian Barometer Survey, only 9 percent of respondents reported somewhat low or low levels of trust in the government. The number was similar at 10 percent for the party. However, while citizens may not distinguish between the party and the state in the abstract, I argue that delegation leads to the salience of two leaders, one who leads the party and one who leads the government. With two salient leaders, it becomes easier for the party to blame the *leader* of the government without damaging the overall confidence in the party, party leader, or government.

In the case of Vietnam, as the following chapters show, the leader of the government in the form of the prime minister is the most frequent target of legislative attack. Unfortunately, on this metric, due to restrictions in the context of Vietnam, we cannot ask citizens directly about their confidence level in individual politicians. One of the most sensitive items to ask about in the Vietnamese context is not confidence in the party, but rather support for individual politicians. However, if the measure were available, the empirical implication of the argument would be that these attacks should lead to lower support for the prime minister as an individual without undermining the image of the party.

Empirical Implications for Election Management

How will the theory outlined here impact the operation of elections? Elections can play two primary signaling functions. First, they may have a direct effect in convincing citizens to support the regime. If citizens see that others support the regime, they may decide that they too support it, due to social desirability bias. Second, they can demonstrate the strength and popularity of the regime. By doing so, elections can impact the degree to which citizens think *other* citizens support the regime. They can also signal that the regime has overwhelming strength, and thus resistance is futile. If this is the case, in the context of elections we should see the regime attempt to show that it has won an overwhelming majority of the votes and, where possible, that a large number of citizens participated. This requires *mobilization* and *manipulation*.

The degree to which elections *signal* rather than *inform* depends on the relative balance of manipulation and mobilization with competition. How might election manipulations impact information? Consider some items from Schedler's "menu of manipulation" (2002). Two of the most important forms of manipulation are restrictions on the "object of choice" and the "freedom of supply." With the object of choice, autocrats may restrict competition by only allowing certain positions to be contested or by restricting the power of the position itself. Restriction on freedom of supply refers to the banning or intimidation of opposition forces such that they cannot compete fairly with the incumbent, if at all.

The degree to which the autocrat engages in these forms of manipulation will have an important effect on several forms of information the regime might hope to acquire through elections (Malesky and Schuler 2011). With regard to the "object of choice," if the regime systematically reserves seats for certain officials, it obviously cannot gain information on the popularity of those officials. Reserving seats also impacts the ability to identify leaders in need of co-opting, as the regime will not know if the officials who are co-opted are genuinely powerful. Reserving seats may also impact information on the quality of subordinates if those subordinates effectively guarantee themselves seats. Finally, reserving seats could have an impact on information on government policies, as those leaders with reserved seats will face little bottom-up accountability and therefore will be less incentivized to provide information on citizen grievances.

An additional form of manipulation—restrictions on freedom of supply—will also damage information. Most obviously, by banning parties, the regime will not know the popularity of the opposition. Banning the opposition will also preclude gathering accurate information on the popularity of regime leaders. Similarly, barring opposition parties from running will restrict information on potentially important officials in need of co-optation. It will weaken information on the quality of subordinates by preventing the strongest challengers from running against them. Finally, it will weaken information on government policies, because with a lack of electoral competitiveness, elected officials will face less bottom-up accountability and therefore engage in the effort to acquire information on citizen preferences (Truex 2016; Malesky and Schuler 2010).

An additional form of manipulation that could impact information would be restrictions on campaigns. Schedler calls this a restriction on the formation of preferences. If campaigns are disallowed, then opposition parties cannot raise awareness of potentially unpopular policy pronouncements. Without such campaigns, the public may not be aware of potentially unpopular policies that the autocracy may be planning. As such, the elected delegates may be unaware of potential pitfalls that could await government proposals.

A final form of institutional manipulation that is less often considered could also impact the degree to which autocrats can acquire information. This is the institutional machinery of nominations and election management. Elections are not only used to manage principal-agent relationship; they create additional principal-agent relationships. To run an election, central officials must rely on local officials to set up polling booths, count the ballots, and in some cases create the ballots. This could complicate the ability of autocrats to acquire information from elections. If, for example, the autocrat delegates management of the ballot and nominations to provincial officials, this could compromise its ability to gain information on the quality of those officials. This is because the local officials may stack the ballots in such a way to ensure that they face weak competitors, or what I call "sacrificial lamb" candidates.

Each of these forms of manipulation that damage information are ex ante manipulations. Other items on Schedler's list include ex post forms of manipulation, such as miscounting or manipulating ballots or simply not acknowledging the results. In theory, autocrats could rely on these forms of information without threatening their access to it. For instance, an autocrat could allow opposition parties to compete without interference, gain information on their strength, and simply annul the results. Why, then, do autocrats not rely on these forms of manipulation?

Here an established literature shows that ex post manipulations tend to be either normatively unpalatable or risky in terms of generating antiregime collective action and revealing regime weakness to the opposition. Several studies show how electoral fraud served to galvanize antiregime opposition forces in the Eastern European color revolutions (Bunce and Wolchik 2011; Tucker 2007). In addition, if the regime performs poorly or loses the election and attempts to reverse the results, this could provide information on regime weakness and therefore encourage antiregime protests (Pop-Eleches and Robertson 2015; Magaloni 2006). Furthermore, such obvious ex post fraud would jeopardize the signaling effects to bureaucrats (Gehlbach and Simpser 2015; Simpser 2013). As such, while ex post fraud could theoretically allow autocrats to acquire information while signaling strength, the reality is that the focal point logic of ex post fraud makes this a risky strategy. As such, I expect that autocrats will attempt to avoid relying on fraud.

In addition to manipulation, mobilization also plays an important role in an election's signaling function. Mobilization, in contrast to manipulation, induces citizens to participate in the election. Of course, mobilization and manipulation work in tandem; the regime may manipulate the mobilized to ensure that they vote correctly. However, mobilization serves two propaganda purposes. First, it can have an impact on mobilized individuals, causing them to invest in the regime. If citizens are forced to participate and vote for the ruling party, they may convince themselves they support the regime in order to rationalize their votes (Mertha 2017; Wedeen 2015).

Mobilization may also induce individuals to update their beliefs about the popularity or strength of the regime vis-à-vis the rest of society. If citizens see others participate, they will be forced to conclude one of two things. First, perhaps they will conclude that the regime is strong enough to mobilize citizen participation, and thus that resistance is futile. This logic is similar to the effects of propaganda on protest (Huang 2015, 2018). Alternatively, they might think that other citizens genuinely support the regime, which will have the same effect of leading those individuals to believe that any act of resistance will not win support from fellow citizens.

OBSERVABLE IMPLICATIONS OF THE SIGNALING ARGUMENT FOR ELECTIONS

This discussion carries empirical implications for how a regime should conduct elections if it is primarily driven by a desire to mobilize participation and demonstrate strength. If regimes use elections for signaling purposes, they should keep strong, non-party challengers off the ballot (*electoral design observable implication 1*). Second, they should manipulate elections to ensure that preferred candidates win (*electoral design observable implication 2*). Third, to project a unified front, campaigns should be restricted to ensure that no divisions within the regime emerge in public (*electoral design observable implication 3*). This may require the regime to place explicit limits on the degree to which individual candidates can campaign. Chapter 3 takes up this issue.

Implications for Voter Behavior

The previous section considered the institutional implications for electoral institutions. Perhaps surprisingly given the interest in single-party elections, little research has gone into theorizing how and why citizens participate in such elections.[9] While a number of studies suggest that elections may successfully encourage meaningful citizen input (Shi 1999; Landry, Davis, and Wang 2010; Manion 2016; Wang and Sun 2017), this notion is seldom reconciled with a substantial literature on democratic settings questioning whether citizens are informed (Campbell et al. 1960; Achen and Bartels 2016). Research on the US Congress shows that where information about and knowledge of candidates are poor, accountability is low (Levy and Squire 2000; Snyder and Stromberg 2010). This oversight is an important omission, as the link between voters and delegates is crucial to assessing whether elections serve primarily to mobilize support for the regime or generate bottom-up accountability.

With regard to research on democracies, studies show that a number of factors drive a citizen's decision to vote and inform herself in a democracy.

These include education (Milligan, Moretti, and Oreopoulos 2004; Sondheimer and Green 2010), social networks (Gerber and Green 2000; Gerber, Green, and Larimer 2008), income (Wolfinger and Rosenstone 1980), and district closeness (Simonivits 2012; De Paola and Scoppa 2014; Geys 2006). These variables increase turnout either by affecting an individual's internal costs and benefits (intrinsic benefits) or by impacting her desire for social approval (extrinsic benefits) (Gerber, Green, and Larimer 2008; Knack 1992; Harbaugh 1996).

These observable factors link to two important mechanisms. The first variable of interest is the degree to which the voter has the capacity to make an informed decision (Delli Carpini and Keeter 1996; Lassen 2005; Larcinese 2007). The second factor is the degree to which voters have a preference. Studies show that when voters have a greater preference for a particular candidate, they are more likely to participate (Larcinese 2007). Obviously, having a preference requires some information on the positions of the candidates.

With this in mind, mobilization and manipulation may impact the decision to vote and the level of information conveyed through the vote. I argue that in nondemocracies, the institutional features described in the previous section will undermine the degree to which the participants in the election vote knowledgeably. First, there is a lack of information. Given the bans on campaigns, even when voters are educated, they are unable to acquire information on the preferences of the candidates. Without information on the preferences of the candidates, voters will be unable to acquire information on the candidates themselves. Second, manipulation may impact the degree to which voters perceive a difference between the candidates. If vetting and ballot manipulation render competition meaningless or the outcome a foregone conclusion in the eyes of voters, they may participate due to strong incentives to do so without bothering to acquire information on the views of the candidates.

All this suggests that in terms of behavior, we should expect mobilization rather than knowledge or information to drive turnout. Mobilization, in the context of a single-party regime, refers to the strength of the local party apparatus and individual ties to the regime. Those with greater ties to the regime in areas where the party is stronger should be more likely to vote due to pressure and mobilization from the regime (*electoral behavior observable implication 1*).

However, this electorate should be largely uninformed about the nature of the election and the identity of the candidates for whom they vote. This aligns with some work on compulsory voting, which suggests that forced voting may weaken the content of elections, because reluctant voters unaware of their preferences will participate in elections (Dassonneville et al. 2018; Jackee and Sun 2006). Although some work suggests that mobilizing nonvoters to vote can increase the information those citizens acquire (Shineman 2016), I argue that the uninformed nature of the mobilized electorate will be worse in autocracies because of the lack of information and the lack of competition. Even if motivated, voters simply will not have the same resources available or the incentive to choose between candidates that may appear substantively similar.

An additional implication is that in contrast to democracies, where the closeness of the election (the "Downsian closeness hypothesis") and strategic considerations impact whether and how to vote, these factors should play no role in a single-party election. This is because voters will either not be aware of how close the election is, or if they are, they will not have sufficient information to distinguish between the candidate they prefer and the one they do not. Therefore, rather than voting strategically, they will vote randomly (*electoral behavior observable implication 2*).

Finally, given the lack of information distinguishing the candidates and the importance of mobilization, voters, even when they do vote, should have little awareness of the delegates they selected (*electoral behavior observable implication 3*). This is because even when encouraged to vote, the voters are simply responding to social or regime pressure. In this case, when voters cast their ballots, they may simply vote as instructed or encouraged to by the regime. I test these theories in chapter 6.

Empirical Implications for Legislative Institutionalization

Moving to the logic of legislative institutionalization, this section considers why, despite the priority on signaling, regime leaders may strengthen the legislature. As the theory previously discussed suggests, signaling is incompatible with information or constraints. However, signaling may coexist with rationalization, in which the regime uses the legislature to help relieve the party leadership of the burden of policy making.

When should this occur? The most obvious time at which a regime might rationalize the legislature is when it needs to write more legislation with greater amounts of detail (*legislative institutionalization observable implication 1*). This might occur when a regime is forced to align its legal code with international institutions, such as the WTO. It might also occur when the regime delegates greater responsibility to the state, as laws will be required to ensure that the state abides by edicts issued by the party.

In the abstract, this notion may appear observationally equivalent to information or constraining theories. Under those logics, a regime may face incentives to acquire more information or constrain the autocrat when it needs more cooperation from society or when economic performance is poor. Because these situations, which could occur when there is a dramatic decline in rents available to the regime, may simultaneously spark institutionalization to rationalize the legislature or to generate greater bottom-up information, how can we distinguish between the two?

I argue that the key is how the rationalization is carried out. As previously noted, rationalization concerns the degree to which a legislature can write "high-quality" legislation. Such legislation should be enforceable and consistent with other existing legislation. Importantly, it need not either align with or go against citizen preferences. More important is that it serves the party's purposes, whatever they may be at the time. In this context, expertise and capacity are important because those tasked with writing legislation must be aware of existing laws, which requires time and knowledge.

Expertise, however, carries risks for the regime. By appointing experts and providing them with additional institutional resources, the regime opens up the possibility that these experts could use this knowledge to undermine regime objectives. This leads to a key difference between the predictions of the rationalization logic and the informational or constraining logic. The constraint logic would predict that those granted additional resources through institutionalization should either have more information on citizen preferences or be most likely to check the party leadership. By contrast, the rationalization logic suggests that those given additional institutional resources should be those with the closest ties to the party leadership. Therefore, rather than appointing those with ties to constituents to important positions in the legislature, the party should appoint only those with closer connections to the party center to those positions (*legislative institutionalization observable implication 2*).

In addition to the rationalization logic, there is another factor that might encourage greater institutionalization. Consistent with the theory previously presented, greater separation of the party or the autocrat from direct government control may also lead to greater legislative strength. In such cases, the party may enhance the power of the legislature to shift blame for policy failures to the government (*legislative institutionalization observable implication 3*). Chapter 5 takes up these questions.

Empirical Implications for Delegate Behavior

The theory also carries implications for delegate behavior. If the party is able to use vetting to get its own people in the legislature, and legislative institutions are designed mainly to rationalize party policy and/or damage rivals in the government, this carries implications for how the legislature should behave once seated. In particular, the predictions from the theory suggest that when active, the legislature should primarily *serve the party leader* rather than *check the leader*. Furthermore, due to the constraints of the signaling role, the assistance should be more likely to reflect the party's perspective rather than provide new information for the party.

In terms of predictions, this suggests several observable implications. First, if one of the goals of legislative institutionalization is rationalization, this should mean that those providing input into legislation should be closely tied to the regime center and given greater institutional capacity (*delegate behavior observable implication 1*). With regard to oversight, to the extent that the government is overseen publicly at all, criticism should only be about policies that the party has delegated to the government (*delegate behavior observable implication 2*). On issues controlled by the party, which in Vietnam includes foreign affairs, defense, the police, the judiciary, and appointments, the legislature should be largely silent (*delegate behavior observable implication 3*). Chapter 7 takes up this question.

Empirical Implications for Public Opinion

Finally, an important component of the signaling theory is its impact on public opinion. As noted previously, one of the key predictions would be that criticism from the VNA of government officials should lead to decreased support for those officials without a corresponding loss in confidence in the party. Unfortunately, because of restrictions due to the sensitivity of the question, we cannot ask about confidence in individual politicians.

However, there are other observable implications consistent with the theory. As with empirical findings on propaganda (Huang 2018, 2015; Simpser 2013), the ultimate purpose is to convince the population that resistance is futile. Therefore, exposure to information about the elections and the legislature should reinforce the citizens' perspective that the regime is strong. Alternatively, information about the legislature could generate outcomes more consistent with soft propaganda, which is that citizens observing election returns and activity in the legislature genuinely believe the regime is more popular and legitimate and hence update their opinions themselves. Both of these mechanisms will lead to the same outcome, which is that the citizens will be less willing to oppose the regime (*public opinion observable implication 1*). If the citizens believe that the regime is united or that others support it, resistance is doomed to failure. Chapter 8 takes up this question.

TWO

How Elections Work in Vietnam

> Deputies do not depend on the people, but on those that nominate
> them. . . . They are chosen by those in power, not the people.
>
> —Tran Quoc Tuan, former deputy chair of the Office
>
> of the National Assembly, May 1, 2014[1]

This chapter lays out the structure of Vietnam's electoral system. It provides
an overview of the system and lays out some of the institutions that block
linkages between citizens and legislators. In particular, it focuses on party
management of vetting institutions and the power of the Vietnam National
Assembly Standing Committee (VNASC) and local election boards to
tilt the elections in favor of preferred candidates. The chapter serves two
purposes. First, it provides important background on Vietnam's electoral
institutions. Second, the examination highlights important institutions
that bolster the signaling value of elections and give the regime control of
legislators.

Electoral System

Vietnam has a bloc voting system in which each district has two to three
seats and each voter can vote for as many candidates as there are seats. Beyond that, the election law tasks the Central Election Commission and
provincial election boards with filling in important details regarding the
number of candidates and who appears on the ballot. Regarding the number of candidates per district and the district magnitude (number of seats
available), the 2016 Election Law requires each province to have least three
delegates who work in that province.[2] The exact number depends on the
population and other "special features" of the province, to be determined by
the Central Election Commission (*Hội đồng Bầu cử Quốc gia*). In addition,
the Central Election Commission sends several other candidates nominated

49

by central institutions to compete against the provincially nominated candidates. Given the VNASC's overwhelming control of the Election Commission, this in effect grants it the ability to distribute candidates.

Within these guidelines, the VNASC can decide how many delegates each province receives. While population is an important guideline, the law allows for the VNASC to grant some provinces more or fewer delegates per voter than others. In 2016 the VNASC set a minimum number of seats per province at six. As figure 2.1 shows, the net result is that smaller provinces are overrepresented. Bac Kan province has the most representation, 48,000 voters per seat. At the higher end of the spectrum, Thanh Hoa, Hanoi, Nghe An, and Ho Chi Minh City are the most underrepresented, with more than 210,000 voters per seat. Hanoi and Ho Chi Minh City are outliers on the trend line, although voters in those cities are still underrepresented. It is not clear whether there is any special significance to the malapportionment. It is worthwhile to note that provinces each only get one provincial leader representative in the VCP Central Committee, so the underrepresentation would be replicated in the party institutions as well.[3] At any rate, the malapportionment does indicate the broad discretion the Central Election Commission and VNASC have in distributing candidates to different provinces.

Once the Central Election Commission chooses the number of delegates per province, the provincial election boards then have the authority to divide the province into election districts, which must be announced eighty days before election day. The only restriction in the 2015 Election Law is that no district may be able to elect more than three seats.[4] There is no minimum threshold, so theoretically a district could have only one seat available. In practice, each election since 2007 has involved only districts with two or three seats available.

Until the 2015 Election Law, there were no legal requirements regarding how competitive each district should be. Therefore, it was at the central and provincial election boards' discretion how many extra candidates per seat there would be. In practice, most districts had either two or three more candidates than seats. However, in some elections, such as 2002, there were districts that elected three delegates with only four candidates. In 2015 the law stipulated that each election district must have two more candidates than seats available.[5]

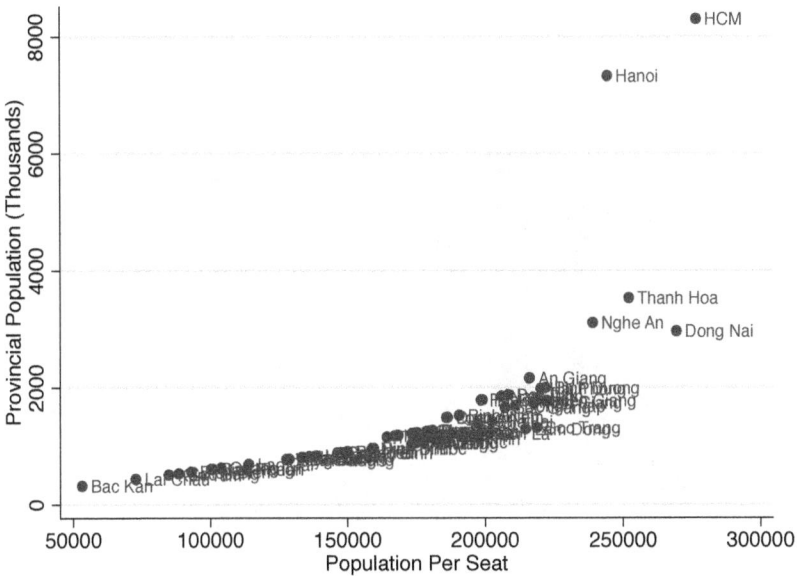

FIGURE 2.1. Malapportionment in the VNA.

While the fact that this number is now stipulated in law may seem important and suggest an increasingly competitive electoral system, it is important to remember a new Election Law is passed with almost every election (the law was amended or rewritten in 1980, 1992, 1997, 2001, and 2015). This means that the law does not really constrain the VNASC, given that it can simply rewrite the law to fulfill whatever objective it has in mind for the upcoming election. Therefore, whether a VNASC decision is issued prior to an election versus or a law is passed is not as critical as it might seem. As figure 2.2 shows, despite the new stipulation in the 2015 law, the number of candidates per seat was slightly below that in the 2007 election, when the ratio was 1.75, compared to 1.74 in the 2016 election. However, just as important, since the 1987 election there has not been a clear trend toward more competitive elections.

Perhaps more important than the number of candidates per seat is the independence of the candidates themselves. While the competitiveness of the election does fluctuate from year to year, so does the *structure* of the

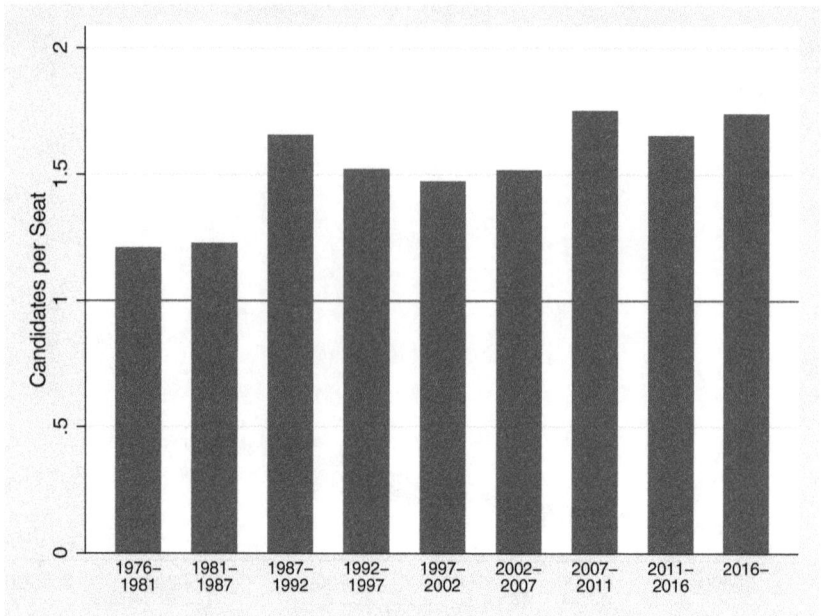

FIGURE 2.2. Candidates per seat in the VNA.

candidates selected. The following section reviews the vetting process in more detail. However, here it is important to note that the Central Election Commission has its first meeting several months before the election, at which it decides on the "structure" (*cơ cấu*) of the legislature. The structure is essentially the number of key demographic groups, such as women, minorities, and model workers, the regime wants to select to the upcoming legislature. While much criticized by those inside and outside the regime, this practice remains in place.[6]

SELF-NOMINEES AND NON-PARTY MEMBERS

In terms of pluralism, the VNA features two types of delegates that could possibly broaden the degree of representation in the legislature. The first are non-party members. The second are self-nominees. While these groups overlap, they are not the same. There are self-nominated party member candidates and non-party members who are not self-nominated. Regarding the non-party, non-self nominated candidates, these include delegates nominated by organizations linked to the Fatherland Front that are allowed to choose a delegate, who nonetheless are non-party members. For example, well-known delegate Duong Trung Quoc is not self-nominated. However, he is a non-party member nominated by the Vietnam Historians Association.

Both non-party and self-nominated delegates are important for giving the VNA a veneer of credibility. Non-party delegates, for example, allow the regime to claim that the legislature is not completely dominated by the party. The self-nominees allow the regime to claim that anyone, in theory, could become a delegate. In addition, reform advocates within the VNA stress the importance of the self-nominees for increasing the degree of choice for voters. Former VNA Office vice-chair Nguyen Sy Dung, for example, has argued that "democracy not only depends on the percentage of self-nominees elected, but also depends more on the ability to choose. If there are more self-nominees then voters will have the more opportunities to choose."[7] However, the number of non-party members in the legislature has never exceeded 15 percent and in 2016 actually dropped to its lowest point since 1976, to less than 5 percent (see figure 4.2 in chapter 4 for details). Furthermore, the number of self-nominees elected has always been negligible. The vetting process is responsible for this.

Vetting: "The Party Nominates, the People Vote"

As has been summarized elsewhere, Vietnam uses a "five gates" system of vetting (Malesky and Schuler 2009; Koh 2006; Salomon 2007).[8] The five gates are the five steps involved in whittling down the list of candidates. The vetting process was first formalized in the 1992 Election Law but was used informally in elections prior to 1992.[9] As this section shows, the vetting process affords the VNASC, through the Central Election Commission, a great deal of power to ensure that the election outcome aligns with its goals. Provincial election boards also have a large degree of power to ensure that election outcomes achieve the desired results.

CENTRAL VERSUS LOCAL NOMINEES

Candidates have two paths to securing nomination. Since the 1992 Electoral Law was implemented, Vietnamese electoral laws have stipulated two types of delegates: central nominees and provincial nominees.[10] The distinction probably results from the fact that from its earliest days, the legislature was supposed to represent all elements of society and the government (S. D. Nguyen 2017, 42–53). Therefore, ensuring that provincial as well as central officials were represented required dividing the task of nominating candidates between central and local election boards.

The central-local distinction is important for the discussion of the vetting process, as the process operates slightly differently for the two sets of candidates. As the following sections show, the central party can more directly influence the nomination of centrally nominated candidates than provincially nominated candidates. The distinction is also important because it affords the central party officials greater control over the nomination of a subset of the candidates. This has important implications for the types of delegates selected to leadership positions and the all-important VNASC, as these are almost exclusively drawn from the centrally nominated candidates.

GATE I: FIRST NEGOTIATION—SETTING THE STRUCTURE

The first step in the vetting, and in many ways the most important, is the "first negotiation" (*hiệp thương*). As previously mentioned, during this step the VNASC sets the structure of the legislature it wants to see elected. While no names are put forward, the first negotiation results in a list of various demographic groups and organizations that will be represented. In 2007, for example, after the first negotiation, the VNASC determined that the VNA should include 150 women, 50 non-party members, 70 delegates under forty years old, and 160 incumbents (Malesky and Schuler 2009, 29). The structure also provides detailed targets for how many members of the Fatherland Front, the government, and the local party apparatus should be selected.

To achieve these targets, the VNASC tasks the provinces with responsibility for meeting different parts of the quota. For example, a province with six delegates will likely be asked to elect two centrally nominated delegates as well as a "notable leader" (*lãnh đạo chủ chốt*) and one of the groups mentioned by the VNASC. One of the issues the structure creates, as noted later, is that it interferes with the ability of self-nominees to win election. If the structure is preplanned, then where do self-nominees who may not fit the province's quota fit in?

This is a concern raised by VNA officials such as Vu Mao.[11] Some have advocated doing away with the structure or at least reducing it, so that 5–10 percent of the seats will be reserved for those nominated outside the structure.[12] Others have suggested that having such a hard structure not only limits the ability of self-nominees to win but undermines democracy itself.

As the late professor Phan Dinh Dieu said: "We should not nominate delegates according to a preplanned structure. If we want a structure, we must find a solution through the negotiation meetings and election campaigns to get the desired structure."[13]

Finally, some suggest that this structure hinders the very representative quality of the legislature in the first place. As Nguyen Sy Dung argues, it effectively turns representation into a lottery, in that a given district, depending on its assigned structure, may be represented by a model worker or an actor regardless of the underlying demographics of the district (S. D. Nguyen 2017). Despite these criticisms, while the types of qualities the structure calls for have varied from election to election, the institution of preplanning a structure has not.

GATE 2: SECOND NEGOTIATION—INTRODUCING THE DELEGATES

Once the first negotiation is complete and the ideal structure is set, the organizations allotted positions in the VNA within the structure are tasked with nominating individual candidates for those positions. To ensure that there is competition for seats, an organization may be tasked with nominating more than one candidate. It is also at this stage that self-nominees (who are not accounted for in the structure) are allowed to submit their applications to run for election. The second negotiation therefore announces the names of the individuals who have successfully completed their applications to run for a VNA seat. As an example, in 2016 Hanoi's second negotiation resulted in eighty-seven candidates, thirty-nine "introduced" (*được giới thiệu*) and forty-eight self-nominated (*tự ứng cử*). One of these self-nominees was noted political activist Nguyen Quang A.[14]

GATES 3 AND 4: MEETING WITH CONSTITUENTS AND MEETING
WITH COWORKERS

After the second negotiation, two meetings are held to assess the qualifications (*tiêu chuẩn*) of the candidate and vote on whether the candidate meets the criteria.[15] For those nominated by a party or state office, one set of meetings is with the coworkers of that nominee. Both the self-nominees and the introduced delegates must also participate in a meeting with neighborhood voters. It is at this stage that many self-nominees are removed from consideration, as the party can decide whom to invite to these meetings and exert pressure on the attendees to vote against candidates the party does not want to run.

For instance, it was at the meeting with local constituents that political activist Nguyen Quang A's nomination was effectively terminated, as his neighbors voted against him sixty-nine to six. The party is able to exert influence over these meetings by controlling the time of day the meeting is held and selectively inviting certain individuals to the meeting. Nguyen Quang A suggested in that meeting that the participants were heavily supportive of the party: "The representatives of the voters at that meeting probably had no information sources outside of *Nhan Dan* [The people's daily], the television, or the party front organizations. Therefore, they likely received very bad information about me."[16]

To assess this possibility, I have used data collected in a survey by the UNDP, which asked whether citizens participated in one of these meetings (UNDP 2017). Tables 2.1 and 2.2 illustrate whether party membership or affiliation in one of the party's united front mass organizations determines participation in the meetings. Table 2.1 shows the raw totals in the survey for the number of citizens in these groups.[17] The survey results show that members of mass organizations and the party are more likely to be invited and to attend the meetings than are the unaffiliated. Combined, party members and mass organization members make up 53 percent of those surveyed, but 64 percent of the total invited and 68 percent of the total in attendance. The unaffiliated make up 47 percent of the total population, 36 percent of those invited, and 32 percent of those in attendance.

Because affiliation is correlated with other factors that could determine participation, such as gender, age, income, and education, table 2.2 examines participation in the meetings in a multivariate regression analysis. Results from the ordinary least squares (OLS) and probit models, controlling for these individual level factors, confirm that regime affiliation is a strong determinant of being invited to and participating in the meetings. Looking at model 3 in table 2.2, party members are 22 percent more likely to be invited than unaffiliated members, and mass organization members are 14 percent more likely. In short, these meetings are heavily influenced by those tied to the party. Further analysis confirms that this stage is an important choke point. As table 2.3 shows, most self-nominees fail. In each of the elections, less than 20 percent of those who self-nominated finally made it to the ballot, and far fewer managed to win election.

TABLE 2.1.
Overall attendance at candidate meetings with neighborhood voters.

	Total in country		Invited		Attended	
Mass organization	7,054	50.16%	4,098	59.24%	3,225	61.94%
Party member	1,616	11.49%	1,139	16.46%	1,162	22.32%
Mass org and/or party member*	7,469	53.11%	4,416	63.83%	3,536	67.91%
Unaffiliated	6,594	46.89%	2,502	36.17%	1,671	32.09%
Total participants	14,063		6,918		5,207	

*The third row is not the sum of the first two rows because some mass organization members are also party members. "Total participants" is the sum of the third and fourth rows.

Anecdotal evidence from previous elections shows that the demise of self-nominees is largely a function of the meetings with voters. In 2007 two dissidents, Cu Huy Ha Vu and Le Cong Dinh, decided to run. Other less controversial but nonetheless independent voices, such as former deputy minister of natural resources and environment Dang Hung Vo and outspoken Ho Chi Minh City People's Council member Dang Van Khoa, also attempted to run. In 2016 a number of high-profile candidates ran for office.

TABLE 2.2.
Determinants of attendance at candidate meetings with neighborhood voters.

Variables	Invited (Model 1)	Attended (Model 2)	Invited (Model 3)	Attended (Model 4)
Party member	0.711*	0.808*	0.228*	0.287*
	(0.0963)	(0.0949)	(0.0280)	(0.0305)
Mass organization member	0.382*	0.439*	0.135*	0.139*
	(0.0466)	(0.0496)	(0.0162)	(0.0155)
Controls	Yes	Yes	Yes	Yes
Region fixed effects	Yes	Yes	Yes	Yes
Career fixed effects	Yes	Yes	Yes	Yes
Constant	−2.245*	−2.591*	−0.265*	−0.301*
	(0.288)	(0.314)	(0.0933)	(0.0966)
Observations	13,039	13,039	13,039	13,039
R-squared			0.161	0.168

Models 1 and 2 are probit models; models 3 and 4 are linear probability.

The dependent variable (DV) in models 1 and 3 is whether or not a voter was invited to a meeting on People's Council or VNA candidate qualifications; for 2 and 3 the DV is attendance.

Standard errors in parentheses.

* = $p < 0.01$

TABLE 2.3.
Self-nominated candidates in the VNA.

Year	Valid applications	Got on ballot	Won election
2007	236	30	1
2011	83	15	4
2016	154	11	2

SOURCES: "11 Người tự ứng cử Quốc hội lọ qua vòng cuối," VNExpress, April 26, 2016, http://vnexpress.net/tin-tu/thoi-su/11-nguoi-tu-ung-cu-quoc-hoi-lot-qua-vong-cuoi-3393717.html; "4 Doanh nhân tự ứng cử trúng cử đại biểu Quốc hội," VNEconomy, June 3, 2011, http://vneconomy.vn/doanh-nhan/4-doanh-nhan-tu-ung-cu-trung-cu-dai-bieu-quoc-hoi-20110603112548667.htm; and "Hai ứng cử viên xin rút khỏi danh sách bầu đại biểu Quốc hội," VNEconomy, April 25, 2011, http://vneconomy.vn/thoi-su/hai-ung-cu-vien-xin-rut-khoi-danh-sach-bau-dai-bieu-quoc-hoi-20110425033334848.htm.

Two of these candidates, Ma Khoi and Nguyen Quang A, were invited by President Barack Obama to a meeting with human rights activists during his visit to Vietnam in May 2016.[18]

As table 2.4 shows, these notable candidates were culled from the ballot in the third gate. News reports and interviews suggest that the meetings with voters were stacked against these candidates, and local officials embarked on door-knocking campaigns to discredit the candidacies of the self-nominated candidates. Indeed, one commentator suggests that the neighborhood meetings are the "red line" preventing truly independent candidates such as Nguyen Quang A from succeeding in their nominations.[19]

GATE 5: THE THIRD NEGOTIATION—DETERMINING THE FINAL BALLOT

At the conclusion of the meetings with voters, the Fatherland Front organizes the third negotiation at the central and provincial levels to assess the results of the meetings with coworkers and voters. It then presents a final report on the evaluation of the candidates to the Central Election Commission and local election boards. The Central Election Commission uses this to determine the final list of candidates who will run in each province. It then sends this list to the provinces to determine the final ballot.

Central Election Commission

An examination of the vetting system shows that the Central Election Commission wields a great deal of power. Therefore, if the party is to influence

TABLE 2.4.
Well-known self-nominated candidates for the VNA.

Year	Candidate	Result
2007	Cu Huy Ha Vu	Failed to win 50% in meeting with voters.
	Le Cong Dinh	Failed to win 50% in meeting with voters.
	Dang Van Khoa	Withdrew name before meeting with voters.
	Dang Hung Vo	Withdrew name before meeting with voters.
	Dang Le Nguyen Vu	Lost election.
2016	Ma Khoi	Failed to win 50% in meeting with voters.
	Nguyen Quang A	Failed to win 50% in meeting with voters.

the selection of candidates, it needs to control this institution. The 2015 Election Law stipulates that the VNA is to select the Central Electoral Commission. However, as is true of many laws in Vietnam, how that is to be done is not clarified. In practice, this means that the VNASC introduces a Central Election Commission chair for the VNA to consider, who then introduces a slate of candidates for the election board. The VNA can then vote up or down on this list.[20] The 2015 election board was led by the outgoing VNA chair, Nguyen Sinh Hung. The four deputy chairs included the deputy chair of the VNA, the country's vice president, the deputy prime minister, and the chair of the Fatherland Front.[21]

The issue of party control over the Central Election Commission was discussed in the debates on the 2013 Constitution, as this was the first time the commission was mentioned in the constitution. Previously, the Central Election Commission was only mentioned in the Election Laws. The stated reason for the inclusion of the Election Commission in the constitution rather than in the law was to "promote democracy and ensure the objectivity of the electoral process."[22] One delegate, Huynh Van Ti, objected to this formulation because it implied that previous elections were "not objective." He argued: "We have had 13 National Assembly and People's Council elections. All the National Assembly and People's Council elections in the past have been democratic and objective, so why use this reason to include the Election Commission?"[23] Others, such as Danh Ut, agreed, suggesting that past elections had gone perfectly fine, so the VNASC should remain in control of naming the election commission.[24] While his argument may appear overly defensive of the previous elections, it does contain a kernel of truth. If the previous election laws had allowed the Standing Committee to set up the election board, how would allowing the VNA to elect it, when the VNASC would likely be in charge of nominating the candidates, substantially change things?

The key reason the Central Election Commission remains dominated by the VNASC is that despite the constitutional change, the 2013 Constitution only states that the commission should be elected by the VNA; it does not stipulate how the candidates should be introduced or voted on. The 2015 Election Law, which clarified these elements, states that the VNA will elect the Central Election Commission chair, who will then nominate candidates for the rest of the board for the VNA to approve. In practice, this gives the VNASC agenda-setting power once again, thus rendering the changes in the 2013 Constitution and 2015 Election Law largely cosmetic. Indeed, the composition of the 2016 Election Commission was virtually identical to the commission that preceded it in 2011.

Regarding the power of the Election Commission, another set of institutions that influences the electoral process is the provincial election boards. Like the Central Election Commission, these provincial electoral boards are not independent of the local power structure. However, in the case of the election boards, they are appointed at the discretion of the provincial People's Committee (the provincial government apparatus), not the provincial People's Council (the provincial legislative body). Therefore, the decisions of the commission are likely driven by the interests of the provincial government and party leaders (S. D. Nguyen 2017).

The provincial boards can influence the division of election districts. While the Central Election Commission has the final approval, Article 10 of the 2015 Election Law notes that the commission approves the districts proposed (*đề nghị*) by the province. The ability to create districts is important because this gives the provincial officials the ability to decide which candidates will compete against each other in a given electoral district. As Nguyen Sy Dung notes, provincial election boards can use this power to tilt the elections in favor of preferred candidates (2017, 52–53).

Provincial boards also influence the selection of the locally nominated candidates and their district assignments. Although provinces must follow the general guidelines set up by the VNASC and the Central Election

Commission, the provincial election board and the provincial offices have influence over the individuals that who fill these roles. Combined with their ability to create election districts, the power to select candidates also gives local officials the ability to tilt the scales in favor of preferred candidates by selecting and appointing weak candidates to compete against preferred candidates. Critically, the degree to which they do so undermines the degree of information and competition in the elections. The next section assesses whether local officials do in fact use their power for these ends.

Possibilities for Manipulation

The preceding analysis shows that under the electoral laws, the party can intervene at several stages to tilt the outcome of the election in favor of preferred candidates. The most important stage, of course, is the ability of the VNASC to set the structure of the legislature. By guaranteeing that a majority of the legislature will be party members, it secures control over the legislature.

However, even within those parameters, it is possible that dissidents or malcontents might slip through the cracks. This could be damaging for the party, as these delegates might disrupt the "public transcript" that the party is unified. It might also afford opponents of the regime a chance to mobilize support. An example can be seen in Egypt, where the Muslim Brotherhood used the opportunity to win seats in the legislature prior to Mubarak's fall as a way to mobilize greater support (Loidolt and Mecham 2013). However, the preceding review shows that the vetting process ensures such potential dissidents may be spotted and removed at an early stage.

A final, more practical concern for the regime is not simply to eliminate the candidates it does not want, but also to ensure the victory of the candidates it *does* want to win. As discussed in the next chapter, even before the first negotiation, the legislative leadership and the party have an idea of whom they want to lead the legislature. Nearly all legislative leaders are centrally nominated by the Office of the VNA. It is therefore important that these delegates win seats if the resulting legislature is to conform to plan. In addition to ensuring that the legislature functions as it should, the elections also should fulfill an important propaganda function for the party. Also competing in the elections are other high-ranking party members, such as the members of the Politburo and Central Committee. For these high-ranking candidates, elections should demonstrate that citizens overwhelmingly back the regime's top leaders.

How, then, does the regime ensure that these candidates win support even when there is competition? Nguyen Sy Dung (2017, 43) suggests that the local election officials "have many ways" to ensure that preferred candidates, such as centrally nominated candidates, win.[25] As occurs in China (Wang 2017), one possible way of securing victory is to nominate "accompanying" candidates to compete against preferred candidates in a given electoral district. Because of provincial control over local candidate selection and placement, the local leadership can decide which candidates compete against one another. These "accompanying" candidates, which I less euphemistically refer to as "sacrificial lambs," are essentially supposed to lose.

To assess whether these sacrificial lamb candidates are used in this way, I have examined the most recent VNA elections to see if powerful candidates are systematically run in districts with weaker competition. The obvious challenge in conducting this test is that it is difficult to create an observable measure of what a "weak candidate" should look like. It is possible that in different local conditions, a weak candidate may look different. In the context of Vietnam, one group of candidates that should be easily observable as sacrificial lambs are *district-level* party officials. District-level party officials hold essentially the same position as provincial-level party officials, except they are the heads of subordinate geographic units. Facing a choice, voters who do not like the provincial leader would have to select a district official, who was most likely appointed by the provincial leader the voters do not like. This places voters in a bind and leaves them with essentially no option.

Another option for electioneering is to avoid having strong candidates run against each other. In particular, if voters prefer candidates such as members of the Politburo or VCP Central Committee, who have greater name recognition and organizational connections, then one way to give an advantage to those candidates is to ensure that they do not run against each other. If, on the other hand, the purpose of elections is to engage in a tournament-like competition, in which election results reveal the relative popularity of these candidates, they should run against each other.

It is also difficult to assess a "strong" candidate. However, similar to the previous analysis, some indicators of what one would assume to be the regime's preferred delegates can be used to assess whether these candidates

should run against each other. To test whether the regime uses these strategies, I collected the biographies and results of all 2,572 candidates for the
VNA in the three elections since 2007.[26] The published lists include the
names of the candidates, the list of the districts, the careers of the candidates, their incumbency status, their party status, and their hometowns. By
examining their careers, I have been able to assess whether or not the candidates are also members of the VCP Politburo or Central Committee. The
lists also show whether or not the candidate was a member of the provincial
party committee. In addition to the candidate lists, I also obtained the list
of candidates nominated by central as opposed to provincial institutions.

This list has allowed me to create the three primary independent variables of interest for the analysis: *central committee, centrally nominated,* and
provincial party secretariat. In addition, I have created a number of other
control variables such as *party member, male, minority, incumbent, education*
(0 = no college; 1 = bachelor's; 2 = master's; 3 = PhD). I have also generated
several important career variables such as *business candidate, military,* and
fatherland front, the last of which assesses whether or not the candidate is a
member of Vietnam's mass organization.

The key dependent variable for the analysis is the quality of the other
candidates in a given candidate's district. If the information theory holds,
we should either see candidates of equal strength facing off against each
other or at the very least, no relationship. However, if the goal of the election
is to signal strength, we should see the preferred candidates run against
weaker candidates. Therefore, I have conducted two analyses. The first
creates a measure of election district strength, which I label the district's
power ranking.[27] To construct the measure, I tallied points for other candidates in the district depending on whether they possess qualities that could
heighten their chance of election. In particular, I added a point for another
candidate's Politburo status, Central Committee status, party membership,
provincial party committee membership, and central nomination status. I
subtracted the candidate's own status along these measures from the district total so that the ranking measures only the power of the opposing
candidates. Based on this measure, the distribution ranges from 0, meaning no other candidate has any of these qualities, to 9, the maximum observed value.

The second variable is the sacrificial lamb variable, which is a measure of
weak candidates who are set up to lose. As I suggested previously, the most

TABLE 2.5.
Impact of candidate quality on electioneering, election results.

Variables	Power ranking (Model 1)	Sacrificial lambs (Model 2)
Centrally nominated	–1.092* (0.0978)	0.306* (0.0519)
Central Committee member	–0.475* (0.108)	0.0915 (0.061)
Provincial party secretariat	–0.440* (0.0782)	0.168* (0.0394)
Controls	Yes	Yes
Constant	5.289* (0.218)	0.526* (0.108)
Observations	2,568	2,568
R-squared	0.149	0.088

NOTE: OLS results with robust standard errors are in parentheses; power ranking is the strength of other candidates in a given candidate's electoral district. Sacrificial lambs are the number of lower-ranking candidates in a given candidate's electoral district.
* $p < 0.01$

obvious types of candidates are district-level officials. These candidates offer no differentiation from provincial or national-level party members but are lower ranking. Therefore, they should have less name recognition and less capability to bring home resources for the district. As such, they should be at a disadvantage compared to the preferred candidates: central committee, centrally nominated, and provincial party secretariat.

To conduct the analysis, I ran OLS regressions using all the returns on the power-ranking measure and the sacrificial lamb measure. If the manipulation strategy is used, we should see the strong candidates systematically facing weaker candidates. The results in models 1 and 2 in table 2.5 show clearly that the preferred candidates are selected into weaker districts. Model 1 shows that the centrally nominated candidates, central committee members, and provincial party officials are less likely to face powerful opponents. Furthermore, model 2 shows centrally nominated candidates and provincial party secretaries are more likely to face sacrificial lamb candidates.[28]

Campaigns

The preceding analyses suggest that the regime can employ a number of strategies to ensure that the election proceeds according to plan. Another critical piece of the puzzle worthy of note are the restrictions on campaigns. Campaigns are particularly important in autocratic regimes, because they enable less well-known opposition candidates to make up for name recognition disadvantages versus incumbents. Greene (2011) shows that in Mexico's posttransition elections, campaigns resulted in increased support for the conservative party due to low levels of precampaign awareness of its policies. Other researchers show that laws increasing campaign spending in Mexico primarily benefited opposition parties because they increased awareness of the opposition parties, while voters were already familiar with the PRI (Larreguy, Marshall, and Snyder 2016).

Similarly, in the United States the effect of campaigns and the party label is greatest in lower-level elections, where uncertainty is the greatest. As Kam and Zechmeister suggest: "In such [low information] contexts where voters are almost blindly casting around for their best guess as to their preferred candidate, cues matter" (2013, 972). As such, the more opposition candidates are allowed to campaign, the better they perform.

Vietnam, like other single-party regimes, is particularly restrictive about campaigns. First, certain institutionally driven logistical factors limit campaigns. These take the form of the limited time between when the ballot is finalized and election day. The 2015 Election Law stipulates that the ballot must only be finalized thirty days before the election, which gives voters about a month to acquaint themselves with the candidates.

More important, the electoral code explicitly bars candidates from raising money or organizing campaign rallies. Although delegates debated this portion of the law extensively in 2015,[29] the 2015 Election Law allows only two forms of electoral campaigns activities. First, delegates may participate in meetings with voters organized by the Fatherland Front. Second, they may participate in campaign activities through the state-run mass media.[30] Article 67 of the law further stipulates that the candidates are only allowed to answer questions from provincial state-run media outlets in their districts or through the National Election website. Furthermore, their comments should reflect what they would do if elected, with the implication being that they will not attack other candidates.

Restricting campaigns to these two forms means that candidates cannot use private funds or social media to mobilize personal support. Although some delegates note that this may limit the knowledge about the candidates among voters,[31] VNA delegates have defended the stipulation by suggesting it ensures the fairness and competitiveness of the election, with the implication that richer candidates will take advantage of looser campaign restrictions. Au Thi Mai, for example, argued: "To ensure fair competition in the election campaign, I propose that the draft law should include an additional stipulation: . . . candidates should not participate in any fundraisers."[32] In short, while restrictions on campaigns limit the competitiveness of elections, few in the VNA have seriously debated changing these restrictions.

Conclusion

This chapter summarizes some of the basic features and functioning of the Vietnamese electoral system. While the chapter stresses the limits on competition, it is worth noting that in comparison to other communist countries, Vietnam's system is quite open. There are more candidates than seats. Furthermore, in contrast to China, citizens vote directly for their representatives. However, the analysis shows that within this framework, the election laws give the VNASC and the party leadership a number of levers to ensure that the outcome conforms to their expectations. Perhaps just as important, the possibility of electoral manipulation and limits on campaigns may dampen enthusiasm for participation. While the regime lauds the high degree of turnout in elections, the actual meaning of that turnout remains suspect. This is important because the voter-politician linkage is a crucial factor underpinning the citizen information theory of authoritarian legislative politics. Chapter 6 examines this link in greater detail.

THREE

"Unconditional Party Government"
Legislative Organization in the VNA

Chapter 2 examined the electoral system, focusing on the ways the party controls the system to ensure that only regime-preferred candidates win seats. This chapter focuses on legislative organization. As chapter 2 showed, the VNA Standing Committee (VNASC) is an important institution within the VNA, almost operating as a legislature within a legislature. Therefore, appointment to this body is critical. In addition to the VNASC, other hierarchies in the VNA impact how the legislature operates, such as full-time delegates and permanent committees. This chapter discusses the powers of each of these subsets of delegates and how delegates are appointed to these positions.

As this chapter shows, the best way to summarize legislative organization in Vietnam is as "unconditional party government." Building on a theory of "conditional party government" developed to explain party control of legislatures in democracies (Aldrich 1995), this chapter represents the VNA as a case of unconditional party government in which the party controls the legislative agenda through the overwhelming control of the VNASC. This power is "unconditional" in the sense that it does not depend on variance in the degree of unity within the legislative party delegation. Rather, VNASC unity in the assembly is enforced and dominance over proceedings is imposed by the central party leadership.

To demonstrate this characterization, I first review the organization of the VNA, focusing in particular on how delegates are selected to the VNASC and other full-time positions. I then discuss the institutions' involvement in legislation and oversight, showing the degree to which the VNASC sets the agenda and controls the proceedings. I also describe an example of the lawmaking process and how it can go awry, using the case of the failed 2018 Special Economic Zone Law. As the chapter makes clear, even in the case of the failed law, the central party leadership exerts dominant control over the VNA agenda through its proxies in the VNASC.

Legislative Organization in the VNA: Unconditional Party Government

Figure 3.1 provides an overview of how the VNA is organized. At the top is the eighteen-member VNASC, which includes a VNA chair, four deputy chairs, and three staff positions held by unelected officials. The VNASC also includes the chairs of the ten permanent committees in the VNA. Within each of the ten permanent committees there are three to five deputy chairs, some additional full-time members, and a larger number of part-time delegates. Finally, in the 2016–2021 VNA there are sixty-two part-time delegates who are not members of any committee. The next section summarizes the role each subset of delegates plays, paying close attention to the mechanisms of party control.

POWERS AND SELECTION OF THE VNASC

As with elections, the most important institution in the VNA with regard to lawmaking and oversight is the VNASC. The VNASC is an eighteen-member body (the exact size and composition depends on a decision by the previous VNASC) that includes the VNA chair, the VNA deputy chairs, and the chairs of the ten permanent committees. The permanent committees, which exist based on the Law on the Organization of the National Assembly, are responsible for substantive issue areas such as finance, education, and defense. The VNASC has sweeping powers over the legislative agenda and the structure of the VNA itself (see table 3.1 for a description of these powers). These include the ability to set the agenda for the two, month-long VNA plenary sessions that occur each year. They also include the ability to set up a special investigation committee, call a vote of confidence, determine the legislative calendar, and set up the electoral commission.

In addition to its powers, the VNASC also derives influence from meeting more regularly than the full VNA. While the full VNA is relatively active

Standing Committee (18 Members)

VNA Chair

Deputy VNA Chairs (4) — Chair Office of VNA* (1) — Delegate Liaison* (1) — Mobilization Chair* (1)

	Finance Comm	Culture Comm	Defense Comm	Econ Comm	Ethnic Affairs	Foreign Affairs	Justice Comm	Legislative Comm	Science Comm	Social Affairs
Chair	Chair(1)	Chair(1)	Chair(1)	Chair(1)	Chair(1)	Chair(1)	Chair(1)	Chair(1)	Chair(1)	Chair(1)
D. Chair	D. Chair (4)	D. Chair (4)	D. Chair (3)	D. Chair (3)	D. Chair (3)	D. Chair (4)	D. Chair (4)	D. Chair (3)	D. Chair (5)	D. Chair (4)
Full-Time Members	Full-Time Members (8)	Full-Time Members (13)	Full-Time Members (9)	Full-Time Members (10)	Full-Time Members (8)	Full-Time Members (10)	Full-Time Members (8)	Full-Time Members (17)	Full-Time Members (10)	Full-Time Members (21)
Part-Time Members	Part-Time Members (32)	Part-Time Members (27)	Part-Time Members (29)	Part-Time Members (28)	Part-Time Members (30)	Part-Time Members (17)	Part-Time Members (25)	Part-Time Members (21)	Part-Time Members (25)	Part-Time Members (24)

Part-Time Non-Committee Members (62)

Full-Time Delegates
176 Members

Part-Time Delegates
330 Members

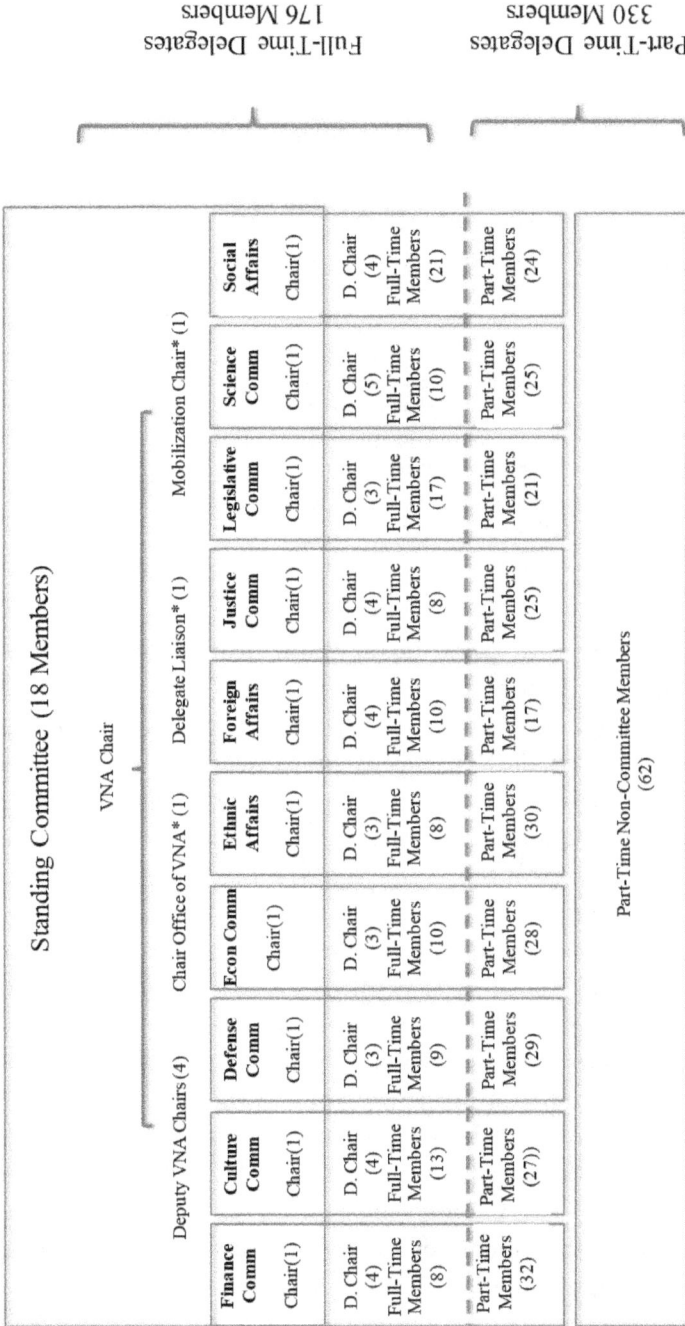

FIGURE 3.1. Structure of the VNA, 2016.

TABLE 3.1.
Powers of the VNA Standing Committee.*

Feature	Power
Agenda control	VNASC determines length of session, which ministers are queried, which laws are debated; which laws voted on; which amendments are considered
Special investigations	VNASC determines whether special committees to investigate government affairs will be set up.
Vote of confidence	VNASC decides whether to approve a petition from the VNA to hold a vote of confidence. This only applies to government leaders.
Professionalization	VNASC members are full-time members of the VNA, unlike 72 percent of assembly members, who are part time.
Meeting times	VNASC meets regularly between full VNA plenary sessions. It may pass directives and hold query sessions at those times.
Legislation	VNASC can issue resolutions when the full VNA is not in session; its resolutions carry the weight of law.
Role in election	VNASC runs the Election Board, which vets candidates and sets the structure for the next VNA.

*Nongovernment, local officials, Central Party Committee leaders.

compared to other single-party legislatures, it is still only in session two months of the year. In between these full meetings, the VNASC conducts additional meetings. For example, in 2015, while the full VNA met for a total of seventy-five days, the VNASC met for ten additional sessions, totaling fifty-three days, between the full VNA sessions.[1] During these meetings the VNASC conducts additional meetings with the government on legislation, conducts query sessions, and plans the agenda for upcoming VNA sessions.

While this overwhelming power would be unusual in a democracy, in theory it need not preclude the VNA from being conceived of as representing the interests of its members. If VNASC members are selected in an open and competitive process that incorporates a variety of organizations and actors, then the VNA may be accountable to its membership. This has implications for the theoretical arguments surrounding the purpose of single-party legislatures. For example, the VNA may serve to protect elite interests if important actors not already represented in the VCP Central Committee are included in the VNASC. Party member business owners, leading members of the mass organizations not included in the VCP Central Committee, and other important local elites keen to protect their interests could, for example, be given a leading role in the legislature. In addition, the legislature could include those who have won large vote shares or non-party member or self-nominated candidates, thus suggesting that the VNASC, and by extension the VNA, indirectly incorporates the views of society in its decisions (Malesky and Schuler 2013).

The degree to which the VNA is likely to perform these functions depends in large part on how the VNASC is chosen. Institutionally speaking, selection to the VNASC is determined by the outgoing VNASC. While the VNA officially votes for the VNASC, because the VNASC nominates the candidates that the VNA must approve through an up or down vote, this effectively grants the VNASC control over selection. If the VNA did oppose the slate of candidates, the VNASC would simply put together a new list.

With this in mind, whom do the VNASC and the VNA choose? Of course the VNASC can only nominate candidates from the pool of elected delegates. Table 3.2 lists the descriptive statistics and features of the VNA delegates discussed here. As it shows, the VNA in each of the three sessions examined in the following discussion includes about 31–36 percent centrally nominated candidates, 8–10 percent from the VCP Central Committee, 34–37 percent provincial party leaders, 3–8 percent non-party members, 2–5 percent businesspeople, and a handful of self-nominated candidates.

With this pool of candidates in mind, if the VCP were looking to create an inclusive legislature representative of citizen interests, it might seek to include non-party members, business leaders, self-nominees, or other locally nominated delegates in the legislative leadership. However, if the party were looking to create a lever of control, it would instead pack the VNASC

TABLE 3.2.
Composition of the VNA, 2007–2021.

	2007–2011		2011–2016		2016–2021	
	Total	Percent*	Total	Percent*	Total	Percent*
Centrally nominated	155	31.5	173	34.6	178	35.9
Central Committee	40	8.1	46	9.2	50	10.1
Provincial party leaders	169	34.3	180	36.0	181	36.5
Non-party members	42	8.5	41	8.2	19	3.8
Businesspeople	16	3.3	24	4.8	12	2.4
Self-nominated	1	0.2	4	0.8	2	0.4
Total delegates	492		500		496	

*The groups in the table are neither mutually exclusive nor collectively exhaustive, so the percentages in the table do not add up to 100%.

TABLE 3.3.
Composition of the VNASC, 2007–2016.

	2007		2011		2016	
	Total	Percent	Total	Percent	Total	Percent
Centrally nominated	18	100	18	100	17	94
Central Committee	16	89	14	78	18	100
Provincial Party leaders	3	17	1	6	1	6
Non-party members	0	0	0	0	0	0
Businesspeople	0	0	0	0	0	0
Self-nominated	0	0	0	0	0	0
Total members*	18		18		18	

The different groups are neither mutually exclusive nor collectively exhaustive. For instance, some centrally nominated delegates are also members of the Central Committee. Therefore, the numbers in the rows do not add up to the total number in the VNASC.

with Central Committee members, who would have far more influence and ability to protect their private interests in the party institutions than in the legislature. Furthermore, membership in the Central Committee could ensure that VNASC leaders are aware of the party line before the VNA meets. Indeed, as discussed later in the chapter, the Central Committee typically meets before the VNASC plans the schedule for a VNA plenary session.

Table 3.3 shows the composition of the VNASC based on the positions the officials held when they were nominated to the VNASC. As it makes clear, nearly all of the VNASC members from 2007 onward were centrally nominated. Furthermore, the VNASC is almost entirely made up of VCP Central Committee members. By contrast, the VNASC includes no non-party members, businesspeople, or self-nominees. With regard to vote share, previous analysis shows that vote totals also do not predict selection into the VNASC (Malesky and Schuler 2013). In addition, only a handful of the VNASC were previously provincial party leaders. What this suggests is that the VNASC is an institution clearly controlled by the VCP center.

POWERS AND SELECTION OF FULL-TIME DELEGATES

Aside from the VNASC, the VNA features another important source of hierarchy, which is the difference between full-time and part-time delegates. Prior to the 2014 Law on the Organization of the VNA, the number of full-time delegates was entirely up to the VNASC. While the VNASC still has some discretion on the upper limit for these delegates, the law now states that the VNA must contain a minimum of 30 percent full-time members.[2] According to the law, full-time delegates are required to spend all of their time working as legislators, while part-time delegates are required to re- serve one-third of their time for legislative duties. Currently, full-time dele- gates make up 34 percent of the legislature. In practice, what the distinction means is that about one-third of the legislature is either permanently in Ha- noi working on one of the permanent committees described her or staffing provincial legislative offices. The other two-thirds only work as legislators during the two, month-long legislative sessions in Hanoi.

As figure 3.1 shows, the VNA has ten permanent committees.[3] Each com- mittee has a chair and several deputy chairs, who are also full-time delegates. The duties of these committees include collecting opinions on legislation assigned to them by the VNASC and conducting oversight on government performance in areas falling within their jurisdiction. In terms of member- ship, not all members of the VNA are members of a committee. About sixty VNA members (mostly part-time delegates) are not members of any com- mittees. Many high-ranking party members of the Politburo and govern- ment ministers, for example, are neither full-time legislators nor members of the permanent committees. Regarding the structure of the permanent committees, each committee has a chair, several deputy chairs, and a num- ber of full-time delegates who are also committee members. According to most commentators, the chairs and deputy chairs perform most of the work in the committees (Harrington, McDorman, and Nielson 1998).

Full-time delegates, therefore, are critical for the theoretical purpose the VNA is supposed to serve. From a power-sharing perspective, if full-time members are chosen from the ranks of the bureaucracy, this may help ensure that different stakeholders in the party and state are represented, in order to check the party center from dictating policy. From the information perspec- tive, the locally nominated full-time delegates are critical. As previous work shows, full-time locally nominated delegates are more likely to speak on the floor of the VNA (Malesky and Schuler 2010). Furthermore, they are tasked with having a closer linkage with citizens. As such, if any delegate is going to channel citizen information, it should be these delegates.

By contrast, if the legislature is to serve a more technocratic, rationalizing function, we would expect to see it staff the full-time committee positions with centrally nominated officials selected by the party. Furthermore, the locally nominated full-time delegates should be selected from among the ranks of the provincial party elite rather than be nominated by citizens.

Table 3.4 shows the types of delegates selected into these different positions. First, it is worth noting that no self-nominees and almost no non-party members are selected for either position. As such, there is strict political control of the full-time delegates. Second, with regard to the full-time, centrally nominated delegates, the Office of the VNA handpicks all the delegates from outside the central party and government leadership. This suggests that the Office of the VNA basically selects experts in key fields, which it appoints to committees to help streamline the legislative process. In short, this selection process is consistent with the rationalization strategy.

Table 3.4 shows that nearly all of the full-time, locally nominated delegates are members of the provincial party leadership. Furthermore, none of these delegates are self-nominated or non-party members. Again, as with the VNASC, this shows that the delegates with the most institutional power are also those most tightly linked to the local party apparatus.

The locally nominated full-time delegates face an additional degree of control. Even after being selected, they are formally given a position as deputy delegation leader. The provincial delegation, discussed later in the chapter, includes all delegates elected from a given province. Importantly, the delegation leader is typically the highest-ranking party member in the provincial delegation and *not* the full-time legislative position. What this

TABLE 3.4.
Selection to full-time positions in the VNA, 2007–2016.

	Full-time central*		Full-time local	
	Total	Percent	Total	Percent
Office of the VNA nominated	219	100	0	0.00
Central Committee	3	1.37	5	2.49
Provincial Party Committee	20	9.13	132	65.67
Central Party leaders	0	0.00	0	0.00
Non-party members	2	0.91	0	0
Businesspeople	3	1.37	1	0.50
Self-nominated	0	0.00	0	0.00
Total delegates	219		201	

*Does not include members of the VNASC. The groups are neither mutually exclusive nor collectively exhaustive, so they do not add up to the total delegates numbers in the last row.

means is that full-time, locally nominated legislators are under the direct supervision of the provincial party leadership.

In practice, the full-time, locally nominated delegate is not likely to speak against the wishes of the provincial party apparatus, an observation confirmed by a former VNA official (D. S. Nguyen 2017). Furthermore, because other positions in the province tend to be more lucrative than the role of permanent member of the VNA, this delegate is likely to behave in a manner that will ensure his or her promotion to another provincial position. In short, while this position may be justified by the VCP as a way to increase citizen input, in practice the provincial party leadership exerts strong control over its selection and subsequent activity.

PERMANENT COMMITTEES

As the preceding sections discuss, the VNASC and the full-time delegates have overwhelming power within the VNA. The VNASC is also closely linked to the party center, which gives the party control over the VNA's proceedings. Given that the chairs of each of the ten permanent committees are members of the VNASC and tightly linked to the party, this means that the chairs provide strong control over the permanent committees. Nonetheless, because these committees are granted substantive areas of control, it is worth considering whether they serve to rationalize lawmaking or provide genuine, bottom-up information.

The VNA has included permanent committees since the 1960 Law on the Organization of the VNA. That early law only established a Legislative Committee and a Budget and Planning Committee, though the VNA was allowed to set up other committees as it saw fit.[4] The 1981 revision to the law expanded the number of committees to seven,[5] and a 2007 amendment expanded the number to the ten we see today.[6] A natural interpretation of this progression is that the expansion of committees follows from the party's greater need for information. However, an equally plausible interpretation is that the legislature needed greater technical expertise to manage the increasing number of laws as the country moved from a system based on government decrees to one based on laws.

One important clue to the role these committees play is how they are structured and who takes the most important roles within those committees. As figure 3.1 shows, each committee includes a chair, who is a member of the VNASC. As established in the previous section and supported by interviews with committee staffers,[7] the chair provides political control over the committee. The deputy chairs conduct much of the substantive work of the committees, which involves conducting investigations into government implementation of laws and providing input into legislation. The deputy chairs are critical precisely because they are full-time members of the committee, but not members of the VNASC, so that they have more time to research the issues before the committees.

Regarding selection of these individuals, the rationalization logic would suggest that these deputy chairs are chosen based on their technocratic expertise. Furthermore, they should be handpicked by the legislative leadership for their expertise. Alternatively, if the committees are designed to ensure that grassroots feedback impacts legislation, we should see, similar to in the United States (Adler and Lapinski 1997), the committee leaders coming from provinces most directly impacted by those issues.

An examination of the backgrounds of these deputy chairs reveals that the former logic applies. Instead of coming from provincially nominated candidates with strong electoral support, the deputy chairs are technocrats handpicked by the Office of the VNA prior to the election to serve on those committees. An example is the deputy chairs of the Economic Committee for the 2016–2021 session. The three deputy chairs are party members and were centrally nominated by the Office of the VNA, which suggests that they were tabbed ahead of time for the leadership positions they would hold. Furthermore, each had a technical background in the field of economic management. Duong Quoc Anh, for example, worked for twenty years in the State Bank of Vietnam.[8] The other deputy chairs, Nguyen Duc Kien and Nguyen Minh Son, also have experience working in economic development institutions with the party and the state. Kien, for example, worked in the Central Committee's Central Economic Commission for nearly a decade.[9] Son has a PhD in economics and worked as a staffer in the Office of the VNA's economic department.

These appointments are not particular to the Economic Committee. The other committees feature deputy chairs with similar profiles. Nguyen Minh Thuyet, mentioned in the introduction, was a deputy chair of the Culture, Education, and Youth Committee, which makes sense from the rationalization logic given his background as a party member and linguistics professor. In short, the deputy committee chairs, who are the workhorses of the committees, are not chosen for their grassroots connections. Rather, they are handpicked by the center for their technical expertise in a given issue area. Indeed, this objective is clearly emphasized by a former official from the Office of the VNA, who specifically argues that the VNA needs more technocratic expertise (D. S. Nguyen 2017).

VNA Legislative and Oversight Processes

Whereas the preceding section discusses the hierarchical organization of the VNA and how the leaders are selected, this section details how the VNA conducts its business. It looks in particular at how bills become laws and how the legislature conducts oversight. Consistent with the previous sections, it demonstrates that the VNASC and the full-time delegates have dominant influence over legislation and the content of the oversight hearings.

LAWMAKING AND THE LEGISLATIVE CALENDAR

In terms of the legislative calendar, while the VNA has the power to pass laws and amend the constitution, the law firmly grants the VNASC power to control which legislation is discussed and the content of the legislation. The Law on the Organization of the VNA stipulates that the VNA decides the agenda for the laws that will be debated in each session "based on the recommendations of the VNASC."[10] The May–June 2018 session provides an example of how this works in practice. Based on the schedule set by the VNASC, the morning of May 23 was set aside to debate both the schedule for laws to be considered in the next two VNA sessions and oversight activities. The afternoon of May 31 was reserved for debate in the full plenary session. In practice, this meant less than two hours of floor time was allocated to debate the legal schedule, allowing only fifteen delegates to speak. Eight days later, the entire VNA passed the resolution on the legal calendar by a vote of 437 of the 448 delegates. In short, the legislative agenda was largely set by the VNASC.

Evidence also supports the notion that the legal restrictions grant the VNASC extreme power over agenda control in practice. Despite the fact that the VNA has steadily increased its time in session, the legislature has actually cut back one of its regular hearings. Prior to its official opening, the VNA holds a "preparatory session" in which members discuss the VNASC's proposal for the schedule of debates for that session. According to a senior VNA official, prior to the May 2008 session, this meeting lasted a full morning.[11] However, due to the lack of debate in the sessions, the meeting was cut to thirty minutes. This suggests that in effect the topics of discussion within a given VNA session are decided in a top-down fashion.

This political control has kept some issues off the calendar. Some delegates, such as Duong Trung Quoc, have clamored for a Law on Associations and a Law on Protests to clarify the limits to the constitutional right to protest, as the police have clearly intervened in several cases of protests since the promulgation of the 2013 Constitution. [12] However, despite the desire in some quarters for such legislation, the law has so far not been debated because, as one delegate suggests, the government has not yet agreed upon the "fine line" between allowing protests and controlling them. Because it has not yet found the proper balance, the government is ultimately fearful of opening the issue up to public debate.[13] The VNASC, through its domination of the agenda, wields the power to keep these laws off the agenda.

The power of the VNASC over the legislative calendar also means that nearly all laws are drafted by the government. Although the Law on the Organization of the VNA gives individual delegates the ability to propose legislation,[14] in practice the government writes nearly all the draft laws, because individual delegates have few resources to draft their own legislation. Furthermore, even if they do manage to draft a law, the VNASC may oppose putting it on the agenda. This means that the delegate will have wasted considerable time and effort in a futile effort to have legislation put forward.

As an example of why few delegates attempt to initiate legislation, consider delegate Nguyen Thi Quoc Khanh's quixotic attempt to put forward a Law on Public Administration. With a small team, she wrote a draft numbering hundreds of pages, which she presented to the VNASC in 2017 and 2018. However, in each case the VNASC refused to put the law on the agenda for plenary debate and passage because it was deemed either unnecessary or in conflict with other laws. For this reason, the VNASC ultimately "highly praised her effort" but rejected it because it "overlapped with other legal codes."[15] Given Khanh's time and effort spent on a draft law that was never even debated, it is no wonder that others do not bother.

In sum, the VNASC, in line with the government and the party leadership, sets the legislative agenda. The key role of the legislature once the draft law is submitted is to "rationalize it" to ensure that it meets party guidelines and is consistent with other legal codes. The VNA is not intended to introduce new issues onto the agenda.

HOW A BILL BECOMES A LAW

VNASC dominance does not conclude with the setting of the agenda. Once bill is introduced, the VNASC still maintains strong control over its passage. According to the Law on the Promulgation of Legal Documents, for a law to be considered, it must first be included in the agenda for the upcoming year. Although individual VNA delegates can attempt to put laws on the schedule, the Ministry of Justice collects a list of law proposals from the ministries each year and, after coordinating with the Office of the Government, submits the list of proposed legislation to the VNASC. [16] If the VNASC approves the list, it is then submitted to the full VNA for a vote.

After the list of laws is set, the VNASC, in consultation with the Ministry of Justice, sets up a drafting committee for the legislation. According to the Law on the Promulgation of Legal Documents, the drafting committee for government-introduced legislation is led by the ministry and does not have to include any members of the legislature.[17] In terms of consultation, the drafting committee is required to garner opinions from "concerned agencies/organizations and the direct objects of the legal documents" in the form of written comments or workshops.[18] Upon completion of the drafting process and the comment process, the drafting agency then submits the draft to the Ministry of Justice for it to confirm the constitutionality and compliance of the law. If the Office of the Government and the Ministry of Justice approve the law for submission, they then send it to the VNASC prior to the opening of a plenary session.

Once the law reaches the VNASC, in coordination with the leadership of one of the permanent committees, it reviews the law in a VNASC meeting before the full plenary session. Only after this process does the full VNA see the law. The Law on the Promulgation of Legal Documents then stipulates that the full legislature must conduct at least one full hearing on the floor of the VNA prior to a vote on the legislation. In practice many laws are heard in two sessions, with the first session reserved for comments and the second session reserved for passage (after a chance for the VNA to provide additional comments). In addition, to give the VNA some time to prepare, the law must be submitted to the full legislature at least twenty days in advance of the session. In terms of the ability to introduce amendments, once again the VNASC plays a critical role. While the law does allow for separate majority votes on portions of the law "where different ideas still remain," such votes occur only at the "request of the VNASC."[19]

IS THERE ROOM FOR INPUT?

What, then, does the VNA substantively change during this process? Most often, bills proceed through the process in a relatively seamless fashion, with the full VNA hearing a bill twice before passing it with more high levels of support. However, bills sometimes explode on the floor of the VNA. While these instances are important in their own right, they also raise the possibility that the threat of a challenge could compel the government to seriously consider potential VNA objections, thus leading to major changes in legislation. A notable example of a law or project that did not proceed according to plan is the proposed Special Economic Zone Law, which was pulled in 2018 due to major public protests. Other examples are the 2008 decision to merge Ha Tay province with Hanoi and the 2010 proposed high-speed rail project linking Hanoi to Ho Chi Minh City. In the case of the Hanoi merger, the proposal was passed in 2008 despite an initial straw poll that reportedly showed a majority of delegates opposing the measure.[20] The same body then rejected the high-speed rail project in 2010. Do these cases demonstrate that the VNA provides more input than my theory suggests?

Although the remaining chapters provide more evidence, a cursory examination of these cases suggests the key reason for the different outcomes was the lack of unity within the party. In the case of the Hanoi merger, the party was united and able to overcome internal VNA opposition with 92 percent of the vote (Malesky, Schuler, and Tran 2011). By contrast, in the case of the high-speed rail project, the government tried to force the proposal through without winning consensus in the Politburo.[21] Therefore, as Koh suggests regarding the high-speed rail case: "The Political Bureau of the Vietnamese Communist Party still calls the shots. If it had felt that the project had to go ahead no matter what the cost, the politburo would have activated its marketing and mobilization agents to persuade the Assembly and the nation that the railway was essential to the country's interests."[22] Evidence provided later in this book, particularly in chapter 6, further supports the contention that the VNA serves at the behest of the party rather than as an independent veto player.

However, while the party may be able to shepherd its preferred laws to passage, does the VNA provide any meaningful information, even in these contentious cases? The failed 2018 Special Economic Zone (SEZ) Law, which led to widespread protests, can provide some insights into the typical functioning of the VNA and the type of input it generally provides. Indeed, the bill was actually debated twice on the floor of the legislature, and several times in the VNASC. If the VNA provides valuable information about or changes to the content of the law, we should see evidence in the evolution of this bill. Furthermore, an examination of the law might provide some insight into the types of activity the VNA generally engages in.

Table 3.5 provides a timeline of the progression of the SEZ Law from its initial proposal to its demise on June 10, 2018. Like nearly all VNA legislation, the SEZ Law was introduced at the behest of the government. The first mention of the law was in May 2017, when the minister of planning and investment said that the government would introduce a law to create enhanced SEZs in three provinces in Vietnam.[23] Although Vietnam already has eighteen coastal SEZs, the new proposed SEZs, which were slated for Quang Ninh, Khanh Hoa, and Kien Giang provinces, would have provided

TABLE 3.5.
Timeline of passage of the Special Economic Zone Law.

Date	Timeline
May 11, 2017	VNASC proposes the SEZ Law be considered by full VNA.[1]
May 31, 2017	VNA debates the revised schedule; no delegate opposes inclusion.[2]
June 8, 2017	VNA approves SEZ Law inclusion in revised legislative calendar.
September 11, 2017	VNASC introduces and discusses the draft law.[3]
November 22, 2017	The SEZ Law is debated on the VNA floor.
April 4, 2018	Special meeting of full-time delegates debates the SEZ Law.
April 16, 2018	VNASC meets to discuss the comments on the legislation.[4]
May 21, 2018	VNA passes the schedule for the May 2018 session and schedules debate on the SEZ Law for May 23 and passage of the law for June 15, 2018.[5]
May 23, 2018	VNA debates the SEZ Law.
June 9, 2018	Protests erupt across Vietnam opposing the law.
June 11, 2018	VNA votes to delay passage of the SEZ Law.[6]

[1]See National Assembly Decision 34/2017.

[2]See the May 31 VNA debate, http://quochoi.vn/hoatdongcuaquochoi/cackyhopquochoi/quochoikhoaXIV/kyhopthuba/Pages/bien-ban-ghi-am.aspx?ItemID=33241.

[3]Duy Anh, "Exclusive Incentives for Economic Zones Recommended," *Vietnam Economic Times*, September 12, 2017, http://vneconomictimes.com/article/vietnam-today/exclusive-incentives-for-special-economic-zones-recommended.

[4]See the VNA website for a summary of VNASC Meeting 23, http://quochoi.vn/UBTVQH/cacphienhop/quochoikhoaXIV/phienhopthu23/Pages/chuong-trinh-lam-viec.aspx?ItemID=35039.

[5]See the VNA website, http://quochoi.vn/hoatdongcuaquochoi/cackyhopquochoi/quochoikhoaXIV/kyhopthunam/Pages/chuong-trinh-lam-viec.aspx?ItemID=35563.

[6]See Hai Le, "Vietnam's SEZ Protests, the Causes and the Results," *VNExpress*, June 18, 2018, https://e.vnexpress.net/news/news/vietnam-s-sez-protests-the-causes-and-the-results-3765066.html.

increased incentives in the form of lower taxes, the construction of casinos to attract tourists, and most controversially, ninety-nine-year land leases for investors.[24] Although it was not included in the bill that was introduced, there was also a proposal from the VNASC leadership to allow red light districts in the SEZs to provide further incentive for investment.[25]

Almost immediately after the law was introduced, great concern arose over the ninety-nine-year lease provision, which led some to argue that the law would allow Chinese investors to acquire land in strategically sensitive regions in Vietnam. Indeed, this objection is what ultimately led to the protests in June 2018 (Vuving 2019). Did the VNA highlight these concerns, as the information theory suggests?

An analysis of the debates shows that while some delegates may have had reservations, they did not raise the issue in plenary sessions. There is evidence that at least two delegates raised the issue in a meeting of full-time delegates organized by the VNASC. In particular, in an April 4, 2018, meeting arranged by the VNASC, delegates Nguyen Nhu Khue and Le Thanh Van raised concerns about the implications the law held for Vietnam's sovereignty. Khue said: "We allocate large tracts of land for foreign investors, along with land use rights for 90 years or more. How will our children and grandchildren deal with this if security situations arise concerning these concessions?"[26] Le Thanh Van raised similar concerns in the same meeting.

While these comments could be interpreted as channeling information to the party, these concerns were not news to the party leadership at the time. Almost immediately after a draft law was released and discussed within the VNASC in September 2017,[27] blogs such as *Danlambao* decried the law as selling Vietnam out to the Chinese.[28] These concerns were also raised at a September 2017 meeting organized by the Vietnam Union of Science and Technology Associations (VUSTA), a mass organization underneath the party-led Fatherland Front.[29]

Despite these concerns, the law proceeded unhindered. In the first full VNA plenary session in November 2017, the VNASC presented the full VNA with a draft that included the ninety-nine-year leases. Furthermore, the delegates were instructed to choose among three versions of the bill that varied on administrative matters unrelated to the core issue of national security and sovereignty. Demonstrating the importance of the VNASC's agenda-setting power, the three versions did *not* include a vote on differing lease lengths, as delegate Duong Trung Quoc called for in May 2018. These versions of the bill discussed whether the zones should be administered under provincial authority or directly under the national government. The decision by the VNASC to use the legislature in this way fits in with the rationalization logic of the VNA perfectly, as this administrative matter concerned the consistency of the legislation with the constitution.

In the full VNA debate in November 2017, no delegates raised the issue of sovereignty. Even Le Thanh Van, who had expressed concerns earlier, merely noted that "it seems that all delegates are in support of the law" and confined himself to discussing issues pertaining to the administration of the zones. The May 23, 2018, hearing just weeks before the protests emerged proceeded largely along the same lines. Delegate after delegate discussed how the zones would be administered but did not raise the sovereignty issue. Some delegates, such as Duong Trung Quoc, did raise the issue of the ninety-nine-year lease, but he did not explicitly address the sovereignty issue in his comments. He merely called for a separate vote on the law and on the length of the lease term, which would require VNASC approval.

It appears, therefore, that even on this controversial law the VNASC leadership did not see the VNA as a venue to discuss its sensitive elements. To the extent that the VNA was involved in the substance, it was to adjudicate the constitutionality of the law and consistency with other regulations. Furthermore, it is not clear that the delegates provided any information other than what the leadership would have already been able to gather from the media or other civil society groups and mass organizations. When the VNA was called to debate the law, it was conspicuously silent on the most explosive element.

Perhaps highlighting the overwhelming power of the VNASC and the party over the VNA, even the decision to delay passage of the law on June 11, 2018, shows the preeminence of the VNASC and the government. Despite delegates professing their support for the need for the law in each of the two debates, at least publicly, the decision to pull the law was made by the VNASC with no debate. Deputy VNA chair Uong Chu Luu and chair of the VNA Legal Committee Nguyen Khac Dinh suddenly announced a vote on a decision to delay passage of the SEZ Law to a later session. Again, despite VNA delegates publicly supporting the law in the previous two sessions, the passage was delayed without debate based on an "agreement" between the government and the VNASC, according to Uong Chu Luu.

The VNA duly approved the measure, with 97 percent of the 432 delegates attending approving the delay.

While the SEZ episode is extraordinary in exemplifying an atypical end to an attempt to pass a law, it nonetheless also highlights how laws generally proceed. The government and the VNASC put bills on the agenda in cooperation with the party. They then provide the VNA with a narrow range of issues to debate on technical matters, which the VNASC can take under consideration. Delegates generally view laws proposed by the VNASC as a fait accompli. In the event that there is VNA opposition to the law, the Politburo can ram it through as long as it is united. The key difference with the SEZ Law is that public protest caused the Politburo and VNASC to pull the bill in a top-down fashion, despite the VNA's acquiescence to the law at each stage along the way.

OVERSIGHT

In addition to lawmaking duties, the VNA also has significant oversight responsibilities. The constitution and the relevant laws grant the VNA the ability to oversee government officials,[30] cast votes of confidence in government ministers,[31] and decide legislation and the constitution.[32] However, within the seemingly broad powers granted to the VNA, the more detailed laws governing the implementation of these powers reveal how the VNASC dominates the assembly. With regard to query sessions, while delegates have the right to question government officials, the VNASC still determines which ministers will be queried *and which subjects* will be discussed. As Article 15 in the Law on National Assembly Oversight Activities states clearly, while delegates can submit requests for the issues they want discussed prior to the session, " the VNASC decides the group of issues to be queried and the individuals that will be queried."[33] This power over oversight activities extends to the regular inspection of different issues. In each session, the legislature will investigate government performance on a different topic. Similar to the query sessions, the VNASC will solicit input on the content of the topic under investigation but retains the ultimate power to put forward an investigation program, which the entire VNA may either vote up or down on.[34]

This clearly allows the VNASC to tilt the content of oversight toward the wishes of the party. Although one cannot know the full range of topics delegates and citizens would prefer to debate, there are clear instances in which some portion of the electorate or the VNA membership wanted to debate topics of laws that were ultimately kept off the agenda. One particular instance occurred ahead of the June 2014 VNA session, in which the legislature was locked in a standoff with China over the placement of a Chinese oil rig within two hundred miles of Vietnam's coast.[35] One delegate requested that the issue be raised in the query sessions.[36] However, that request was ultimately denied, and the VNA had to content itself with a closed-door meeting with the government.

Similarly, the VNA did not debate police abuse in 2014 or management of the build-operate-transfer (BOT) road construction schemes in 2017, despite much demand from the public and some provincial delegations.[37] Although the VNA did ultimately question the minister of transportation on the BOT issue in June 2018, the process by which ministers are selected for query sessions is ultimately opaque and under the discretion of the VNASC.[38]

On the votes of confidence, while delegates have the power to vote on government ministers, a vote may only be called when there is a request from 20 percent of the VNA. Given that provincial delegations are explicitly discouraged from coordinating across provincial lines by requiring that the provincial delegations meet with different provinces in each VNA meeting,[39] gathering a petition of 20 percent (approximately one hundred delegates) is a tall order. However, the law also stipulates that a minister may face a confidence vote if explicitly recommended by the VNASC or one of the VNA's ten permanent committees. Even the power of the permanent committees reinforces the power of the VNASC, given that the chairs of the ten committees are also members of the VNASC.[40]

ADDITIONAL PARTY CONTROL MECHANISMS

To add another layer of party control, the party also holds Central Committee plenums directly prior to the VNA sessions. Typically, less than a month before the VNA session, the party will hold a Central Committee plenum, where it will issue a resolution. The resolution will contain some instructions regarding party affairs for the Politburo to implement. However, it will also discuss economic and social affairs, which will provide some guidance for the VNASC and the full VNA plenary session. This allows the party to provide more direct instructions to the VNASC on how to manage the upcoming VNA session.

An additional element of the organization of the legislature is the penetration of the party into the leadership structure. In addition to the

VNASC, the VNA contains a VNA Party Committee. This caucus includes most members of the VNASC. In the 14th VNA (2016–2021), this includes all but two of the members of the VNASC.[41] The VNA Party Committee, like the VNASC, also includes a member who is simultaneously a member of the VCP Organization Committee, which is the party's key personnel management body. In the 14th VNA, for example, Tran Van Tuy is simultaneously the head of the VNA Delegate Affairs Committee and deputy chair of the VCP Organization Committee.

Like other party bodies, this group rarely publicizes its meetings and does not disclose its membership. However, based on information from interviews, this group typically meets prior to the full sessions of the VNA as well as sessions of the VNASC to finalize the agenda. This group is also involved in personnel decisions, such as whom to promote to leadership positions in the following assembly and how to staff the VNA offices.[42] The fact that a member of the VCP Organization Committee is both a member of the VNASC and the VNA Party Committee ensures that the party may exert its nomenklatura power within the VNA.

Unconditional Party Government

A review of the VNA legislative institutions shows that the party, through its control of the VNASC, can effectively dictate the VNA's legislative calendar, its oversight activities, and the content of legislation. In addition, because each of the chairs of the ten permanent committees is a member of the VNASC, there is political control of the permanent committees as well. Returning to the theory of "conditional party government," the VNASC wields near total control over the legislature. However, in contrast to that theory, the strength of the VNA is not conditional on the unity of the VNA party membership. Rather, the strength of the VNASC is unconditional; it is imposed by the VCP.

FOUR

Explaining the Evolution of the VNA

The previous chapters have reviewed the structure of the VNA and VNA elections. In that review I suggest that the party exerts influence over the VNA through its tight control of the VNASC. As such, the role of the legislature, under the leadership of the VNASC, is to provide technocratic expertise, all while operating under the constraint that the legislature should project the unity of the party. While an examination of VNA institutions provides support for this view, it does fly in the face of many characterizations of VNA development.

Many accounts of legislative development in Vietnam suggest that the VNA developed in the way revisionist theories suggest. That is, responding to economic deterioration and a legitimacy crisis in the 1980s, Vietnamese reformers liberalized the legislature to provide a check on the party and provide greater information. The VNA is thus a crucial case for the binding or citizen information theories, as it faced the conditions assumed to be propitious for legislative development and appeared, at least on the surface, to follow the path suggested by existing research (Gerring 2007). This would suggest that economic reformers pushed for liberalization of the VNA in order to improve economic governance. Alternatively, seeking greater information, the regime opened up electoral procedures to allow more diverse voices to have a say in policy making. I argue that the latter is a misreading of the VNA's development.

In making my argument, this chapter details why Vietnam exhibited the characteristics of a country that should have created a binding, informative legislature in 1985, according to existing theory. After making the argument that Vietnam is a compelling "crucial case," I then explain the logic of the legislative reforms that took place, showing that the proponents of *Doi moi* (Vietnam's economic reform program) were not the strongest advocates of legislative reform. Rather, officials most commonly seen as skeptical of economic reforms supported legislative institutionalization. Rather than enhancing the ability of the legislature to check the party, legislative institutionalization was intended to restrain the prime minister. At the same time, the necessity of projecting unity required the regime to continue to place restraints on grassroots accountability within the legislature. The result was an empowered, technocratic legislature used by the party to challenge the state, rather than a responsive legislature checking or informing the party on the behalf of citizens.

Conditions Favoring a Binding, Informative Legislature

Why do some authoritarian regimes increase the power of their legislatures? Research on authoritarian legislatures largely suggests that regimes require institutions when they cannot rely on "easy money" in the form of foreign aid or natural resource rents, or if there are strong challenges from society. This is so because the primary logic of institutions in these accounts is to protect private property (North and Weingast 1989; Gehlbach and Keefer 2012) and increase economic productivity (Gandhi 2008). Research on authoritarian institutions commonly operationalizes this logic in terms of access to natural resource rents (Wright 2008; Gandhi and Przeworski 2007, 2006). An alternative view is that autocrats bolster institutions when they face an increased revolutionary threat from society (Truex 2016, ch. 7).

Starting with the private property and economic growth argument, in these accounts natural resources are a proxy for the need to generate higher levels of economic production in society. Therefore, theoretically, any contextual factor either generating the need for increased resources or cutting off access to easy money should increase the need for a robust legislative institution.

Natural resources are not the only source of "easy money." Another important source of nontax revenue is foreign aid. As Morrison (2010) notes, the same linkages between institutional underdevelopment and natural resources can be applied to foreign aid, with cross-national research suggesting that foreign aid does negatively impact governance quality (Knack 2001;

Djankov, Montalvo, and Reynal-Querol 2008).[1] Therefore, one condition predicting the rise of binding authoritarian institutions is *lack of access to easy revenue in the form of either natural resources or foreign aid.*

Although existing research primarily focuses on access to resources, a broader range of factors could also impact the degree to which a regime needs to engage in economic productivity and good governance. Societal demands and security threats may also be important intervening factors. If a regime can sustain itself through narrow appeals to an ethnic minority, for example, it may be able to remain in power even without access to easy revenue. Consistent with selectorate theory (Bueno de Mesquita et al. 2004), when the winning coalition is larger, the government will be required to provide more public goods. This will require additional resources. The potential for narrower coalitions is also one of many reasons ethnically diverse countries have lower levels of public goods provision (Alesina, Baqir, and Easterly 1999; Miguel and Gugerty 2005; Easterly and Levine 1997). This dovetails with a more general argument that regimes will improve governance when the threat of revolution from society is greater. Using the case of China, Truex (2016, Chapter 7) argues that the NPC's capacity to deliver constrained representation increased after the regime faced challenges in the Tiananmen Square crisis.

Societal pressures could have an additional effect on the need for institutionalization, particularly if one segment of society excluded from the regime holds greater wealth that the regime needs for budgetary reasons. Indeed, whether the money is to be used to engage in war or productive economic development, the central tenet of the co-optation model is that inclusion in a legislature will encourage wealth holders to contribute to economic development and tax receipts (Gandhi 2008; North and Weingast 1989). Therefore, a second condition predicting the rise of binding authoritarian institutions is *strong societal pressures,* particularly from segments of the society that can generate wealth.

Finally, a security threat also plays an important role. While the actual outbreak of conflict may simultaneously reduce the degree to which a country engages in productive economic activities and maintain robust institutions, the *threat* of such conflict could generate a positive incentive. As Doner, Ritchie, and Slater (2005) note, a security threat requires that a regime devote greater resources to military spending than would otherwise be necessary. If the same regime faces societal demands and lacks natural

TABLE 4.1.
Factors that should lead to a binding or informative legislature: logic.

Determinants of a strong legislature	Logic
Low natural resource rents	Legislature facilitates cooperation from domestic actors to improve economic output and overcome lack of access to "easy money."
Low foreign assistance	Legislature facilitates cooperation from domestic actors to improve economic output and overcome lack of access to "easy money."
High security threat	Legislature facilitates cooperation from domestic actors to improve economic output and overcome lack of access to "easy money."
Broad societal demands	Broad societal demands place additional pressure on the regime for side payments, thus creating need for legislature to facilitate cooperation. Alternatively, demands from excluded wealth holders might encourage regime elites to incorporate them in times of economic need.

resources, its only choice is to improve efficiency. Borrowing from the logic of authoritarian institutionalization, which suggests that fewer resources mean greater institutionalization, this would imply that increased security threats should increase the need for stronger representative institutions. Therefore, a final condition that could predict the need for binding authoritarian institutions could be a *military threat*.

Legislatures are implicated in each of these threats because theory suggests that while they may be costly or limit the power of the autocrat, they can improve governance or productivity. Autocrats will therefore construct legislatures when they face this combination of threats. Table 4.1 provides a summary of the variables that are linked with greater legislative institutionalization under authoritarian rule.

Contextual Factors and Legislative Reform

As this section demonstrates, Vietnam in 1985 faced each of these conditions when it began to reform its legislative institutions. In particular, facing sudden coalitional demands due to economic mismanagement and the inability to generate revenue to meet these demands, the country was also spending heavily on the military to support its occupation of Cambodia. Perhaps most important, during this period its major source of "easy money"—Soviet aid—suddenly evaporated, and oil revenues were not sufficient to fill the gap. This almost certainly led to Vietnam's decision to embark on its *Doi moi* economic reforms. The question this chapter addresses is whether it also caused the regime to use the legislature as a way of constraining the party or providing it with citizen information.

VIETNAM AND DOI MOI

While economic reforms began in earnest after 1986, Vietnam's economy was already in tatters as early as 1979. Due to poor harvests (Nyland 1981), the imposition of central planning in the South (Stern 1985), and the expropriation of private businesses after unification (Nyland 1981), the Vietnamese economy faced goods shortages, inflation, and budget shortfalls. The economic situation was exacerbated by security concerns. Vietnam responded to Cambodian leader Pol Pot's border attacks in 1978 by deposing the Khmer Rouge, and the subsequent invasion required the Vietnamese to maintain a large presence in Cambodia for several years (Woodside 1979).

The economic and security problems were compounded in 1979, when China launched a retaliatory attack on Vietnam. Vietnam had to devote significant resources to dealing with the Cambodian threat. This not only drained limited state resources but also prevented agricultural production in fertile border areas at a time when weather conditions were causing widespread crop failures (Nyland 1981, 444).

In terms of policy, during this crisis the party had to temporarily suspend efforts to impose central planning in the South. In addition, it had to tolerate off-plan activities throughout the country. These concessions were necessary in order to keep the economy functioning and were a tacit acknowledgment of illegal economic reforms that were already occurring at the provincial level (Fforde and de Vylder 1996, 130–131).[2] Therefore, by 1979 the party was forced to slow down imposition of central planning and private business expropriation in the South (Stern 1985; Nyland 1981). This led the party, in a Central Committee plenum in 1979, to institute limited reforms acknowledging the necessity of the market while still trying to maintain the plan, which some point to as the real beginning of Vietnam's economic reforms (Fforde and de Vylder 1996, 13).

While the situation was dire in 1979, several factors resulted in the economy plunging to a qualitatively new level of dysfunction in 1985. First, an "awkward" compromise in 1982 whereby state-owned enterprises were allowed to operate off plan as well as on plan was unsustainable (Riedel and

Turley 1999, 16). As prices in the nonplanned sector outpaced those in the planned sector, state employees demanded wage increases to match the off-plan price increases. The state gradually did this by increasing wages and printing more money, thus increasing inflation. The government attempted to deal with the issue in one fell swoop in 1985 by simultaneously introducing currency reform, higher state prices, and increased wages (Fforde and de Vylder 1996, 142). The reform was such a disaster that the army suggested a key proponent of the reform, Tran Phuong, be removed, or he would be shot (Dang 2008; Fforde and de Vylder 1996, 165n27).

In sum, Vietnam's economy in 1985 was spent, and its security situation imposed heavy budget demands that prevented it from being able to easily placate a restive society with resources from the budget coffers. Consistent with work on authoritarian institutionalization, Vietnam had several options to deal with these threats if it hoped to avoid strengthening the legislature: rely on foreign aid or natural resource revenues, or attempt to cater to a narrower set of supporters. Unfortunately for Vietnam, these also were not tenable options.

NATURAL RESOURCES

Starting with natural resources, Vietnam does have oil natural resources. During the mid-1980s, Vietnam's oil industry was an important source of income, but still in its infancy and insufficient to meet energy demands. In 1986, Vietnam and the Soviet Union began developing the White Tiger oil field under the auspices of the Vietsovpetro joint venture (Cotton 1989). By 1993 the latter had entered agreements with several firms from countries including the Great Britain, the Netherlands, and Japan. Vietnam was also actively courting US companies (Cotton 1989; England and Kammen 1993).

However, these resources were not sufficient in 1985 to meet Vietnam's budget crisis. First, these resources did not come online until 1986.[3] Second, while oil was an important source of export revenue, Vietnam ultimately had to import refined oil, which was still not enough to meet its energy demands (England and Kammen 1993). Furthermore, despite the promise of more potential reserves, technical difficulties in extracting the oil from difficult geological conditions, combined with continuing political difficulties related to the disputed Spratly Islands, meant that this potential remained unrealized (England and Kammen 1993). In short, Vietnam had oil and the promise of more, yet it was not a source of cash from which regime elites could stuff their pockets or meet the demands of the citizens.

Despite the difficulties, at least until 1989 Vietnam had access to an important resource that helped paper over its fiscal cracks: Soviet aid. Riedel and Turley summarize the situation in the late 1970s well: "[Vietnam's] economy was exceptionally aid-dependent, partly because of the war and partly because the DRV, with a predominantly agricultural population but chronic food deficit, lacked the capital, resources, and institutions needed to sustain central planning" (1999, 13). According to statistics they cite, from 1966 to 1975 foreign assistance accounted for *63.2 percent of the non-military state budget.*

The aid came in two forms. First, the Soviet Union and Eastern Bloc's Council for Mutual Economic Assistance (CMEA) provided direct assistance as nonrefundable grants. Second, these countries also increasingly provided "trade as aid," whereby the communist bloc would sell the Vietnamese goods at subsidized rates or provide them with favorable loans with which to purchase the goods. This assistance helped in two ways. First, the concessional loans obviously provided important inputs at subsidized rates, which helped the regime staunch the budgetary bleeding (Beresford and Dang 2000, 26). Second, it ensured that Vietnam could fill at least some of the important input shortages for industrial production. Because of the dysfunctional nature of the centrally planned pricing structure and the overall weakness of the economy, key industrial sectors in Vietnam lacked crucial inputs, which effectively shut down production. Subsidized imports from the Soviet Union and Eastern Europe helped fill this gap (Beresford and Dang 2000).

Soviet assistance was not only important for Vietnam's fiscal position; it was also important for its defense posture. Of course Soviet assistance helped Vietnam maintain its military budget. However, Soviet assistance was also important to the management of Vietnam's military. For example, the Vietnamese air force relied on Soviet technicians to help maintain Vietnam's fleet of MIG aircraft during its occupation of Cambodia (Guilbert 1990; Light 1991).

For these reasons, even through the economic difficulties of the early 1980s, Vietnam was able to limp along while still sporadically attempting to reinstate central planning in the South. Despite disputes about whether Vietnam's

reforms began in 1979, 1986, or 1989,[4] most agree that 1989 represented a major turning point. While the 6th Party Congress in 1986 represented a rhetor-
ical shift, some components of central planning remained in place. However,
with the collapse of the Eastern Bloc in 1989, the remaining vestiges of central
planning disappeared. Riedel and Turley argue that "[u]p to the late 1980s,
Viet Nam approached reform in gradual steps, but in seeking immediate solutions across several policy areas the measures adopted around 1989 qualified as
a 'shock'" (1999, 22).[5] Even the more skeptical Fforde and de Vylder suggest
that 1989 marked the point of no return for central planning.[6] In short, whatever ability the VCP had to cling to the hope of returning to central planning
disappeared with the fall of the Berlin Wall.

SOCIETAL DEMANDS

Amid these fiscal difficulties, the VCP also found it difficult to play one
group off of another or to narrow its coalition of support in order to grab
resources or shed some of its financial burden. Vietnam is a relatively ho-
mogenous country, in which most of the people speak the same language.[7]
Furthermore, unlike other countries in Southeast Asia, which evolved from
"mandala"-style political entities with fluid boundaries (Wolters 1983), Vietnam has a shared sense of historic identity with a relatively firm conceptu-
alization of where it sits geographically in relation to its neighbors. As one
study notes, this shared sense of identity was "a factor that had proved a valuable asset in many battles in the past and should have facilitated the struggle
for economic and social development" (Fforde and de Vylder 1996, 11).

The one potentially important cleavage that the regime might have activated in order to manage the economic crisis was the North-South divide, which was important after gaining independence from the French in
1954. The North and the South have different histories, with present-day
southern Vietnam ruled by the Champa kingdom and Angkor Kingdoms
throughout Vietnam's centuries-long "southward march" (*nam tiến*). It was
not until 1802 that a Vietnamese ruling authority controlled most of what
is today southern Vietnam, including present-day Ho Chi Minh City. The
distinct economic organization of the South, which was less heavily popu-
lated and relied more on plantation-style agriculture, in part led France to
impose more direct administration in the South than in the North.

Given these differences, one plausible approach from the party leadership could have been to starve the South of resources and funnel them to

the North. Indeed, after the war the ruling Communist Party did repress some groups in the South, at least partially. After reunification, the regime opened reeducation camps to indoctrinate former South Vietnamese officials (Thayer 2009a, 426). Furthermore, escalating tensions between Vietnam and China caused the mass exodus of thousands of ethnic Chinese in southern Vietnam, disrupting the economy in Ho Chi Minh City, where they were most prevalent (Unger 1988; Woodside 1979).[8] Indeed, the party instituted a policy to expropriate private businesses in Ho Chi Minh City in 1978. Unofficial persecution also followed, with ethnic Hoa (Chinese) émigrés reporting widespread looting (Stern 1985).

However, as a general solution to Vietnam's financial difficulties, fleecing the South or ethnic Chinese for the benefit of a narrow coalition loyal to the regime leaders was not an option. First, the imposition of central planning on the South was in part responsible for the economic tailspin, thus depriving the regime of important sources of revenue and food. However, just as important was the fact that southern communists were instrumental in the victory over the Americans and the Republic of Vietnam.

Furthermore, many of these southern communists, while supportive of the regime, were nonetheless more skeptical of central planning and opposed many of the policies implemented after 1975. This skepticism eventually manifested itself in the form of the Club of Former Resistance Fighters (CFRF). This group, led by former generals from the South, formed in 1986 as a "self-help" group for veterans. It quickly shifted from a purely social grouping to a political organization when it engaged in a campaign to force the regime to replace Prime Minister Pham Hung, himself a southerner who died in 1988, with another southerner, economic liberal Vo Van Kiet (Abuza 2001; Duc 2012).

While the regime managed to disband the CFRF and force some of the more moderate members to reconstitute themselves under the party-backed Fatherland Front (Khng 1993), some members of the Politburo sympathized with the group's objectives. In particular, top leaders such as Vo Van Kiet opposed the rigid imposition of central planning on the South. Furthermore, the "fence-breaking" provincial authorities, once again primarily from the South, also increasingly flouted central edicts. These factors placed internal political constraints as well as practical constraints on the ability to completely redistribute wealth from the South to the North, even if the regime had desired to do so.

Finally, it should be noted that the pressure from the South is particularly pertinent given co-optation theory, which suggests that the purpose of a legislature is to incorporate the wealthier segments of the population to encourage them to engage in economically productive activity. In this context, southern Vietnam is more economically productive in terms of agriculture and industrial development. Thus, given the logic of co-optation, the need to placate southern party elites and social groups nicely fits the theory. Co-optation would predict that providing disgruntled southern officials with a greater say in policy through inclusion in a legislature might have encouraged greater productivity in the South, which declined rapidly under the ten-year period of socialization.

The coalitional demands were not limited to elites. Throughout 1988 and 1989, the regime also faced protests from important sectors of the economy. Indeed, in 1988 protesters descended on Ho Chi Minh City, objecting to land confiscations. Similar protests occurred in Hanoi in 1989. Furthermore, disgruntled farmers, fishermen, and coal miners protested labor conditions and wages in provinces such as Thanh Hoa, Thuan Hai, and Quang Ninh throughout this period. In each of these cases, the protesters were not "bourgeoisie" whom the regime could easily dismiss, but rather important pillars of the Communist Party's supposed core constituency (Vo 1990).

In short, important actors critical to the regime's ability to project influence throughout its newly unified territory posed a credible constraint on the ability of central officials to respond to the economic crisis with repression or redistribution. Furthermore, these important actors were sensitive to the rapid deterioration of economic conditions, particularly in the southern parts of the country. Indeed, as Thayer (2009a, 428) notes, "the [CFRF] appealed to a large group of party and army veterans whose basic material needs were not being met by the state." Facing an economic crisis from sectors with close ties to those within the regime itself, the party required additional resources that it could not easily muster. Existing theories would predict that co-opting those elites into a legislature is a natural response.

With all this in mind, as table 4.2 shows, some of the main factors that should lead to a strong legislature in an authoritarian regime were present in Vietnam. Vietnam in the 1980s featured low natural resource rents, declining foreign aid, security threats, and broad social pressures. Each of these factors, theoretically, should have led to an increase in the constraining power of the VNA.

TABLE 4.2.
Factors that should lead to a binding or informative legislature:
Vietnam, 1986–1989.

Determinants of a strong legislature	Vietnam, 1986–1989
Low natural resource rents	Yes
Low foreign assistance	Yes
High security threat	Yes
Broad social pressures	Yes

The Response in the VNA: From "Decoration" to "Forum"

In summing up the preceding discussion, in 1989 the VCP, facing broad opposition from organized groups and social sectors with ties to the regime, particularly in the economically productive South, suddenly ran out of access to "easy money."[9] As noted previously and more extensively elsewhere in this book, this forced a change to its economic policy in the form of *Doi moi.*[10] While this shift is well documented, this section considers more explicitly how existing accounts from Vietnam explain reforms to the VNA that also occurred during this period. In short, both existing theory and several conventional explanations from Vietnam suggest a similar story: the VCP reformed the VNA in order to provide a check on the party and generate greater information.

However, using detailed accounts from key institutional changes to the VNA, I show that contrary to these accounts, the reforms are actually more consistent with the signaling and rationalization arguments. Where the reforms went further, it was due to a strategy of deflecting blame toward the government for governance failures. Throughout these reforms, contrary to competing arguments, the VCP did not meaningfully increase the competitiveness of elections or relax control of the VNA in a way that created a constraint on the party or generated new channels of citizen information.

Timeline of Legislative Reforms in Vietnam

This section details the evolution of the VNA and the dominant explanations for the changes that occurred. Different authors fix different dates to the changes. Some accounts focus on formal changes to regulations. Bui Ngoc Son (2007, 190), for example, suggests four eras for the VNA, with the most recent period beginning after the constitutional revision in 1992. He suggests that at this point the legislature moved past its "formalism" and "old thinking" to something more representative and active. Others, however, suggest that changes began earlier. Abuza places the beginning of the reforms at the 6th Party Congress in 1986 (2001, 102–103). Huy Duc (2012) suggests that the transition of the VNA from a "decoration" to a "forum" started as early as 1981, with chair Nguyen Huu Tho's decision to ask members of the Politburo to stand down from the dais. This decision, Duc argues, empowered legislative leaders rather than party leaders to take control of the proceedings.

Similar to arguments about Vietnam's economic reforms, I also argue that some piecemeal reforms were instituted beginning perhaps in 1981. However, I also contend that much of the evidence of increased activity in the VNA at this time is largely anecdotal. Instead, I look for evidence of sustained changes to the way the legislature functioned as evidence of a reform. Using this approach, I argue that there was a gradual change in the way the legislature operated starting in 1986. These reforms were not sudden but occurred gradually, with some reforms being implemented as late as 2012. This suggests that the VNA did not reform suddenly but rather has evolved since 1986. Importantly, the logic of this evolution does not cohere with the predictions of existing theory.

"OLD THINKING" IN THE VNA

In summing up the purpose of the VNA before 1986, former deputy chair of the Office of the VNA Nguyen Sy Dung nicely explains how it followed from the old Soviet model. Under the Soviet model, the purpose of the legislature was to formalize the party line, maintain the solidarity among citizens, and ensure the support of citizens for the party (D. S. Nguyen 2017, 38–39). He points to several features that ensured the VNA would fill those roles. Those included the electoral structure (see chapter 2), which required the legislature to descriptively represent the social sectors that the party deemed relevant. The Soviet model also explained the strong degree of control exercised by the VNASC and the strict limits on the days the VNA operated (see chapter 3).

With that said, Vietnam, even during the old period, did have some features that differ from other communist legislatures. In contrast to the Chinese NPC and Cuba's National Assembly, Vietnam's legislature has always been directly elected. This is at least partly the legacy of the first National Assembly elected in 1946, which at that time included members of nationalist parties as well as the Communist Party. In the first election, voters were allowed to vote for multiple candidates, with provinces as the electoral districts.[11] The more pluralistic character of the 1946 Constitution was due to the need to build a large coalition at a time "when the nearest major communist armed forces were almost three thousand miles away" (Fall 1960, 158). However, the inclusiveness was short lived. Less than a year after the first meeting of the VNA, the number of representatives in it dropped from 403 to 291 (Duc 2012, 188). Most of those culled were noncommunist members.

In North Vietnam, the pretense of pluralism was officially abandoned in the 1959 Election Law and subsequent election laws, which granted the Election Board and the Fatherland Front broad authority to screen candidates.[12] Therefore, in the first election in 1960 in North Vietnam after independence, votes for senior leaders ranged from 98.75 to 99.6 percent (Fall 1960, 157). While a number of features of the election law have changed, the power of the VNASC over vetting through its control of the Election Board remains largely unchanged to the present day. Even after the reforms in the late 1980s and early 1990s, the "five gates" system of electoral vetting summarized in chapter 2 remains in place.[13]

In terms of legislative power, the 1959 Constitution also formally declared the VNA "the highest organ of state power in Vietnam."[14] Each subsequent constitutional revision (1980, 1992, 2002, 2013) has repeated this general formulation. However, to ensure party dominance over the body, the 1959 Constitution and the 1960 Law on the Organization of the National Assembly once again granted broad powers to the VNASC. The key powers include the ability to schedule the plenary sessions, decide what laws will be debated, and decide how long and what form oversight duties will take. Until 1989, the VNASC used its power to ensure that the legislature met no more than two weeks a year.[15] Furthermore, during these sessions, if laws or government performance were debated, those meetings occurred in small groups rather than the full plenary sessions. These groups, which were borrowed from a similar institution from the Supreme Soviet (Duc 2012, 188), were organized based on provincial delegations and were rotated every session so that the same provinces did not meet twice in a row.

The lack of open debate on the floor of the legislature on laws or government oversight persisted as late as June 1988. In that famous session, in which a number of delegations from the south introduced Vo Van Kiet to compete with the Politburo's nomination of Do Muoi as premier,[16] the legislature still only met for four days, debated no legislation, and conducted its two days of oversight of the government's work report in small groups rather than on the floor of the VNA. The only hearing conducted on the full floor was the query session of government ministers, which at that time was only half a day, as opposed to the three to four days that has been common since 1998.[17]

At this point it is worth discussing the unprecedented introduction of Vo Van Kiet as a competitor to Do Muoi in the 1988 session, as this might be an indicator of a legislature keen to challenge the party. Indeed, many in the VNA itself laud the 1988 vote as evidence of a more democratic VNA largely because of its near rebuke of General Secretary Nguyen Van Linh's decision to appoint Do Muoi as prime minister (D. N. Nguyen 2005). With regard to the competition between Vo Van Kiet and Do Muoi in that session, it bears pointing out that this incident did not speak to any conscious change in the design of the VNA but rather to dissension within the party that spilled onto the floor of the VNA. While some media outlets such as *Lao Dong* and *Tuoi Tre* mentioned the competition between Do Muoi and Vo Van Kiet (Porter 1993), the party mouthpiece, *Nhan Dan* (People's daily), did not mention the competition in announcing Muoi's eventual selection.[18]

The unprecedented challenge was due in part to the influence of the CFRF. This group had strong ties within the party, including to General Secretary Nguyen Van Linh himself, and was strongly critical of the regime's attempts to impose central planning on the South. Therefore, it actively lobbied the VNA to support Vo Van Kiet over Do Muoi, who was a key cadre in charge of implementing central planning in the South after unification in 1976.[19] In addition, the response by the southern delegations inside and outside the VNA was "anticipated" by Linh.[20]

It is therefore more accurate to say that the VNA's activity in this incident occurred *despite* institutions clearly designed to limit the visibility of the VNA and its ability to challenge party decisions. The underlying reason for the dissent was a failure to reach consensus within the party prior to introducing Do Muoi to the VNA. As Porter noted in the 1990s regarding occasional divisions on draft laws in the VNA: "Occasionally, the assembly has divided sharply on a draft law, but such a vote indicates internal divisions within the party apparatus rather than genuine autonomy from the government" (1993, 76). Perhaps more important, the legislature ultimately failed to overturn the general secretary's decision. Much like the Tiananmen Square "Signature Incident" or the Three Gorges Dam vote in China, in which the National People's Congress *almost* disapproved of party policy, ultimately the VNA fell in line (Hu 1993).

INITIAL REFORMS: EXPANDING TECHNICAL LEGISLATIVE CAPACITY

Even as late as 1988, the legislature largely operated as it always had. With the VNASC firmly in control of the electoral proceedings and the legislative sessions, the full VNA had little opportunity to assert itself. The examples of assertiveness that exist were in the form of occasional outbursts from delegates. One example is delegate Dao Thi Bieu "tossing out" her prepared speech in 1985 during a query session and berating the government for the disastrous wage-price-money reforms (Porter 1993; Duc 2012). However, this exception highlights the rule at the time, which was that outside of the small group meetings, the speeches on the VNA floor were vetted and planned to ensure that were no "deviations" (*lệch lạc*) from the public transcript (Duc 2012, 82).

As a sign of the changes to come, in 1987 General Secretary Nguyen Van Linh delivered a speech to open the eighth VNA suggesting that the legislature should act more assertively. This is notable because in a typical session, the chair of the VNA opens the session. Linh's speech, which he reprised in the June 1989 session after the fall of the Berlin Wall, suggests he was serious about bolstering the activity of the VNA. In the 1987 speech, Linh explicitly linked his intention for a reformed VNA to *Doi moi*, the "renewal" policy decided upon at the 6th Party Congress. Whether branding or substantive, Linh invoked *Doi moi* in the speech in imploring the legislature to speak "honestly and directly."[21] He said the legislature "must *renew* [*đổi mới*] its way of thinking and its way of working across all range of activities" in order to strengthen the country and stabilize the economy.[22]

Several facts support the notion that he and the party leadership were serious. Immediately following the 1987 election, Linh intervened directly in the appointments to the VNA leadership by surprisingly appointing Ngo Ba Thanh, a lawyer with ties to the Republic of Vietnam, to chair the Law Committee (Duc 2012, n362). Perhaps more important, the Council of State, which between 1980 and 1992 was the name of the VNASC, issued a flurry of directives to increase the resources available to the VNA. These resolutions increased the per diem account for delegates and the salary for overtime work, changes critical to enabling the VNA to meet for longer sessions.[23] In addition, in terms of involving the VNA more in lawmaking, this required increasing the number of staff in the Office of the VNA as well as the quality of the staff. Therefore, the State Council also issued a series of directives increasing the number of full-time staff working in the Office of the VNA.[24]

Regarding increasing the quality of the staff, in 1990 the National Assembly for the first time passed regulations governing the activities of the VNA's permanent committees. These regulations stipulated that some portion of the committee should work for the committee on a full-time basis, and the leadership should meet at least once every three months. Some of these changes, which required only the approval of the Council of State, were then codified in the 1992 Constitution and the 1992 Law on the Organization of the National Assembly. In particular, those two documents strengthened the role of committees and called for more full-time members with technical expertise.

What was the effect of these early reforms? As figure 4.1 shows, the legislature did indeed become more active, at least in terms of the number of days it was in session. A review of the length of the plenary sessions indicates three periods when the session lengths increased. The first was in 1989, when the two plenary sessions met for more than ten days. The second cut point was in 1993, when the number increased to more than twenty days per session. Then, in 1998, the number increased further to its current level of about thirty-five days per session.

Each of these cut points in aggregate activity represented a substantive change in the functioning of the legislature. As discussed, the increase in days in 1989 followed from Nguyen Van Linh's desire for the legislature to become more active, which was backed up by increased resources for the committees and the delegates. Thanks to the additional resources, the legislature was now able to debate legislation for several days before eventually passing the measures.

The typical VNA session from 1975 to 1986 consisted of about five days of meetings. The first day would include the opening ceremony, at which the VNA chair would give a speech and the prime minister would deliver the work report. The next day the VNA would retire to small groups to discuss the work report. On a third day, the VNA might meet to hear the

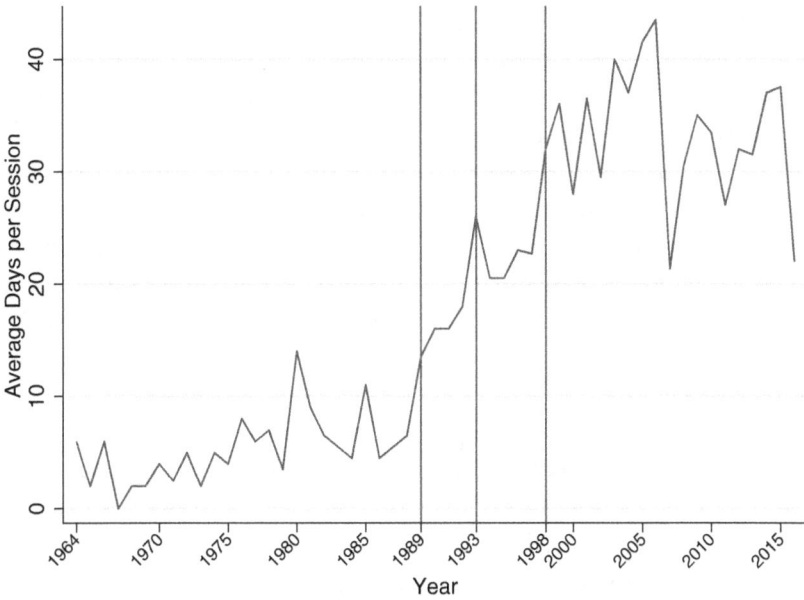

FIGURE 4.1. Days per session of the VNA, 1964–2015.

draft of a law, then adjourn to small groups to discuss the draft law. On the fourth day, the legislature would conduct the query session of the government, which at that time was a heavily scripted affair. On the final day, the VNA would meet to pass any laws introduced in that session and hear the closing speech. While there was some variation on this theme depending on the number of laws, this was the general setup.

What changed in 1989? The June 1990 session, which lasted sixteen days, highlights where the increased time went. In contrast to previous sessions, at which laws were less frequently introduced, in June 1990 six laws were discussed. Furthermore, each law was discussed in small groups and on the floor. An entire day of floor time, for example, was reserved for discussion of the Criminal Code. An additional day of floor time was used to discuss the Law on Foreign Investment and the Maritime Law. It is important to note that at this point, oversight hearings nonetheless remained largely perfunctory. While there was more debate on legislation, the query sessions in the December 1990 session still lasted only one day. In addition, there was also only one day of debate on the floor for the government's socioeconomic plan report.

The second cut point occurred in 1993, which was the first set of sessions after the enactment of the 1992 Constitution. The 1992 Constitution increased the number of session days by writing into law increased substantive activities for the VNA permanent committees. In addition, the 1992 Constitution and subsequent law on the organization of the VNA also stipulated that the VNA would have more full-time delegates. As a former chair of the Office of the VNA notes in his personal documents, the decision to professionalize the legislature came from the VCP Central Committee in November 1991, when they decided that "[i]n the future, the National Assembly will change to work on a permanent basis and increase the number of fulltime delegates."[25]

Although codifying this change into law proved to be contentious, it was nonetheless included in Article 37 of the 1992 Law on the Organization of the VNA that "some of the National Assembly deputies shall work in accordance with the specialized duty system and some with the non-specialized duty system."[26] The goal of these "specialized" delegates was clearly to increase the technical capacity of the VNA in order to help it pass coherent legislation and provide oversight.

As figure 4.2 shows, the VNA has lived up to the spirit of the 1992 Central Committee resolution. Prior to 1992, the number of delegates in the VNA on a full-time basis was negligible. Starting in 1992, with the passage of the 1992 Law on the Organization of the VNA, the number increased to 5 percent. Then, in 2002, the number of full-time delegates surged to 20 percent, and it has steadily increased to nearly 35 percent in the current VNA. Part of the reason for the surge in full-time delegates in 2002 is that a change in the 2001 Law on the Organization of the VNA provided for all provincial delegations to have at least one full-time delegate (Ngo 2005, 154). Previously, all the full-time delegates were handpicked by the center and were centrally nominated.

The full-time delegates were important because they also invigorated the committee structure. On this front, the 1981 Law on the Organization of the National Assembly actually did move past the previous 1960 Law by specifying eight permanent committees.[27] The 1992 Law retained these committees, some with slightly changed names. However, the addition of more full-time members ensured that it was not simply handpicked party leaders staffing these committees (Bui 2007, 201).

These changes have had important effects. Most notably, the professionalization of the legislature coincided with an increase in laws passed. As

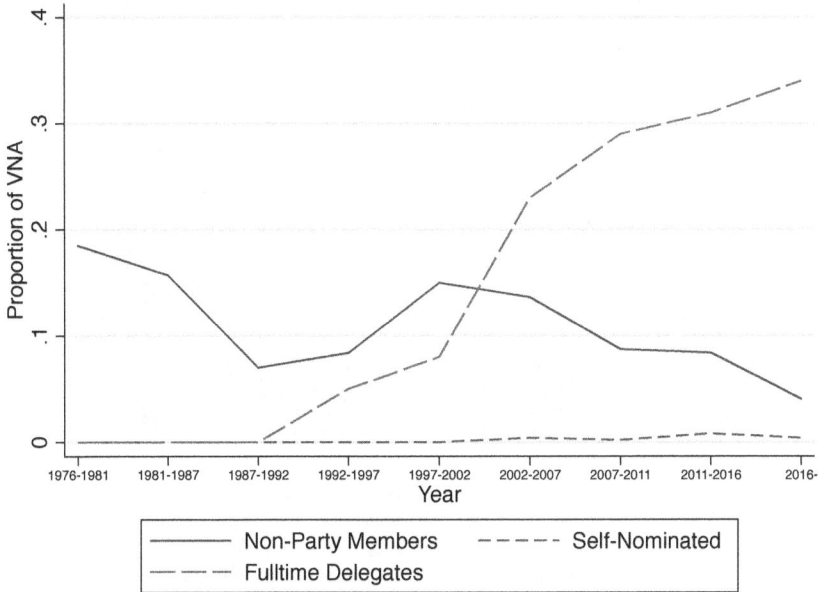

FIGURE 4.2. Percentage of delegates in the legislature full time, 1976–2016.

figure 4.3 shows, the number of laws passed per year has expanded from an average of less than one per year prior to 1989 to nearly ten per year by 2015. The first surge occurred in 1989 with the dismantling of central planning. However, the professionalization of the legislature and the committees further increased the number of days the legislature met and the number of laws passed. This was in part a response to shifting management of the economy from the party to the government, which required the creation of a series of laws to formalize government management. In addition, opening the economy to foreign investment required a legal infrastructure for foreign governments to navigate. For this reason, many of the laws passed between 1989 and 1992 pertained to management of the economy and taxation.[28]

Figure 4.3 also reveals an important dynamic in the evolution of the VNA. As the VNA first embarked upon reforms, its capacity to contribute to such legislation was limited by the weak expertise in the legislature aside from the VNASC. As such, at least initially the VNASC also increased the number of directives it issued in the late 1980s. These decisions related to new complex economic demands foisted upon the country by its economic opening. A number of these directives related to economic and trade issues,

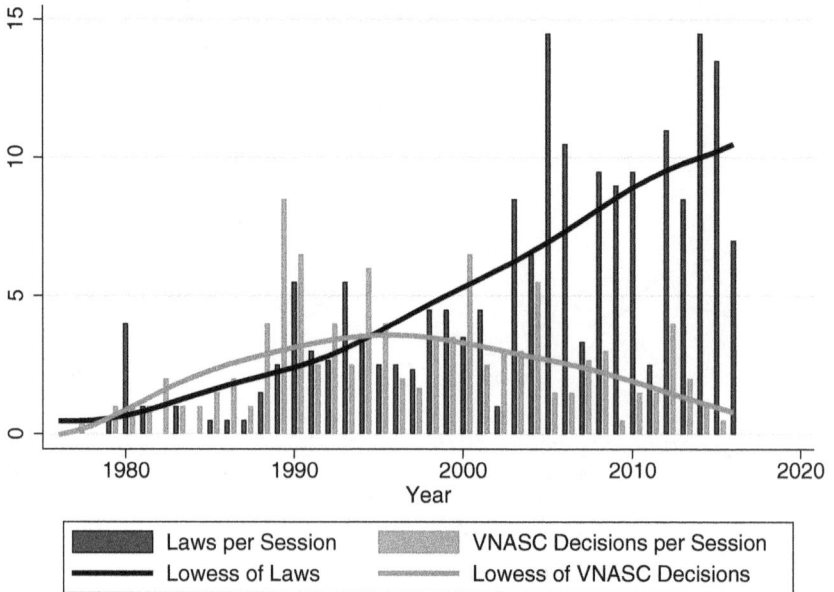

FIGURE 4.3. VNA laws and VNASC decisions passed per year, 1975–2016. Note: The lowess line is a smoothed trend line generated by taking a weighted local mean of the laws and VNASC decisions in a given year.

such as the Directive on Accounting and Statistics (1988), the Directive on Economic Contracts (1989), and the Directive on the Transfer of Foreign Technology into Vietnam (1989). Simply put, given the momentous changes to the Vietnamese economy, the legal system was overwhelmed, thus requiring the VNASC to issue regulations that the VNA, with its infrequent sessions, was unable to address.

As Figure 4.4 shows, as the VNA sessions have grown longer and the VNA committee system has become more professional, the legislature has become better able to issue more detailed legal regulations. Therefore the VNASC has not been called upon to issue as many direct regulations as during the initial stages of liberalization from 1989 to 1992. By 2015 the VNASC was issuing very few directives, and the full VNA is now able to hear and pass legislation with sufficient detail and timeliness to meet the demands of the economy. This reduces the burden on the VNASC so that it can engage in other activities, such as managing the flow of legislation and the legislative calendar and engaging in direct oversight of the government.

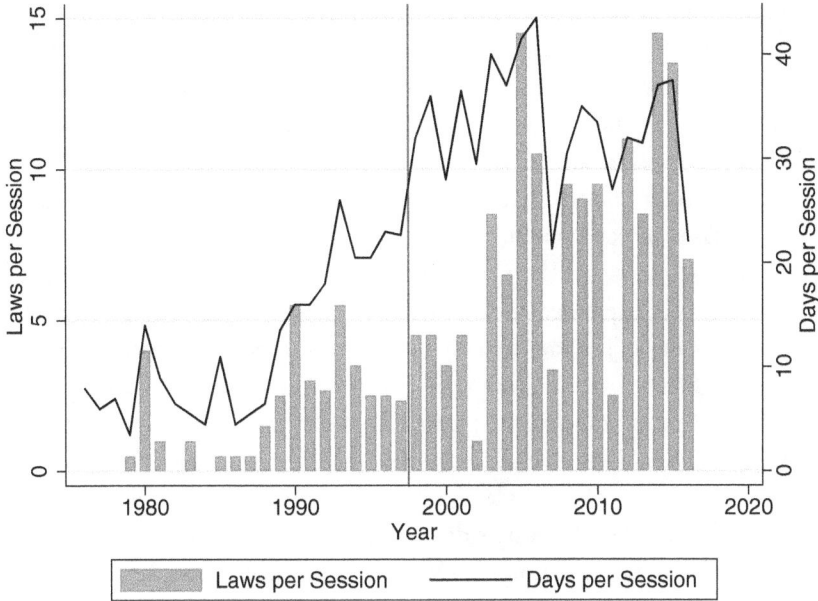

FIGURE 4.4. Days in VNA session and laws per session, 1975–2016.

The rare VNASC directive now pertains to the management of the VNA and not to substantive legal issues related to the economy, as was the case during the late 1980s and early 1990s.

This discussion shows that the increase in days that the legislature met and the increase in laws was largely a result of the initial reforms by Nguyen Van Linh in 1989 and formalization of these reforms in the 1992 Constitution and Law on the Organization of the VNA. The subsequent steady increase in the number of laws versus decisions has resulted from a steady increase in the professionalization of the legislature and the ability to meet the demands of accession to the global market economy. This explains much of the change in the operation of the VNA.

LATER REFORMS: EXPANSION OF OVERSIGHT DUTIES

Figure 4.4 also shows another cut point that occurred in 1998. At that point, the average number of days in session increased from about twenty-two to more than thirty. Some of this increase can be attributed to the steady increase in legislation passed by the VNA. As figure 4.4 shows, the number of meeting days certainly followed the number of laws passed. However, as it also shows, there was a substantial increase in average activity in the VNA after 1998 that preceded the increase in legislation passed after 2003 and 2004, as Vietnam prepared to join the World Trade Organization (WTO). What led to this increase in days in session after 1998?

An important change that occurred in 1998 was the decision to televise query sessions of government officials. The number of days devoted to the query session remained largely unchanged until the October 1998 session, when they were expanded to 3 days. Before October 1998, they were typically 1 to 1.5 days. The fact that this expansion occurred in the session *following* the first televised query session in June 1998 lends credence to the Huy Duc's contention that the greatest beneficiary of the change was VNA chair Nong Duc Manh, who could now appear as a statesmanlike politician on television (2012, 235).[29] Indeed, rather than presenting a challenge to the party, it was those on the party side, such as General Secretary Le Kha Phieu and Manh, who benefited, not Vo Van Kiet's protégé, Prime Minister Phan Van Khai. The fact that the VNA expanded the number of days for the televised query sessions after the first experiment shows that its leaders clearly viewed the experience of the first televised session as a success.

Before discussing the logic of the changes, it is important to note that although 1989, 1992, and 1998 represent important cut points, other reforms did occur outside of these periods. One important reform was the decision to add a regular vote of confidence in government ministers. Introduced in 2012, this resolution required an annual vote of confidence in all officials elected by the VNA. In practice, this means all the ministers, including the prime minister as well as the VNA leadership. Notably, it does not include key party leaders such as the VCP general secretary or the leaders of the Central Committee organizations. Different than a normal confidence vote, this vote asks delegates to assess whether they have "high confidence," "confidence," or "low confidence" in the official under question. If an official receives more than 50 percent "low confidence," that official may be asked to resign, or a subsequent actual confidence vote may be held. Perhaps most important is that the votes are made public. While the vote was initially supposed to be held twice per VNA session (two times every five years), it is now only held once per year.

These new oversight duties have clearly changed the way the public and the media view the legislature. Huy Duc writes that Le Quang Dao's treatment of the finance minister in 1991 would likely not have caused public interest if *Tuoi Tre* had not reported it. The interest in the story, he suggests, led to more newspapers, particularly those from Ho Chi Minh City, sending reporters to the VNA sessions: "Instead of relying on official news sources such as the Vietnam News Agency or Nhan Dan, the newspapers—especially from Saigon—began to send journalists to the capital. Politics was no longer seen as tedious so the number of papers such as Tuoi Tre, Thanh Nien, Lao Dong increased with each National Assembly meeting" (Duc 2012, 192).[30]

Existing Explanations

Why did Vietnam reform the legislature in 1989, in 1998, and again in 2012? This section reviews some theories explaining legislative reforms in Vietnam and China. The first argument concerns legitimation. With hyperinflation in 1985 exposing the failures of central planning, some suggest that the Vietnamese leadership hoped to generate support for the party by giving the legislature greater power and openness (Turley 1993, 263; Le 2012, 162). This argument maps on most neatly to classic arguments about the purpose of authoritarian legislatures, which is to legitimize the regime. Presumably, prior to Vietnam's economic collapse the leadership felt less need to legitimate their rule through a costly institution.

A second potential reason is liberalization (O'Brien 1990). In Vietnam during the time of reforms there were potential advocates of greater political reforms. In Vietnam, Tran Xuan Bach was ultimately eliminated from the Politburo for espousing the virtues of multiparty democracy. However, liberalization need not mean full democratization. In the context of Vietnam, several legislative reformers, including Vu Mao and the newspaper *Tuoi Tre*, advocated for increasing the number of non-party members in the interests of increased democratization (Abuza 2001, 101).

A third reason is more tactical. Research suggests that similar to the situation in China, there was initial hope from advocates for economic reform that an enhanced legislature would be an ally in such reform. Tanner argues that in China, "Deng Xiaoping and many of his fellow economic reformers probably valued an open legislature more instrumentally—as a vehicle to forge consensus behind economic reform—than intrinsically, as a proper way to make policy" (1999, 53).[31] One finds similar arguments in Vietnam, where some suggest that at least initially Vo Van Kiet and Le Kha Phieu felt that the VNA would provide support for economic reforms (Vasavakul 2019).

Similar to more general power-sharing theories of authoritarian legislatures, a fourth reason that legislative reform may have dovetailed with economic reform relates to bureaucratic inclusion. In Vietnam, the party in 1985 was more centralized than at any other time in the regime's history.[32] Party Secretary Le Duan had been in power since 1966, and national economic and political policy was centralized under party authority, with the government less autonomous than it would become.[33] As Premier Pham Van Dong said as early as 1980, Vietnam needed a stronger legislature to combat excessive bureaucratism in the party and government (Turley 1980, 184). Perhaps the enhancement of the VNA was a way to check the influence of party leaders.

The final logic, and the one most frequently espoused by reformers in China and Vietnam, was the need to "rationalize" laws and the lawmaking process (O'Brien 1990). This logic aligns with the vast literature on the need to establish "rule of law" in both countries (Rose 1998).[34] Relatedly, rationalization also aimed to ensure that laws were consistent with each other to facilitate the management of the state. Indeed, this is one area that also appealed to government officials in Vietnam, whose prime minister, Vo Van Kiet, emphasized in 1993 the need for clear laws delivered by the VNA (Rose 1998, 105).

In looking at the reforms already described, they seem clearly consistent with the regime legitimacy and rationalization arguments. That is, the regime, facing pressure from the economic collapse and the need to reform central planning, also decided to increase the visibility of the legislature. However, support for the citizen input argument or citizen information arguments is weaker. If the goal was to generate greater citizen input, the electoral institutions should have been reformed to allow greater choice and greater interaction between citizens and legislators. Indeed, the Soviet Union instituted reforms that did just that ahead of its fateful 1989 elections in order to increase the responsiveness of legislators to citizens (Marples 2015).

A deeper look at the reforms might suggest an additional explanation, which is that the legislative reforms were actually designed by the political leadership in the party to restrain what they perceived as extreme economic reforms in the government. This suggests an alternative interpretation linking political and economic reforms in Vietnam. In short, the reforms are linked because the opponents of economic reform desired a way to *restrain* the independence of the economic reformers in the government, rather than economic reformers desiring a mechanism to inform and improve their performance. This interpretation would cast a more complex light on the nature of VNA activism, which is that it is not necessarily a force for economic reform but rather for economic conservatism. Does this interpretation find support?

Explaining the Reforms in Vietnam

The previous sections show that there were two major legislative reforms. The first was to professionalize the legislature. The second was to increase legal and government oversight. This section evaluates how well alternative theories explain these reforms compared to my argument, which focuses on increasing the technical capacity of the legislature and its ability to check the state.

REFORM TO PERSONNEL: TECHNOCRATS NOT CRITICS

Starting with the pluralism and citizen information arguments, how do the VNA reforms square with this explanation? Indeed, a number of changes suggest the possibility of increased pluralism in the legislature to generate greater bottom-up accountability and more citizen information. Figure 2.2 in chapter 2 shows a modest increase in the number of candidates per seat. Furthermore, in 1997 the VNA introduced the institution of self-nominated candidates. Finally, in 2001 the legislature added full-time, locally nominated delegates. Prior to 2001, all full-time delegates were centrally nominated (Ngo 2005). Is it possible that these changes were introduced in order to increase citizen input into legislation and oversight through increased influence over legislators?

A useful place to start in understanding the purpose of the reforms is to focus on the leader most responsible for the initial changes to the VNA: General Secretary Nguyen Van Linh. Several authors point to Nguyen Van Linh as a key figure sparking the initial reforms (Abuza 2001; D. N. Nguyen 2005). Indeed, he was the general secretary in 1989 when the legislature increased its activity. Furthermore, he made two speeches on the floor of the VNA during his tenure, a rarity for a general secretary. Ahead of the *Doi Moi* reforms, Nguyen Van Linh wrote to the Office of the VNA that it should "not become a decoration" (D. N. Nguyen 2005, 129).

What were his intentions? Nguyen Van Linh was clearly supportive of limited economic reforms. Indeed, his reformist credentials were bolstered when he was removed from the Politburo in 1982 due to differences of opinion over the pace of economic reforms. The *Far Eastern Economic Review* notes that it "was certainly no accident when Nguyen Van Linh—one of the leaders most closely identified with the reforms in the south—was unprecedentedly reinstated as a member of the politburo in June 1985. He was dropped in 1982, ostensibly for health reasons, but in fact for his unconventional economic approach."[35] At the same time, his decision to replace Prime Minister Pham Hung with Do Muoi instead of Vo Van Kiet in 1988 led to great opposition from southern, economic-reform-minded officials.

Scholars are therefore ambivalent about characterizing his approach to the economy. Similarly, his approach to strengthening the role of the VNA is consistent with several logics. In one part of his speech to the VNA in 1987, he seems to support the rationalization or the binding logic: "[I]n our country today, we have a lack of laws to govern the country. Regarding the laws that we already have, many people do not understand them. The work of issuing laws is also not taken up seriously. . . . Those are some among many reasons that have led to an increase in scandals, crimes not decreasing, and discipline not being maintained, and the security of the society not adequately protected."[36] Consistent with the rationalization logic, he expresses concern that party and government officials are breaking the law because of a lack of clarity about what the law actually is. However, at the same time it could be consistent with a binding logic, wherein party officials should be constrained by a more active legislature from breaking the law.

Later in the speech he voices arguments consistent with the rationalization logic and the citizen information logic. Consistent with the latter, he argues that increasing citizen participation in legislative activity will improve government accountability. Invoking Lenin, he suggested: "Long ago, V.I. Lenin raised the question of why Russia had so many laws but there were so many crimes. He answered: 'Only when individual citizens help, will the struggle be complete.' Of course, citizens understanding laws will help them have an additional powerful tool to fight this disadvantageous situation."[37]

Despite the several possible interpretations of Nguyen Van Linh's agenda derived from his words, the actual reforms suggest that his goal was not to generate greater bottom-up information. Rather, they indicate that he was more interested in improving the technical capacity of the legislature and its ability to educate citizens on the laws. One of the first important actions that allowed the VNA to assume greater lawmaking responsibilities was the selection of two former advisers to South Vietnam to the VNA. Lawyer and legal expert Ngo Ba Thanh, who was elected to the VNA in 1976, was selected to chair the Law Committee of the VNA. According to Duc, this selection "surprised more than a few delegates" (2012, 236). Furthermore, Duc suggests her selection was due to Linh's *direct intervention*. Duc quotes VNA delegate Le Van Triet as saying: "When General Secretary Nguyen Van Linh met with the Ho Chi Minh City VNA delegation, Thanh started to cry [because she was not selected to a leadership position]. Linh sat with her and the next day Ngo Ba Thanh was selected as chair of the Law Committee" (2012, 231n362). The other delegate selected was Nguyen Xuan Oanh, a former deputy prime minister for South Vietnam who had a PhD in economics from Harvard University. Oanh was instrumental in developing the foreign investment law. Indeed, the promotion of these delegates was not the result of bottom-up pressure, but of Linh's desire to increase the lawmaking capacity of the body. In particular, he wanted the expertise of those with experience in market economics to assist in the wave of economic laws that would pass through the VNA between 1988 and 1992.

Furthermore, it is clear that his inclusion of these officials was not out of a desire to undermine strong, single-party control. As Duc lays out in detail, Linh was clearly opposed to any political reforms that might open the door to multiparty democracy. Indeed, it was Linh who disbanded the nominally democratic parties in Vietnam in 1988 (Duc 2012). Furthermore, after "solving the multiparty problem," he also sought to stamp out further "pluralism" in the party (Duc 2012, 60). In an opening speech to the 6th Central Committee Plenum in March 1989, Linh emphasized that one could only see pluralism as a "reactionary plot by class enemies of the people" (Duc 2012, 60). It was in this context that one such promoter of "pluralism," Tran Xuan Bach, was purged from the Politburo in 1990. Seen in this light, Linh's promotion of Oanh and Thanh to leadership roles in the VNA is better interpreted as a desire for expertise rather than for greater information from previously unrepresented segments of the Vietnamese population.

Other evidence also points to the same explanation for the strengthening of the VNA. The key changes to the 1992 Constitution and the Law on the Organization of the VNA were not to expand the level of competition for elections or allow additional parties to compete. Rather, the major changes were, first, to strengthen the role of the committees by requiring them to meet more often and giving them staff. Second, and more important, the party leadership committed to increasing the number of full-time delegates in the VNA. In speech at the 7th Vietnam Communist Party Central Committee meeting in 1991, Muoi said it was the long-term goal of the party to have the VNA operate on a permanent basis. Although codifying this into law proved to be contentious, it was nonetheless included in Article 37 of the 1992 Law on the Organization of the VNA. The goal of these "specialized" delegates was clearly to increase the technical capacity of the VNA in order to help it pass coherent legislation and provide oversight. Because he most clearly states this objective, an interview response by former VNA chair Le Quang Dao is worth quoting at length:

> The National Assembly should have a legislative agenda and regard legislation as a scientific undertaking to be put in the charge of really knowledgeable people. These people should be paid and their work presented to the National Assembly only after it has been 'tested' and proven to be satisfactory. If necessary, foreign specialists may be invited to help. . . . The National Assembly library should have been well-stocked with all the laws of nations, but, at present, it is just a small book collection. In our country, state management is still being administered according to resolutions and directives, not totally in accordance with the law. This is a practice that must be corrected.[38]

The quoted response further suggests that the increased role of the VNA was most intended to increase the technical quality of legislation and to ensure that the government abided by those laws.

Additional evidence from those most intimately involved in crafting the reforms for Politburo approval also points to the technocratic nature of the reforms. Indeed, proponents of reforms to the electoral system have often voiced a desire for the elimination of the structure for selecting the legislature. At the same time, rather than promoting an alternative of open elections, they seem to suggest increasing the technical capacity of the legislature. In arguing against seeing representation as descriptive, Nguyen Minh Quang writes: "Representation means that the representative has 'heart', 'intelligence', and 'courage.' A scientist can have heart for farmers, can have intelligence to understand the issues of farmers, and can have courage to speak strongly for farmers in the National Assembly so why can we not see them as representative of farmers?" (2005, 75–76).[39]

Some scholars recognize that the reforms passed by the VNA to increase professionalism have confused technocratic specialization with political skills. Specialists have a particular ability in a subject but are not necessarily able to channel citizen input into the process of generating laws and conducting oversight. Selecting those with political skills requires increasing the number of self-nominated candidates, as this is the only way to identify those with political skills (D. S. Nguyen 2017, 60). However, as figure 4.2 shows, there has been no substantive increase in the number of self-nominees allowed to compete.

Furthermore, as figure 4.5 shows, the Election Board limits choice either by reducing the number of independent candidates or by reducing the total number of candidates. The fluctuation in non-party members is important, because they are an additional layer of security by which party leaders can exert their influence, particularly in contentious votes (Bui 2007). Figure 4.5 shows that the relationship between the candidate-to-seat ratio and non-party member candidates is negatively correlated, suggesting a substitution effect. The more diversity in the candidates, the more the Election Board restricts the number of options to choose from.

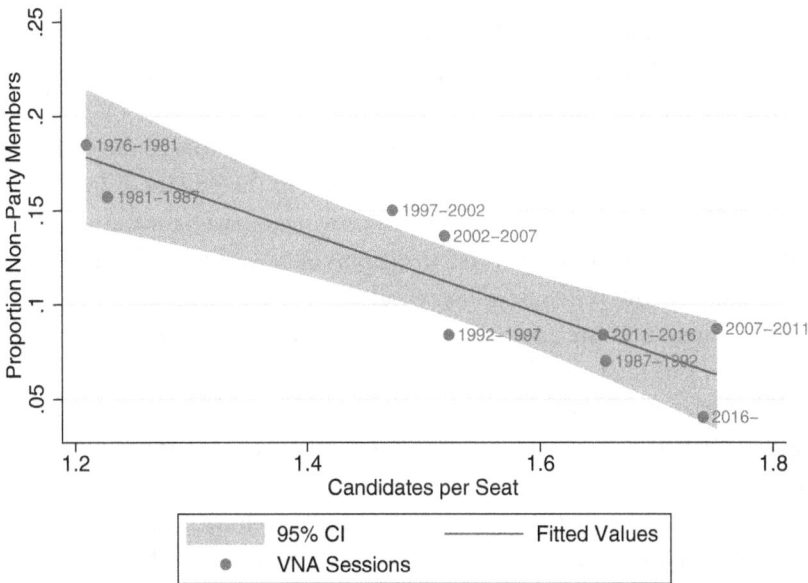

FIGURE 4.5. Relationship between candidates per seat and non-party members, 1976–2020.

While the two elections in 1976 and 1981 were outliers, the relationship still holds even for the more recent election. The obvious conclusion is that the more candidates the regime nominates, the more tightly it controls the candidates selected. Therefore, each election is controlled one way or another by the party leadership. While there has been a clear increase in professionalism, there has been little subsequent increase in the competitiveness in elections. This suggests that the changes to the legislature have increased the technical capacity of the legislature but have not dramatically increased the ability of citizens to choose their representatives.

A potential challenge to this rationalization argument is the addition of full-time, locally nominated delegates. These delegates, instituted in 2001, potentially support the citizen information argument, as their explicit purpose is to "reflect the wishes of the voters to the local officials and the center" (Ngo 2005, 158). Indeed, the fact that these delegates speak most often on the floor of the VNA lends some credence to the notion that the legislature is establishing this vital linkage between citizens and the center (Malesky and Schuler 2010). While this is possible in the abstract, a closer look at how these delegates are selected and controlled shows a different logic. First, the decision about the identity of the full-time locally nominated delegates is made by the head of the provincial delegation, who is the highest ranking local party member in the delegation. Once selected, the local, full-time delegate will then assume the role of deputy delegation head, under this higher-ranking party official.

Therefore, a more convincing interpretation of the role of the full-time locally nominated delegates is that they represent the provincial legislative committee, which is dominated by the provincial party apparatus. These delegates face strong pressure to toe the provincial party line because their future jobs in the province will depend on it. Furthermore, they do not want to offend ministers for fear of being cut off from government largesse.

Former Office of the VNA deputy chair Nguyen Sy Dung lays out this problem clearly in his discussion of provincially nominated full-time delegates: "[I]f [the provincial fulltime delegates] challenge the Center, this will definitely impact the province. Therefore, in the next election, the local leaders will ensure that those delegates are not reelected" (D. S. Nguyen 2017, 47).[40] Dung relates a story about how in one instance when a centrally nominated member of a delegation criticized a minister, the head of the provincial delegation said that the delegate was centrally nominated and therefore had nothing to do with the province. This is why most of the critical delegates such as Nguyen Minh Thuyet are centrally nominated. With this in mind, while locally nominated full-time delegates may speak frequently on the floor, their activity is better seen as a reflection of provincial leadership views than information on citizen preferences.

REFORM TO LEGISLATIVE INSTITUTIONS: BINDING THE PARTY
OR CHECKING THE GOVERNMENT?

Another key set of reforms was to empower the legislature through additional resources for committees, more meeting times for the legislature, and greater oversight powers. One interpretation of these reforms, consistent with the binding theory, is that they were designed to restrain a party that had mismanaged the economy. The argument in this book is that maintaining the signaling role of the legislature prevents its being a meaningful check on the party. Instead, this section suggests that the real goal of increasing the role of the VNA was to prevent reformists in the government from initiating reforms that deviated too far from the party line. That is, rather than constraining the party, the goal for the party was to use the legislature to manage potential rivals in the government. The following sections examine this argument in the context of two important reforms: the decision to televise query sessions and the decision to institute a vote of confidence in elected officials.

TELEVISING QUERY SESSIONS

The decision to televise query sessions in Vietnam is unique for several reasons. First, Vietnam is one of the few countries to subject government ministers to live questioning. China and other Eastern European communist regimes did allow some measure of oversight of the government. However, the most unique feature of the VNA query sessions is that they are televised live. During the day, observers can watch the proceedings on VTV1, Vietnam's primary state-run channel. The highlights of these proceedings are also carried on the evening news programs. China does not allow such sessions. The Soviet Union did briefly, but only shortly before the regime collapsed (Marples 2015). Why the difference in Vietnam?

If the "allies in reform," citizen information, power-sharing, or liberalization theories hold, we might expect those pushing for economic reforms within the government to also support the televised query sessions. Eager to gain input on their performance, they might push conservatives in the party to allow more open debate. From the power-sharing perspective, government leaders might fight for greater influence through the legislature to weaken the influence of the Politburo. Alternatively, if the party deflection theory is correct, we should find those in the Politburo whose primary position is in the party most likely to support the change. In addition, those in the government—particularly the prime minister—should be most likely to oppose the change.

What happened? In 1998, when the decision to televise was made, the leaders of the party and the government were Le Kha Phieu and Phan Van Khai, respectively.[41] In terms of the "reformer" or "conservative" label, there is no clear distinction. To the extent that one of the leaders could be labeled a reformer, it would be Phan Van Khai, who was linked to the previous prime minister, Vo Van Kiet. For context, in June 1997 some of the largest protests the regime had seen since unification occurred in Thai Binh province. These protests, which reached more than forty thousand participants, were largely directed at provincial and district officials involved in land seizures. Such was the degree of concern that the party passed the Grassroots Democracy Decree, increasing local governance measures, the following year (H. H. Nguyen 2016).

Vu Mao, who was at that time the chair of the VNA, relates the story of the passage of the reform. Mao initially put forward the reform proposal to the Politburo.[42] He claims it was a result of discussions with the interparliamentary union and development aid officials from Australia. The Politburo accepted the proposal. As is often the case, it is difficult to know who supported and who opposed the measure, as the Politburo simply assented to it by consensus.

While we do not know who supported the reforms in the Politburo, debates that preceded the rollout of the measure provide more evidence that the party leaders who were more opposed to economic reforms spearheaded the change. Ahead of the first day on which the sessions were to be televised, VTV got cold feet (Duc 2012). In particular, some within the Ministry of Information and the prime minister himself were concerned about the measure. At this stage, Vu Mao went directly to the Politburo to gain reauthorization to have the measure go forward, which it ultimately did.

This evidence suggests that, consistent with the theory, General Secretary Le Kha Phieu pushed for the change, not Phan Van Khai. Why? A newspaper interview with the general secretary ahead of that legislative session and the content of the debates provide clues. Ahead of the legislative session, in an interview with the newspaper *Lao Dong*, Phieu said in reference to the lack of democracy in Vietnam: "That is a problem we must firmly resolve. When we hear people speaking, we find that cadres (not only at the grassroots level, but also at higher levels) are far from the people."[43] This suggests that he was blaming not only the local government for the protests but also the central government. The topic of debate at the query session is consistent with this conclusion. The main subject under discussion was management of agricultural land.[44]

One additional point worth mentioning regarding the nature of the reform is that the VNA query sessions only apply to government officials, not party officials. Therefore, the prime minister, deputy prime minister, or ministers may be queried. However, the general secretary, whose office was not merged with the presidency at that time, could not be queried. Nor could other members of the party leadership, such as the chairs of the Central Organization Committee or the Central Propaganda Committee. This further suggests that the party leadership was not threatened by the change to the same degree as the reformers in the government. In short, the best evidence available suggests that party economic conservatives supported televising the query sessions over the reluctance of the more economically reform-minded government leaders.

VOTE OF CONFIDENCE MEASURE

A second instance in which the legislature gained power was in 2012, with the institution of the vote of confidence measure. Again, my theory would suggest that the party leadership should support the institution of the vote of confidence measure. Alternative theories would suggest that the creation of this measure would be designed to win legitimacy for the regime or signal greater openness.

In terms of the split between the party and state, the evidence is much clearer that in 2012 there was a split between General Secretary Nguyen Phu Trong and Prime Minister Nguyen Tan Dung. As has been well documented, Trong and the Politburo attempted to oust Dung in 2012, only to be dramatically rebuffed by the Central Committee in October of that year (Vuving 2013; Schuler and Ostwald 2016). Regarding the orientations of the two leaders, while it is difficult to point to a clear "reformer-conservative" cleavage, Trong does not fit anyone's definition of a reformer (Vuving 2010; H. M. Nguyen 2016). A former party ideological theorist trained in the Soviet Union, Trong's orientation has been to ensure the strength of the regime.

Dung, by contrast, at least had the image of reformer, whether or not he had the substance. His major policy initiatives involved streamlining bureaucratic procedures to ensure greater business efficiency. He was also credited in some quarters as instrumental in pushing through the Bilateral Trade Agreement between the United States and Vietnam. Finally, his son-in-law, an American citizen, opened the first McDonald's in Vietnam in Ho Chi Minh City. The allies-in-reform or citizen information thesis would predict that Dung should support the reforms, while the logic presented in this book suggests that Trong should support the reforms to shift blame for governance failures onto Dung.

In this case, the evidence is clear that the vote of confidence measure was spearheaded by Trong to damage Dung (Malesky 2014; Vuving 2013). In a speech before constituents in 2013 after the first confidence vote was held, Trong explicitly linked the measure to the self-criticism campaign initiated by Central Committee Resolution 4 in 2012, which led to the attempt to oust Dung: "In speaking with constituents about the confidence vote . . . Nguyen Phu Trong agreed with the opinion that the results reflected the true conditions of the country's economic, defense, security, foreign relations and legal situation. This is *part of the implementation of Central Committee Resolution 4 (11th Term)*."[45]

Why Did the Government Agree? Why Didn't the Party Reassert Direct Control?

A potential question about the preceding account is why, if the southern leaders had sufficient power to carve out independent space in the government, did they allow the legislature to gain increased power. Alternatively, why, if the party leaders had the power to strengthen the legislature, did they not reinstitute party controls over the economy instead of leaning on the legislature?

Part of the answer potentially lies in the sequence of the reforms. With the constitutional revision and the selection of Vo Van Kiet as prime minister, 1992 was the pivotal year for separation of the party and the state. In terms of legislative institutionalization, in 1992 the main push was to professionalize and rationalize, not to institute oversight. There was less conflict between the general secretaries and the prime ministers regarding rationalization. While this chapter shows that general secretaries Nguyen Van Linh and Do Muoi pushed rationalization, as Vo Van Kiet's letter to the Politburo shows, he was not opposed to rationalization, as a more competent VNA could assist in government lawmaking. Therefore, it was not unreasonable for him to support these early attempts to strengthen the VNA in exchange for greater independence.

The question is why Phan Van Khai would consent to allowing the VNA to engage in critical query sessions in 1998 if he had sufficient power to defend the independence of his position as prime minister. Alternatively, why would the party not simply directly reassert control over government policy by reinstituting party committees if it was dissatisfied with government performance? A potential answer to the first question has to do with the distribution of voting authority in the Politburo at the time. While the government does have several positions on the Politburo—generally the prime minister, a deputy prime minister, the minister of public security, the foreign minister, and the minister of defense hold positions on that body—the party also has several members. On the party side, aside from the general secretary, the Politburo includes the chairs of the Central Organization Committee, the Propaganda Committee, and the Central Inspection Commission. Other positions that are less clearly aligned with the party or the state are the secretaries of Hanoi and Ho Chi Minh City.

Aside from these positions, in 1998 there were also two positions closely aligned with the interests of the VNA: the chair of the VNA and the chair of the Fatherland Front, the mass organization in charge of vetting candidates for the VNA. Given this distribution of interests in the VNA, although no voting data are available, it is entirely possible that the party and the VNA, only recently having devolved power to Vo Van Kiet and his protégé, Phan Van Khai, were reluctant to reassert direct control over the government's economic portfolio. Indeed, the southern contingent may have mobilized resistance if the party had attempted to reinstate party economic committees. A better strategy would be to apply pressure through subtler means, such as through proxies in the VNA. From the government's side, while enhancing the power of the VNA was potentially embarrassing, it was likely not sufficiently destabilizing to push the southern leaders into open dissent. Therefore, while the government likely did not support the increased power of the VNA in 1998 and again in 2012, it was also not willing to engage in open dissent to challenge the decision.

Reinterpreting the Institutionalization of the VNA

This chapter highlights why Vietnam is a compelling, crucial case for the competing theories of authoritarian legislative development. At precisely the time the regime faced an economic crisis due to a series of poor policy decisions and the cessation of Soviet aid, the regime strengthened committee structures and allowed the legislature to meet for a longer duration, suggesting that the party was either tying its hands or wanted to acquire better information on the preferences of the citizens. Furthermore, the economic growth after 1989 suggests these reforms played an important role in improving economic outcomes. The important question here is whether these increased resources served to incorporate more divergent views into the legislature or it was simply done in order to "rationalize" policy making under the party's general direction while retaining the essential features of the VNA's propaganda function.

This review provides some hints about why, despite the apparent need for more information, the rationalization and blame deflection theories may be the best explanation. First, while the party increased the number of professionals in the legislature, the degree of pluralism in the assembly dropped, if anything. This suggests that as the regime was devoting more resources to the legislature, it was simultaneously using other levers to control behavior in the assembly. This is partly because despite the various iterations of the electoral law (2015, 2010, 2001, 1997, 1992), the five gates vetting system has remained essentially unchanged. The one key change was the self-nominating candidates in 2002 (Abuza 2001). However, despite the fanfare, this institution has had limited impact on the actual composition of the VNA.

In addition, in the various legal changes to the constitution (1992, 2001, 2013) and the legislature (1992, 2001, 2007, 2014), the essential dominance of the VNASC remains unchanged. While its role in lawmaking has undoubtedly expanded since 1989 due to its increased resources and professionalism, it still remains a "legislature within a legislature." Furthermore, as the following chapters note, this legislature within a legislature remains firmly controlled by the center due to Vietnam's unique electoral system and patterns of appointment. Therefore, while it may appear the party has delegated lawmaking to the VNA, it may be more correct to say that the party has delegated lawmaking to the VNASC.

Another puzzling feature of the developments described here is the fact that, at least initially, there were few moves to enhance the oversight function of the legislature. The visibility of the oversight mechanisms increased slightly in 1992 but really did not change dramatically until 1998 with the televising of the query sessions. After that point the legislature not only televised the sessions but also extended them from one day to three or four days. In this vein, it is instructive that the legislature moved first to institutionalize its lawmaking responsibilities before doing the same for oversight duties. As concrete evidence of this, in 1988 the State Council passed a directive on the promulgation of laws, which was converted into a law in 1996.[46] Among other things, the law specified in detail the steps laws must follow before they are passed. By contrast, the first Law on the Oversight Activities was not passed until 2003.[47] This suggests there were other reasons than simply improved performance driving the move to increase the legislature's public oversight role. The impetus behind these later reforms of the VNA was to restrain the independence the government had gained from the party in the initial wave of institutional reforms from 1986 to 1992.

FIVE

Mobilized or Motivated?
Voting Behavior in Vietnamese Elections

> People shouldn't think that "Vietnamese do not care about politics"; it is more correct to say that they are not allowed to care.
>
> —former VNA delegate Nguyen Minh Thuyet[1]

The previous chapters of this book have discussed the electoral and legislative institutions in the VNA and how they map onto existing theories. This chapter moves in a different direction and considers how these institutions impact electoral behavior. As chapter 1 discusses, electoral behavior is integral to my overall theory that the purpose of the VNA and its elections is to signal strength. This theory suggests that citizens should care little about electoral outcomes. That is, if elections are stage managed to demonstrate regime strength, we should not see citizens informing themselves about the election. Furthermore, citizens should not take their votes particularly seriously. This argument contrasts with other work on single-party electoral behavior, which suggests that citizens *do* care about participating in elections (Landry, Davis, and Wang 2010; Shi 1999; Wang and Sun 2017). Indeed, this is a critical link in information theories that suggest single-party elections serve to elect candidates more closely aligned with citizen preferences.

More specifically, I predict that citizens will exhibit little knowledge of candidates and not vote based on the types of incentives that predominate in democratic elections. In particular, because of the lack of interest in elections and lack of knowledge of the candidates, both a result of campaign restrictions imposed by the regime, the closeness of the elections should have no impact on electoral turnout. Instead, consistent with the logic of this book, party strength should mobilize turnout. An additional implication of this is that in contrast to democracies that use similar electoral systems, in Vietnam we should see no strategic voting. This is because strategic voting implies that citizens know the difference between candidates and care about who wins.

To test this theory, this chapter relies on a unique dataset. In a first for a single-party regime, Vietnam published vote totals for the winning and losing candidates in its 2016 National Assembly election. I matched these returns to a national survey of fourteen thousand people that asked questions about vote turnout and candidate knowledge. Analysis of this unique dataset shows results consistent with the signaling argument. In short, mobilization, not the closeness of the election, drives turnout. Furthermore, citizens do not vote strategically. Finally, those who do vote do not vote knowledgeably. This suggests that elections contain little information but do serve to rally the faithful to demonstrate regime support at the polls.

The Impact of Knowledge, Turnout, and Competitiveness on Electoral Information

Do citizens vote knowledgeably in Vietnam? This is a crucial component of the alternative logics of authoritarian legislatures. In short, the idea that an elected legislator should represent citizen interests to a greater degree than an unelected bureaucrat rests on the assumption that elections generate an electoral connection. However, there are reasons to be skeptical that this will be the case. First, even in democracies, many are skeptical that voters are informed (Achen and Bartels 2016; Delli Carpini and Keeter 1996). In addition, research on the US Congress shows that where information is poor, a situation endemic to single-party regimes, knowledge of candidates and accountability are low (Levy and Squire 2000; Snyder and Stromberg 2010). Finally, research on turnout suggests that *caring about the outcome* matters for participation. Where citizens feel the stakes are higher, they are more likely to turn out due to the psychological costs of not participating (Aytac and Stokes 2019).

Each of these factors that inhibit meaningful electoral participation in democracies should be exacerbated in a single-party regime. Citizens will likely perceive few differences between candidates who have gone through the vetting procedures discussed in chapter 2. Also, manipulation should depress interest or participation in the election due to concerns about the meaning of people's votes. Finally, voters may simply lack information on the candidates, which will impact the degree to which they care about the election. As chapter 2 shows, Vietnam, like other single-party regimes such as China (Chen and Zhong 2002, 182), Syria (Varulkar and Winter 2007), and the Soviet Union (Hill 1976), features restrictions on campaigning that pale in comparison to even the most information-poor election districts in the United States. In short, if voters in democracies are not sufficiently informed, what hope is there in a single-party setting?

Empirically, existing evidence that single-party elections may contain information is open to competing interpretations. One set of studies uses downstream indicators of legislative behavior, showing that national- and local-level representatives in China and Vietnam reflect preferences consistent with the views of their constituents (Manion 2016; Truex 2016; Malesky and Schuler 2010). While this is consistent with the premise that elections provide information on citizen views, it could also be the case that both the elected officials and constituents are generally concerned with similar topics because of a shared geography. Critical behavior could also reflect intraregime dissent instead of genuine citizen preferences (Lu, Liu, and Li 2019).

In other research, Manion (2016) shows that locally nominated delegates are more likely to be "good types" than "governing types," suggesting that voters provide meaningful input. Unfortunately this does not rule out the possibility that the entire exercise is stage managed. For example, it is possible that the regime preplans two separate types of delegates: those in charge of the legislature and others tasked with providing a link between citizens and the regime. To increase the legitimacy of the latter group, the regime may formally ask for local approval for those candidates, while directly nominating the governing types. This scenario is consistent with accounts of single-party settings such as Vietnam and China, where centrally nominated candidates fit a different profile by design (Malesky and Schuler 2009; Wang 2017).

Finally, some studies show that voters take their votes seriously, suggesting that votes contain information (Landry, Davis, and Wang 2010; Shi 1999; Wang and Sun 2017). This evidence is compelling because it shows that rather than simply being mobilized to vote, some voters actually respond to electoral conditions. At the same time, these findings suffer from an important limitation. Measures of district competitiveness are based on a respondent's perceptions rather than objective indicators, which is problematic because self-assessments of district competitiveness may not align with actual competitiveness. A more direct test would follow similar research from democracies examining the impact of actual district competitiveness on turnout (Geys 2006; Cancela and Geys 2016). It is important to note that existing research acknowledges this and is forced to use survey data because of data availability concerns.

Observable Implications of the Signaling Theory

Before assessing Vietnam specifically, what has an impact on voting behavior in other contexts? Research on democracies shows that a number of factors drive the decision to vote in democracies, including education (Milligan, Moretti, and Oreopoulos 2004; Sondheimer and Green 2010), social networks (Gerber and Green 2000; Gerber, Green, and Larimer 2008), income (Wolfinger and Rosenstone 1980), and district closeness (Simonivits 2012; De Paola and Scoppa 2014; Geys 2006). These variables increase turnout either by affecting an individual's internal costs and benefits (intrinsic benefits) or by impacting one's desire for social approval (extrinsic benefits) (Gerber, Green, and Larimer 2008; Knack 1992; Harbaugh 1996).

For the purposes of this chapter, it is not important whether intrinsic or extrinsic motivations obtain in Vietnam. What is important is whether these motives drive voters to acquire information and vote. The signaling theory would predict that only the mobilization channel drives turnout. Namely, the party apparatus raises the cost of not voting (or increases the direct benefit of voting) by pressuring citizens to go to the polls. Indeed, in democracies, research on vote buying (Hicken 2011; Desposato 2007), civic virtue (Galston 2001), and knowledge (Delli Carpini and Keeter 1996; Campbell et al. 1960) raises the concern that voting behavior operates primarily through the mobilization channel.

Alternative theories generate different predictions. For citizen information theory, one observable implication is that voters have some knowledge of the candidates. Informed voting leads to two additional observable implications. Research from democracies also shows increased turnout in competitive districts (Simonivits 2012; De Paola and Scoppa 2014; Geys 2006). Indeed, for this to be the case, voters require some information on the competitiveness of the candidates. This is why citizen information theorists have used the link between competition and voting as evidence of informative elections (Landry, Davis, and Wang 2010; Shi 1999). This leads to an additional observable implication of informed voting: election district competitiveness should increase turnout.

A final piece of evidence, consistent with table 5.1, is that informed voters may behave strategically. Strategic voting occurs when voters abandon their first-choice candidate for a candidate with a better chance of winning. When districts have a sufficiently small district magnitude, strategic voting occurs (Cox 1995). Critically, as with the link between district closeness and turnout, strategic voting also relies on some information about the viability

TABLE 5.1.
Observable implications of information and signaling theories
for voting behavior.

Theory	Observable implications
Information	Strategic voting
	Competitiveness drives turnout
	Knowledge of candidates
Signaling	No strategic voting
	Party mobilizes turnout
	No knowledge of candidates

of the candidates. Therefore, the presence of strategic voting constitutes evidence of informed voting.[2]

By contrast, as table 5.1 shows, when the information channel is cut off, the other factors that flow from it—strategic voting, responsiveness to competitiveness, and knowledge of the candidates—also disappear. This means that voters should not vote strategically, district competitiveness should have no impact on turnout, and voters should have little knowledge of candidates. At the same time, key evidence in favor of the signaling argument would be that the strength of the local party apparatus drives voting behavior. While voters may not care who wins, the ability of the local party leaders to drive citizens to the polls should increase turnout.

Empirical Evidence

Table 5.1 outlines three sets of observable implications of informed voting versus mobilized voting: strategic voting, competitiveness and turnout, and voter knowledge. The following sections present testable hypotheses and results for each of the implications.

STRATEGIC VOTING

This section tests for strategic voting. Tests of strategic voting rely on two sets of indicators: patterns in district-level vote outcomes (Cox 1995; Cox and Shugart 1996; Moser and Scheiner 2009) and survey data (Niemi, Whitten and Franklin 1992). Because survey data on strategic voting are not available for Vietnam, this section relies on election district-level outcomes. A standard measure of strategic voting is the election district-level distributions of the SF ratio, the ratio of the vote share between the second loser and the first loser (Cox 1995; Cox and Shugart 1996; Moser and Scheiner 2009).

Where strategic voting occurs, we should see a bimodal distribution of SF ratios. This is because in moderately competitive districts, voters abandon the second loser in favor of the first loser or one of the winning candidates in order to have an impact on the outcome, thus shifting districts that would have had a middle SF ratio to a low SF ratio. However, when there is no clear difference in the viability of two or more of the losing candidates (hence a high SF ratio), voters do not abandon either of the losing candidates. Therefore, districts with high SF ratios do not change.

Turning now to the data, because the predicted SF ratio distribution under Vietnam's block voting system has not been confirmed in democratic contexts, to demonstrate that the tendency holds, panel 2 of figure 5.1 shows the SF ratio for Thailand's block voting electoral districts in 1996 and 1995.[3] As the figure shows, there is a mode near one, where voters fail to coordinate on a viable contender, and another near zero, where strategic voting occurs. This demonstrates that as theory would predict, strategic voting occurs in democratic contexts using the block voting system. For Vietnam, I examined the patterns from the 2016 election. Panel 1 of Figure 5.1 shows a remarkable difference. In contrast to Thailand, there are no election districts where the ratio is less than .35, meaning there are *no* election districts where voters abandon a losing candidate for a more competitive trailing candidate.

Of course, while failing to find strategic voting is consistent with mobilization theory, it does not rule out the information argument. One possible reason for the lack of strategic voting is that voters do not coordinate because the popularity of the winners is so extreme that voters preferring likely losers do not bother to abandon their first preferences (Cox 1995). Under this logic, the votes still contain information because votes for the winners are sincere. However, another interpretation is that some districts are noncompetitive because of electioneering. That is, some districts have a higher SF ratio because those districts are manipulated. In this case, the electoral outcome contains little information on citizen preferences. To assess whether manipulation or genuine popularity contributes to the lack of strategic voting, I examined the relationship between manipulation and the competitiveness of the districts.

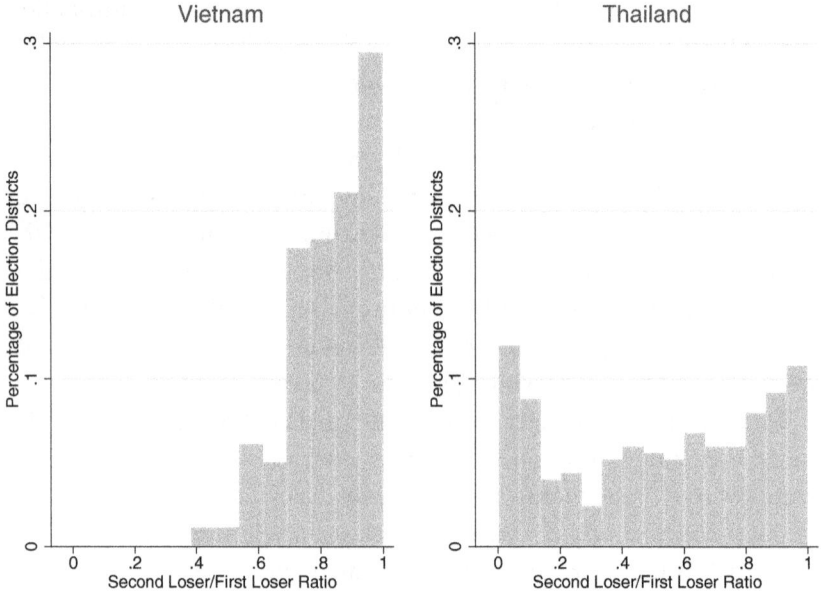

FIGURE 5.1. SF ratio in Vietnam and Thailand.

To identify uncompetitive districts, I calculated an additional measure, the FL ratio, or the "first loser/last winner" ratio. This is essentially the same as the measures of competitiveness used in single-member district elections (Geys 2006), except that instead of looking at the difference between the winning and losing candidate with the largest vote share, I measured the difference between the winning candidate with the lowest vote total and the most popular losing candidate. The higher the ratio, the more competitive the district.

Using these two measures, figure 5.2 presents a hypothetical distribution of election districts and the implications for the information and mobilization arguments. The bottom half of the figure shows districts with strategic voting. The top left square includes uncompetitive districts, which could be consistent with genuinely popular winners or manipulated districts. The top right shows competitive districts with no strategic voting. These districts could be consistent with the information theory if voters turn out in greater numbers. However, they could also be consistent with random voting patterns.

Looking at the cases examined here, figure 5.3 shows that while Thailand features a number of districts that demonstrate patterns consistent with strategic voting, in Vietnam there are virtually no districts that demonstrate

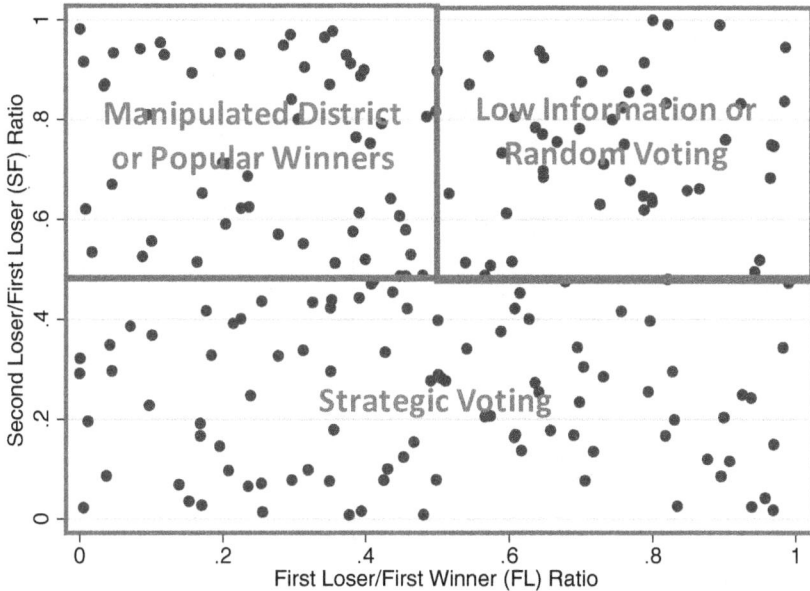

FIGURE 5.2. Hypothetical distribution of SF ratio, FL ratio, and implications for behavior.

patterns consistent with such behavior. Indeed, in almost every district the two losing candidates had vote shares very close to each other. Where there is variation in Vietnam is in the difference between the winning candidates and the losing candidates. In some districts (the top left), the winning candidates vote percentages were significantly higher than the losing candidates. In others (the top right), the winning and losing candidates had roughly equal vote shares. If the signaling theory holds, we should see the difference between the top-left and top-right squares driven mostly by electioneering. If information theory holds, it could be that citizens in the top-left districts genuinely preferred the winners, and thus there is no relationship between victory differentials and electioneering.

To identify electioneering, I used the proxy measure developed in chapter 2, which is the number of "sacrificial lamb" candidates. As described in chapter 2, sacrificial lamb candidates are those who only work at district-level (as opposed to province-level) offices. To validate this measure, tables 5.2 and 5.3 show that voters punish sacrificial lambs. Controlling for a range of factors, the results show that these candidates have a 13 percent lower chance of election and receive about 7 percent lower vote shares. Between

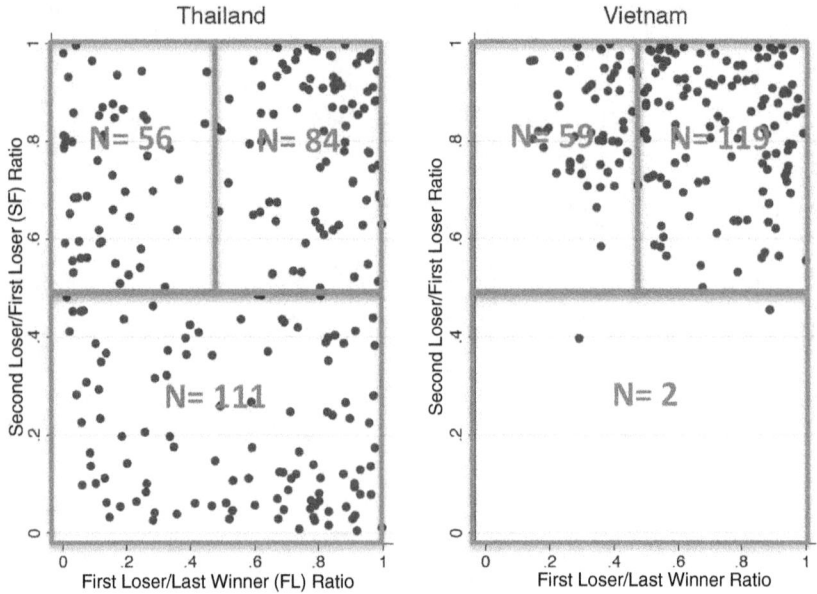

FIGURE 5.3. SF ratio and FL ratio in electoral districts, Thailand (1995 and 1996) and Vietnam (2016).

2007 and 2016 only 26 percent of the district-level candidates won election, compared to 63 percent of the rest of the candidates. If electioneering drives the high vote totals for the top left quadrant, we should see more of these sacrificial lamb candidates nominated in those districts than in the top-right square of figure 5.2.

Table 5.4 tests whether electioneering drives districts into the upper left quadrant of figure 5.2. Using an OLS regression, the dependent variable is the FL ratio, and the key independent variable is the sacrificial lamb variable, which is the sum of the total district-level candidates in an election district. To account for other factors that could drive election district competitiveness, the model includes other factors such as local party capacity, which is a measure of the number of party members per capita in a province (Thayer 2015). Unfortunately, these data are not available annually and therefore this factor is measured only in 2010. However, party strength is likely a slow-moving variable and should be a reasonable proxy for local party capacity in 2016. The model also includes Malesky and Schuler's (2011) measure of electoral district strength, which is an additive measure of

TABLE 5.2.
Sacrificial lamb candidates, descriptive statistics (2007, 2011, 2016).

	Sacrificial lamb candidates*	Other candidates
Total	**345**	**2,227**
2007	*128*	*748*
2011	*101*	*726*
2016	*116*	*753*
Election Winners	91	1,398
Winning %	26.38%	62.78%

*Candidates whose highest position is in the district level (rather than province).
Boldface numbers are cumulative.

TABLE 5.3.
Model of candidate election, voting percentage.

Variables	Results (Model 1)	Percentage Vote Share (Model 2)
Sacrificial lamb candidates	−0.122*	−7.052*
	(0.0338)	(2.001)
Controls	Yes	Yes
Constant		22.69
		(3.751)
Observations	2,569	867
R-squared	0.359	0.54

NOTE: Model 1 is the marginal effects of a probit model for 2007, 2011, and 2016 on whether or not a candidate won; model 2 is the results of an OLS model on the 2016 election where the vote percentage is the dependent variable (2011 and 2007 not included because no percentage totals available for the losing candidates).

Robust standard errors in parentheses.

* $p < 0.01$

characteristics popular with voters.[4] Provincial GDP per capita is included to account for any wealth effects. Finally, because district magnitude can impact the coordination, the model includes a magnitude measure, which indicates whether two or three candidates were selected from the district.

Table 5.4 confirms that noncompetitive districts (top-left quadrant of figure 5.2) are far more likely to have sacrificial lamb candidates. Model 1 shows that having one district-level candidate reduces the FL ratio by .09, and two candidates reduce it by .18. A one standard deviation shift in the FL

TABLE 5.4.
Impact of electioneering on district competitiveness (FL ratio).

	FL ratio (Model 1)	FL ratio (Model 2)
District-level candidates	−0.0982** (0.0188)	−0.0668** (0.0189)
Power index		−0.0199 (0.0123)
Party members per capita		−0.0465** (0.00999)
GDP per capita		0.000886* (0.000375)
District magnitude		0.173** (0.0377)
Constant	0.677 (0.0201)	0.476 (0.0998)
Observations	181	181
R-squared	0.133	0.346

NOTE: The dependent variable is the ratio between the first losing candidate and the last winning candidate. A lower FL ratio means the election was not close; a higher number means the election was closer.
Robust standard errors in parentheses.
* p < 0.05, ** p < 0.01

ratio is about .24, so the effect is substantive. Model 2 shows that the addition of controls does not change the coefficient, indicating that the result is robust. The results in model 2 are also consistent with a mobilization story, that provincial party membership also reduces the FL ratio. This is true even after controlling for electioneering, suggesting that the noncompetitive districts are those with more party members. This is consistent with existing findings from hybrid regimes showing that manipulation is greater where the party is stronger (Rozenas 2016; Rundlett and Svolik 2016). Importantly, as Rozenas (2016) argues, this means that the information from such manipulated districts will be minimal. Therefore, if information is to be found, it is in the competitive districts.

VOTER TURNOUT

While the previous section shows there is no strategic voting and that noncompetitive districts are subject to more intense electioneering, thus undermining information from those districts, it may be that in the competitive districts (top-right quadrant of figure 5.2) the vote totals are more meaningful. However, those districts are also consistent with the story that voters are simply not informed, do not care about the candidate they elect in those districts, or are not told whom to vote for. Furthermore, it is a lack of mobilization to vote for the party's preferred candidate that drives the seeming competitiveness of the districts, rather than genuine citizen preferences.

As identified in the literature, one way to distinguish between these two possibilities is to see whether voters respond to increased competition by voting in greater numbers (Shi 1999; Landry, Davis, and Wang 2010). If voters care about the election, they are more likely to vote in competitive districts. This section looks at this question by matching the election returns from the previous section to the 2016 Vietnam Provincial Governance and Public Administrative Performance Index (PAPI). PAPI is a nationally representative survey that also features representative samples down to the provincial level. PAPI is useful because it reaches 142 of the 182 election districts across the country. In each district where the survey is conducted, at least sixty respondents answer the survey. For the dependent variable, the survey asks respondents whether they *personally* voted in the election.

Similar to China, in Vietnam, although the government officially reports turnout of near 99 percent across the country, because of proxy voting, in which family members vote on behalf of other members, the number is actually far lower (Wang and Sun 2017). According to the PAPI survey, 71 percent of respondents in 2016 said they voted personally. Of the 29 percent who did not vote, the vast majority said they asked a family member to vote on their behalf. If voters turn out in greater numbers in competitive districts, this is consistent with the notion that voters are informed and care about the outcome. If signaling theory holds, the party may directly mobilize turnout during elections. Alternatively, party mobilization could be indirect, in that the party co-opts citizens into regime-linked organizations, then pressures voters to turn out through membership in those organizations.

To measure competitiveness, the key independent variable is the election district FL ratio discussed in the previous section. To assess signaling theory, I included other variables that would indicate direct and indirect mobilization. For direct mobilization, I included the provincial party membership data from the previous section. For indirect mobilization, I included individual-level variables identifying a link to the party. These include whether or not the respondent is a party member and whether or not the respondent is a member of a party-affiliated mass organization.[5] I also included other controls such as education and income. On the one hand, it could operate through the information channel if education, age, gender, and ethnicity are considered.

For the model, I used a probit model with multiway clustering (provincial, district, commune, and village) to account for the multitiered, clustered design of the survey. In addition, because one province is the source of oil revenues, I dummied out Ba Ria-Vung Tau's provincial effects to account for its abnormal gross domestic product (GDP) levels.[6]

Table 5.5 shows the results of four models. When individual-level factors are excluded, provincial party capacity positively predicts turnout (models 2 and 3). For the mobilization theory, model 4, which includes the individual-level factors, shows that party capacity is mediated through the co-optation of individuals into party-led organizations. Obviously the increased number

TABLE 5.5.
Probit model of turnout in Vietnam's 2016 election.

Variables	Party capacity Model 1	District competitiveness Model 2	Province controls Model 3	Individual controls Model 4
FL ratio (higher more competitive)	−0.341** (0.0809)		−0.229* (0.0894)	−0.187* (0.094)
Provincial party members per capita		0.0596** (0.0107)	0.0491** (0.0115)	−0.0126 (0.0133)
Provincial GDP per capita			0.000544 (0.000884)	−0.00116 (0.000955)
Party member				0.875** (0.0834)
Mass organization member				0.356** (0.0381)
Education				0.191** (0.0172)
Income				0.0108 (0.0154)
Other controls	No	No	No	Yes
Constant	0.783 (0.0538)	0.333 (0.0438)	0.496 (0.0817)	−0.509 (0.144)
Observations	6,845	6,975	6,845	6,372

NOTE: Results are from a probit model, with standard errors using multiway clustering with an individual's decision to vote personally as the dependent variable.

* $p < 0.05$, ** $p < 0.01$

of party members accounts for some of the effect of local party capacity. However, the presence of civil society groups is also positively associated with party capacity, and these individuals are also more likely to vote. The results also show that the provinces with greater party capacity are more likely to have highly educated respondents, who are more likely to vote than less educated respondents. As model 4 shows, once these factors are accounted for, the direct impact of party capacity disappears, showing that the impact of party capacity works through individual-level incorporation into party-led organizations and education.

Regarding competitiveness, the FL ratio is significant, but in the opposite direction. That is, the *less competitive* the district *the more likely the respondent is to vote*. These findings hold in the models that also include individual-level factors, such as model 4. These results suggest that competitiveness does not drive turnout. Turning to other individual-level factors, political awareness and education are both correlated with voting. These variables could be consistent with both the information and the mobilization story, depending on the degree to which those voters are more informed. Assessing that possibility is the focus of the next section. However, the results in table 5.5 show that contrary to the revisionist arguments, district competitiveness does not increase turnout.

VOTER KNOWLEDGE

The previous sections show no evidence of strategic voting or that district competitiveness drives turnout. Both results are consistent with a mobilization story. However, one potential remaining conclusion consistent with the citizen information argument is that while voters do not vote strategically or respond to district-level competition, they could still have knowledge of the candidates. Therefore, a final test of information concerns the degree to which voters are informed about the candidates running.

The most common measure of voter knowledge is recall or recognition of candidate names (Mann and Wolfinger 1980; Levy and Squire 2000; Schulhofer-Wohl and Garrido 2013; Snyder and Stromberg 2010). Unfortunately, two limitations prevent replicating previous work in this area. First, the PAPI survey does not ask respondents to recall candidate names for office. Second, the PAPI survey filters only ask *voters* about the candidates running. Therefore, one cannot compare voter knowledge to nonvoter knowledge.

However, the survey does allow for two alternative tests that could indicate voter knowledge. First, the survey includes two questions about whether the election district had a female candidate or a non-party candidate.[7] By matching responses to these questions to the actual districts, I can assess the degree to which voters could correctly identify candidate backgrounds. It is important to note that due to the strict vetting, no district had more than six candidates, so this measure does not ask voters to identify obscure candidates with no chance of winning. Using these data, as a first test, I can assess whether respondents had a greater than 50/50 chance of correctly identifying the gender and party status of candidates running in their district.

The second hypothesis relies on the assumption that educated voters should be more likely to correctly identify candidate features than uneducated voters. Research in democracies shows that educated voters are more informed about the candidates (Jackee and Sun 2006). Theory suggests this knowledge lowers their cost of participation, thus leading to greater turnout. This interpretation would be consistent with the results in table 5.5, which shows a strong increase in turnout based on education. If this is the case, uneducated voters, whose votes are based more on mobilization pressures, should have less knowledge of the candidates than the educated voters, who are partially induced to vote due to their information advantage. To demonstrate the plausibility of the assumption that educated voters are more knowledgeable than less-educated voters, I show in the following discussion that educated voters are in fact more likely to correctly answer knowledge questions about issues *other* than the election candidates than are less-educated voters.

An alternative mobilization view is that more-educated voters are more likely to be mobilized because of their connections to party officials and because they feel more pressure to vote. While such voters may be more knowledgeable generally, they will be no more likely to invest energy in learning about the candidates than uneducated voters. This is because the lack of information and genuine competition undermines their willingness and ability to acquire information. As such, the mobilization theory would not predict a difference between educated and uneducated voters.

To test these hypotheses, I ran a probit model on whether or not the voters correctly identified whether or not a non-party member or female candidate was running in their district. To account for any confounds based on gender, ethnicity, or provincial characteristics, I used the same controls as those in table 5.5. The only additional variable is a measure of whether or not there actually was a female member or non-party member in district. This is to account for the fact that voters are far more likely to say there is a female candidate or a non-party candidate than not, regardless of the actual district characteristics.

Before proceeding to the test and the results, I first demonstrate that educated voters are in fact more politically knowledgeable than uneducated voters regarding general political knowledge. To address this, the PAPI survey includes four knowledge questions. The first is an open-ended question that randomly divides the respondents into four groups, asking them to name the general secretary, the prime minister, the president, or the National Assembly chair. These responses are aggregated into a single indicator. Other questions ask respondents to self-identify if they are aware of the Trans-Pacific Partnership, the Access to Information Law, or the Anti-Corruption Law.

Figure 5.4 shows the predicted probability of a correct response by education on these political knowledge items among voters. As it clearly indicates, educated voters are more politically knowledgeable than uneducated voters. Reassuringly, the result on correctly identifying the leader, which is an open-ended question, fits this trend, thus ensuring the results are not simply due to the fact that educated voters are more likely to answer the questions. This suggests that consistent with the assumption underlying the second hypothesis, educated voters are more knowledgeable about general political issues than uneducated voters.

Turning now to candidate knowledge, I ran the same model as in figure 5.4, except with the dependent variable measuring whether or not respondents correctly identified their district candidates' features. Figure 5.5 includes the results when all voters are included and the "don't knows" (DKs) are treated as incorrect answers. For the estimated effects, all control variables are held to their means except the district female and district non-party members. These are held to .5 to normalize the results to a .5 probability of being in either district type. Figure 5.5 clearly shows that for both dependent variables, educated and uneducated voters are no more likely than chance to correctly identify the candidates' characteristics. This suggests that the first hypothesis—that voters should have a better than chance ability to correctly identify candidates—does not hold.

Moving to the second set of hypotheses, contrary to the predictions of the citizen information theory, educated voters are also no more likely to correctly identify the features of the candidates than less-educated voters.

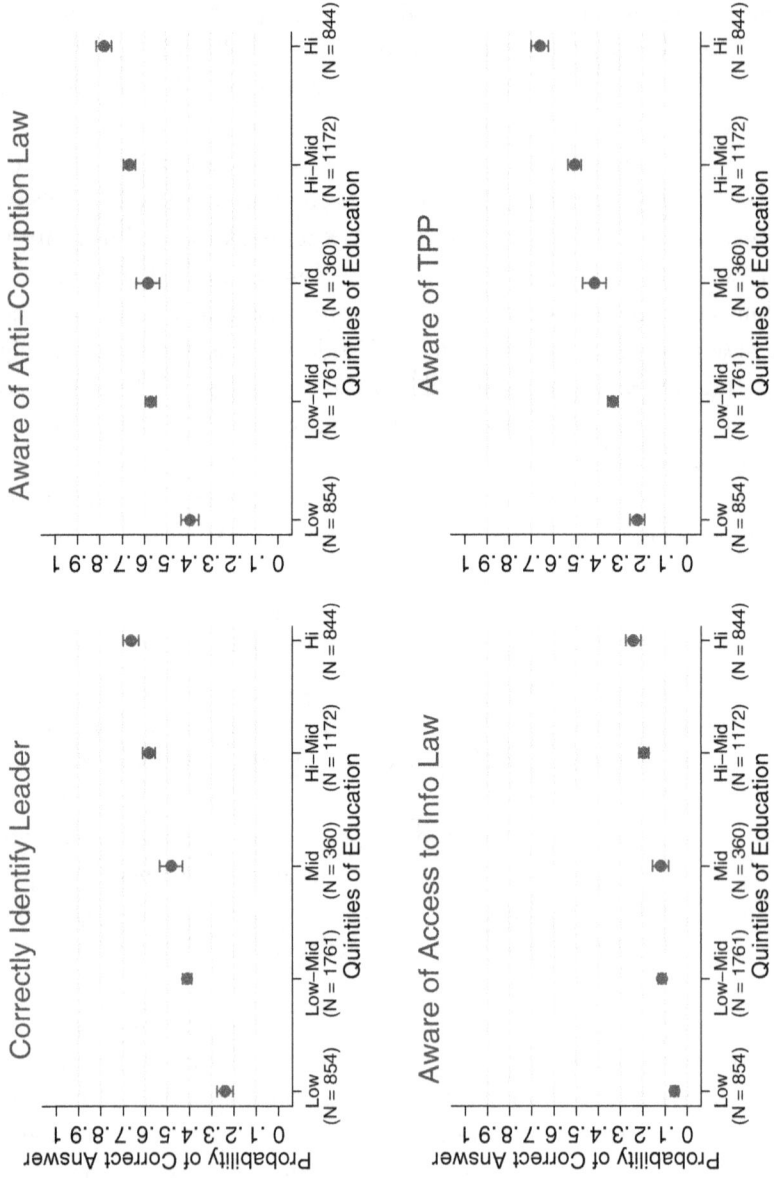

FIGURE 5.4. Education and general political knowledge among voters.

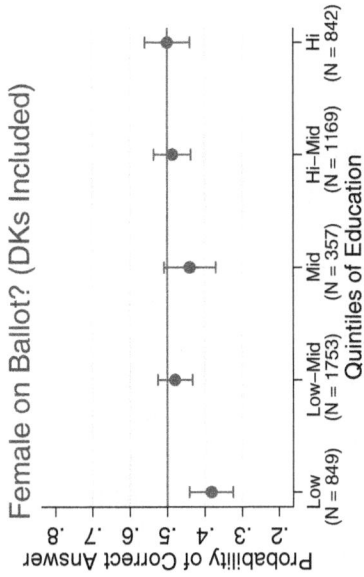

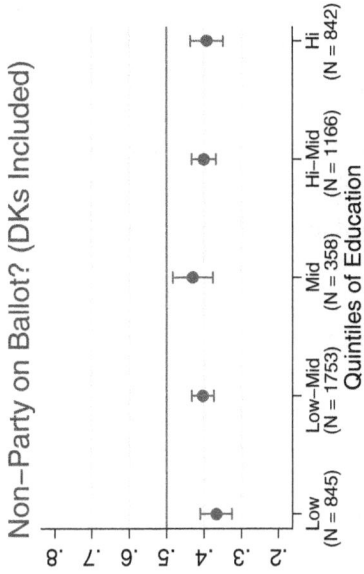

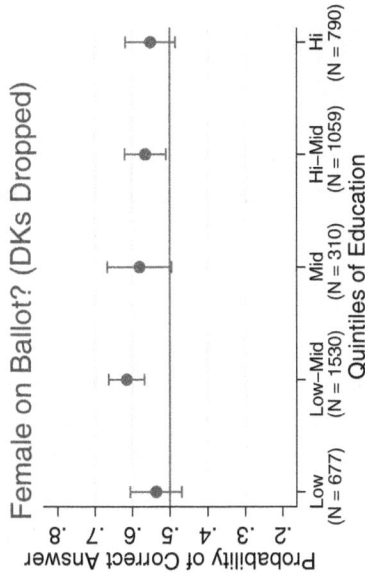

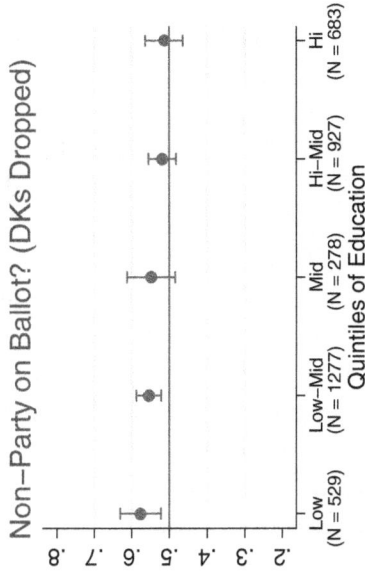

FIGURE 5.5. Education and knowledge of candidates among voters.

Only in the top-left panel is there a relationship between education and a correct response. However, as the bottom-left panel shows, this is largely because educated respondents are more likely to hazard a guess and therefore are guaranteed a greater probability of being near .5 by chance. When the "don't knows" are dropped, the highly educated voters are not much better than chance at correctly identifying the candidates in their district.

These results suggest two things. First, voters on average are ill informed about the candidates. Just several months after the election, respondents were less able than chance to identify basic features of candidates running in their districts. Second, even the educated voters, who we expect to have greater knowledge about candidates, are not more aware than uneducated voters, even though educated voters are more aware about general political knowledge issues. This suggests that while educated candidates are more politically knowledgeable and are mobilized to vote, they are not mobilized to care about the election.

Mobilizing Elections

A lynchpin of theories of democratic governance as well as the revisionist literature on authoritarian elections is that elections provide information on citizen preferences. By contrast, classic understandings of single-party elections and the central theory of this book are that elections are exercises in mobilization. The unique, original data provided in this chapter show that in Vietnam, the evidence is that voters are uninformed and do not respond to electoral conditions when deciding to vote. Rather, voting is driven mostly by the strength of the party and voters' connections to the party.

This makes sense. Given the electoral manipulation detailed in chapter 2, how would citizens express genuine preferences? Just as important, if citizens did care, restrictions on campaigning should make it difficult for citizens to even perceive the differences between the candidates. The facts that there is no strategic voting in Vietnam and that electoral conditions do not drive turnout are consistent with this.

How does a lack of electoral connection impact delegate behavior? The next chapter addresses this question.

SIX

Explaining Oversight Behavior
Position Taking or Position Ducking?

Why don't we see the VNA deal quickly with issues such as Tien Lang-
Hai Phong, Van Giang-Hung Yen? When Chinese fishermen are fishing
in the Cam Rang military zone, why are these issues discovered by journalists [and not the VNA]?

—Duong Trung Quoc, 2012[1]

[D]elegate Tran Thi Suu stood up and said "I have the impression that
there is someone behind the scenes pulling the strings of the VNA." This
prompted [VNA Chair] Le Quang Dao to slam his hand on the table
and say: "[W]ho, who is pulling the strings of the VNA?!"

—(Duc 2012)[2]

All the debates in the VNA still take place within the boundaries set by
the party.

—Phan Dinh Dieu, 1992[3]

The previous chapter showed that the party exercises a great deal of influence over election outcomes in Vietnam. Furthermore, I argued earlier in
the book that the reason for the development of Vietnam's legislative institutions was not to achieve greater openness or provide more information.
Rather, the purpose is to use the legislature to shift blame to the government. I have demonstrated that the major innovations to the VNA—the
public query sessions and votes of no confidence—were introduced to damage rivals. This chapter raises the question of whether the legislature actually
behaves according to the goal of shifting blame in practice.

To address this question, I look at the content of oversight hearings. If
the theory holds, we should see the legislature engage in debate directed at
the government. However, the party should remain inviolable. This chapter

tests this argument using an original dataset of public opinion and legislative behavior in Vietnam. I examine the degree to which hot button issues are debated on the floor of the VNA. My theory suggests that hot button issues pertaining to party-controlled portfolios should not be debated in contrast to issues more tightly controlled by the government. The theory here is that public interest drives legislative debate not because legislators are reflecting the interests of the public, but rather because the party leverages public interest to pressure rivals in the government.

To make this argument, I conducted an automated text analysis of 1,935 speeches made in oversight hearings on the floor of the Vietnam National Assembly between 2007 and 2013. Using the resulting data, I show that the legislature only debates hot topics on issues the government controls, not on issues that the party controls. In addition to the quantitative test, I examine four cases of salient issues to examine whether party control of the issue determined whether the issue was debated or not. For the party-controlled issues—the repression of dissidents and management of the South China Sea—it shows the party had the capacity to influence policy on those issues and prevented the VNA from discussing them. In contrast, on the government-controlled issues—land management and state-owned enterprise (SOE) management—the party had less capacity vis-à-vis the government and therefore explicitly allowed the VNA leadership to engage in oversight behavior. However, critically, this oversight behavior occurred *after* information about the government's behavior had already leaked to the media.

Legislative Debate in Vietnam

Existing work on legislative behavior in authoritarian regimes focuses on who participates and what types of issues legislators raise (Truex 2016; Malesky and Schuler 2010). This work suggests that because of the surprising congruence between citizens and delegates as well as the assertiveness of some legislatures, the legislature may reflect non-party interests. Research from democracies, where the electoral connection should be stronger, suggests that legislative debate is largely performative (Proksch and Slapin 2015; Vliegenthart and Walgrave 2011; Mayhew 1974). That is, legislators make speeches in order to win public support for the ruling party. Therefore, rather than criticizing the party, speeches from copartisans are designed to highlight the successes of the ruling party. What does this say about a single-party regime?

Consistent with the central argument of this book, I theorize that the party will not be keen to use the legislature to challenge itself. However, if there is separation between the party and government, the party may perhaps mobilize the legislature to shift blame for governance failures onto the government. Chapter 4 discussed the separation between the party and the state, showing that during the economic reforms of the 1980s the VCP shifted greater authority to the government. The theory tested in this chapter is simple and intuitive. Because the VCP has delegated greater authority to the government, it should allow the legislature to publicly debate those issues that the party has delegated. On issues where it has not delegated authority, it should limit debate.

To assess this theory, two facts must first be established. First, is there variation in the degree to which the VCP delegates authority to the government across issues? Second, does the VCP have agenda control over the VNA such that it can direct debate away from issues it does not want to discuss and toward issues it does want to debate?

AGENDA CONTROL IN VIETNAM

With regard to query sessions, the party maintains strong mechanisms of agenda control, particularly within the oversight hearings. Vietnam's legislature is extremely hierarchical. While all legislatures feature some degree of hierarchy in order to conduct business (Cox 2006), as chapter 3 discusses, the hierarchy is particularly rigid in the VNA. The eighteen-member Standing Committee wields veto power over the legislative agenda. Individual delegates may suggest legislation or request oversight hearings, but the Standing Committee must ultimately approve any requests. Therefore, the party, through the Central Committee and the Politburo, has the power to determine which issues are addressed on the VNA floor.

PARTY-STATE DIVISION IN VIETNAM

Since Vietnam's economic opening in 1986, the party has increasingly pared back its control of the government. Responding to the criticism that excessive ideological control was contributing to poor policy performance, in 1989 the VCP decreased the number of party committees accountable to the VCP Central Committee (Thayer 1991). As of 2007, the party maintained

TABLE 6.1.
Party control over ministries.

Ministry	Party Committee (2007–2012)	Party control	Times queried *
Defense	Central Military Comm.	Yes	0
Internal Affairs	Central Org Comm.	Yes	2
Foreign Affairs	Foreign Affairs Comm.	Yes	0
Information	Propaganda Comm.	Yes	1
Justice	Internal Affairs Comm.	Yes	2
State Inspectorate	Central Inspection Comm.	Yes	0
Public Security	Central Military Comm.	Yes	1
Labor, Veterans, Soc. Affairs	None	No	3
Agriculture and Rural Dev.	None	No	4
Finance	None	No	6
Industry	None	No	6
Planning and Investment	None	No	3
Construction	None	No	0
Culture, Sports, Tourism	None	No	2
Education	None	No	5
Health	None	No	3
Natural Resources	None	No	3
Science and Technology	None	No	0
State Bank	None	No	4
Transportation	None	No	3

* indicates how many times the minister was required to take questions before the VNA. The shaded rows are ministries with a corresponding party committee.

committees that explicitly paralleled seven out of twenty government ministries. Table 6.1 lists these ministries, which include defense, foreign affairs, information, and internal affairs. At the other end of the spectrum, the public-service-related ministries such as education and health have no explicit party body shadowing them. The only institutions available to make policy in those areas are the Politburo and the VCP Central Committee.[4]

To be sure, the lack of a parallel party institution does not mean the party has no influence over these other ministries. Indeed, through the party's role in appointments and the presence of party cells within all state bodies, the VCP can still provide information on general party policies and fire particularly problematic officials. However, the party cells generally exist within state bodies to provide training on the party line and do not offer independent, portfolio-specific policies. Furthermore, using nomenklatura power to enforce party discipline requires vigilant oversight of state activities to identify those in need of replacing. This task is made more difficult when the party lacks independent policy-specific institutions. With this in mind, I use the presence of parallel party institutions as a proxy for party control (see table 6.1).

With this distinction in mind, I now state the hypotheses tested in this chapter.

> *H1: In oversight hearings, legislators will publicly debate salient issues on portfolios delegated to the government.*

> *H2: In oversight hearings, legislators will not publicly debate salient issues on portfolios the VCP controls.*

Testing the Theory

Testing the theory requires measurement of both legislative and public attention. To create a measure of which topics the legislature considers, I first gathered all the debates in oversight hearings between 2007 and 2013. Oversight speeches cover two types of debate: debates on the government's socioeconomic report and query sessions with government ministers. Critically, for query sessions, only ministers approved by the Standing Committee appeared for questioning. In addition to these four to five ministers, the prime minister or deputy prime minister also appeared in each session. In all, this amounted to 1,935 speeches, all of which were available on the VNA website *and* were carried on live television in Vietnam. Putting this number in perspective, this is more speeches than in many autocracies, where such publicly observable speech is barred. However, the number is far smaller than in democracies such as the United States or the United Kingdom, where legislatures meet more regularly and legislators are allowed greater access to the floor (Maltzman and Sigelman 1996).

To generate a measure of topics that vary over time, I created a mixed-membership topic model, which assumes that each speech is a mixture of multiple topics. Of such models, the latent dirichlet allocation (LDA) model (Blei, Ng, and Jordan 2003) with Gibbs sampling is the most common (Grimmer and Stewart 2013).[5] The basic logic of the LDA model is that all corpora are made up of a latent set of topics, with each document the sum of all topics and each word in the document drawn from each of those topics.[6] The model produces two values of interest. First, it assigns a value to the proportion of the individual document about each given topic. Second, it produces the words that are most associated with a given topic. The words help identify what the topics are about, while the proportions, when aggregated to the session level, provide a measure of how much a session focused on a particular topic. The mixed-membership model was preferable to a single-topic model, such as k-means, a mixture model, because a single speech may raise several questions on different topics.

To conduct the automated analysis, several processing steps are required. First, because Vietnamese, like Chinese, is monosyllabic, automated analysis requires a "tokenizer" to attach different syllables together. Therefore, *gia dình*, which means family, must become *gia_dình*. To tokenize the words, I employed a Vietnamese company that tracks Internet interest in Vietnam. This company has proprietary software that automatically links together syllables that form words. To improve the meaning of the discovered topics, scholars typically drop words that do not contain substantive meaning, such as "if," "and," or "but." For English, such lists come with most natural language processing packages, such as *nltk* for Python. At the time of writing, no such lists were available for Vietnamese. Therefore, I created a list based on the English list, adding words such as *được* and *bị*, which are specific to Vietnamese. Finally, I modified the speeches to ensure that the topics generated were based on the subject of the speech and not the identity of the speaker. One modification was to change all provincial names to the word "province" to avoid having the topics cluster on the delegate from the province rather than the topic of the speech. Through this process, I created the dependent variable, which is the proportion of session k about topic i.

MEASURING PUBLIC ATTENTION

Research on democracies uses various approaches to measure public interest. Some analyze the correspondence between polling data on the most important issue facing the country and debate (Soroka 2002). Some also use content analyses of media reports, which of course measure a distinct phenomenon that may not directly relate to actual public opinion (Vliegenthart and Walgrave 2011; Walgrave, Soroka, and Nuytemans 2008). More recently, scholars have suggested that Internet search data demonstrate convergent validity with these measures (Ripberger 2011; Mellon 2014). In the context of Vietnam, Internet searches are the best available approach because of the lack of polling data.

To generate a dataset of public interest in different issues and match this to legislative debate, I used the three-step process. First, I identified key events through a fine-grained LDA topic model of domestic and foreign media outlets. For the domestic media, I relied on *Tuoi Tre*, which is one of Vietnam's most widely read online and print publications. It is also one of Vietnam's more open-minded state-run outlets. I also chose *Tuoi Tre* because it regularly reports on political events and because its online archives are comprehensive. By scraping its online archives of stories from the domestic news section, I collected 46,603 articles, an average of 25 per day. For the foreign media, I scraped 6,980 articles from BBC Vietnam, which publishes about 2 stories per day on Vietnamese politics. The articles have been processed in the same manner as the VNA speeches.

Using each of these media outlets, I identified events by looking for spikes of interest in specific topics, then reading the news stories associated with those bursts. To identify a spike, I looked for months in which the interest in a given topic was more than three standard deviations above the mean level of interest in that topic. Where the topic did not concern political issues, such as the release of a new movie, or if it explicitly dealt with the VNA, I discarded the event. For the remaining events, I entered search terms related to the event into Google Trends, which measures the number of times Internet users search for a given term on a weekly basis.[7] To ensure that the searches were valid, I only included those for which the timing of the spike corresponded with the timing of the events identified in the media reports. Through this process, I identified 140 unique spikes related to politics during the period under consideration. These spikes ranged from Chinese activity in the South China Sea to the 2009 swine flu scare.

COMBINING THE DATA

The final step in creating a panel dataset of public interest in issues was matching the public interest measure with the topics discussed in the VNA. This required some degree of interpretation. To facilitate the mapping, I used an LDA model with 150 topics on the VNA speeches. This fine-grained level of disaggregation facilitated matching on specific issues by breaking out subtopics. For instance, while debates on Vietnam's economic stimulus and taxes may be grouped under macroeconomics in a low dimensional model, these

Step 1: Identify Important Events	Step 2: Convert to Measure of Public Interest	Step 3: Match it with Legislative Debate	Step 4: Final Product
Identify events based on issue spikes in domestic media using LDA model with 200 topics	Quantify interest through Internet Searches for event on Google Trends	Match with closest topic or topics identified through LDA model of VNA	Panel dataset of public and legislative interest in 38 issues over 12 VNA
Identify events based on issue spikes in foreign media using LDA model with 200 topics			

* The results are replicated using an LDA model of 100, 150, and 200 topics

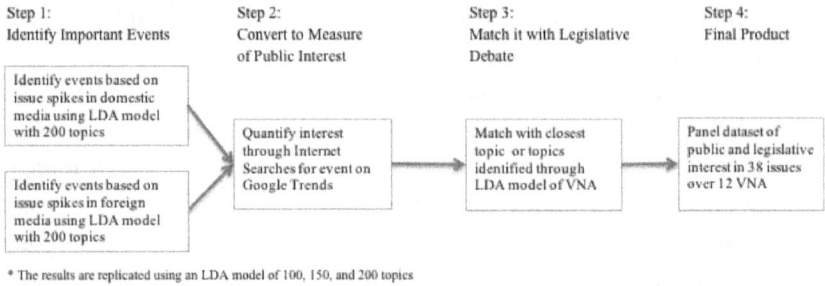

FIGURE 6.1. How the panel dataset was constructed.

topics form distinct topics when more topics are allowed. Because choices on topic numbers can generate idiosyncratic results, I repeated the analysis with one hundred and two hundred topics (Wilkerson and Casas 2017).

Before conducting the analysis, three final steps were necessary. First, measuring whether interest in the issue corresponded to debate in the VNA required a time series dataset in which VNA debate *followed* public interest rather than preceded it. Because the VNA meets once every six months, the measure of public interest was the average Google Search measure in the period between the previous VNA session and prior to the opening of the current VNA session. To ensure that the Internet interest was not driven by debate within the VNA, I did not include measures of public interest during the month the VNA sat. However, because it is possible that even using this lagged structure, anticipation of debate could have sparked public interest, in the validation section I looked at the specific issues to see whether they were exogenous to the VNA calendar.

Second, because Internet interest is highly skewed, with some issues receiving tremendous attention and others less, to account for the diminishing marginal returns of Internet interest, I used the natural log of the Google Search measure as the key independent variable. Finally, to differentiate between issues controlled by the party and those that were delegated to the government, I used the measure of party control from table 6.1 to match specific issues with these ministries.

Empirical Test

I now turn to the empirical test. The central hypothesis of this chapter is that public attention should positively predict VNA attention, but only within the subset of issues where the party delegates authority to the state.

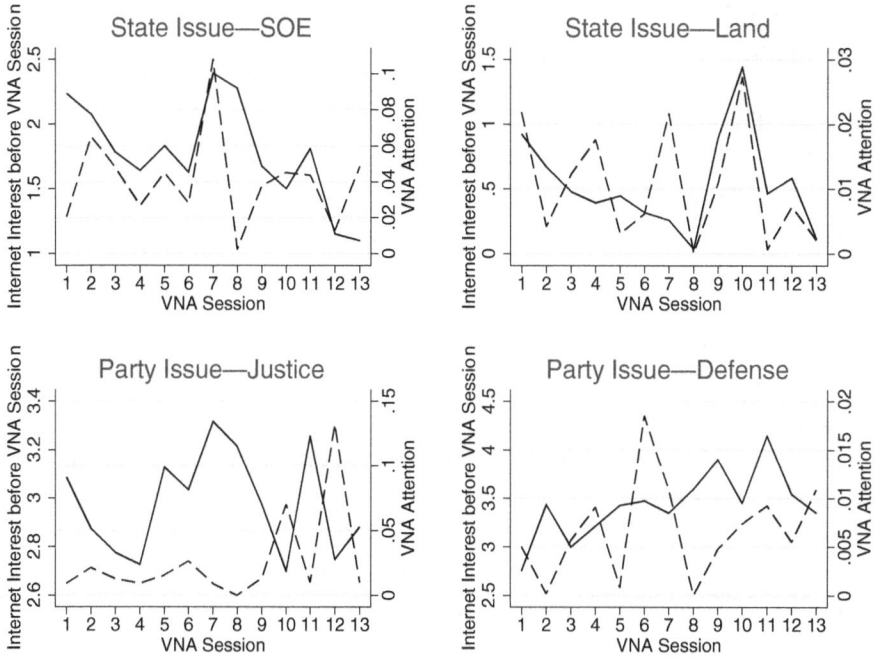

FIGURE 6.2. Change in VNA oversight attention/Internet interest on selected issues. Dashed line is VNA attention; solid line is Internet attention.

There should be no relationship between public interest and VNA attention within the nondelegated issues. This prediction follows from my theory that the party will mobilize public attention to salient issues to pressure the government and deflect blame from the party when the government controls the issue. However, the party will seek to dampen public attention when the public is focused on an issue the party controls directly.

Figure 6.2 provides some initial visual evidence of a relationship between Internet interest and VNA attention. For SOEs and land, issues that are delegated to the government, spikes in interest were followed by increased attention in the VNA. For SOEs, the notable spike occurred prior to the seventh session, when Vinashin, a major SOE, was found to be $4.4 billion in debt. During the seventh session, the minister of transportation and the prime minister were grilled on their responsibility for the issue. Similarly, for land the VNA considered this issue more extensively after an incident in February 2012 involving a farmer firing on security forces attempting seize his land. Contrast these two issues with party-controlled issues related to justice and national security (defense). As the bottom two panels of figure

6.2 show, VNA attention to justice or defense was not connected to spikes in interest in the arrest of prominent dissidents or the South China Sea. What attention was paid to these issues related to oversight of lower level court officials and budget resources for defense.

Before moving on, it is important to note that figure 6.2 also shows two features of the data critical for the analysis. First, there is a great deal of unexplained variation in the VNA. Other factors that this model cannot pick up also influence the oversight speeches, such as party priorities, delayed attention to past issues, and local issues. For example, land spiked as an important topic in the VNA during the seventh session despite relatively low levels of public interest in the topic. This may have occurred either because the government was responding to calls from the VNA to more fully consider such issues months after an incident or because it was responding to events not picked up by the procedures used here. Such unexplained variation should bias all the results toward a null finding.

The second point is that VNA attention has some time dependence. For oversight hearings, although there is no formal rule, it appears that the VNA focuses on different topics in different sessions. Therefore, if an issue is considered in a given session, it is less likely to be discussed in a subsequent session. To account for this, the models used one-session lags for VNA debate. For the tests, I used two models. Because the dependent variable is a fraction, the main model is a fractional probit regression:

$$\ln(L) = \sum_{i=1}^{N} y_{i,t} \ln \Phi(\beta_1 x'_{i,t} + \beta_2 y'_{t-1} + \alpha_i) +$$

$$(1-y_{i,t}) \ln\Phi(\beta_1 x'_{i,t} + \beta_2 y'_{t-1} + \alpha_i)$$

where $y_{i,t}$ is the level of attention paid to topic i during session t and $\beta_1 x'_{i,t}$ is the level of Internet interest in topic i immediately preceding session t. The fixed effect for VNA interest in topic i is α_i. The lag of VNA interest is $\beta_2 y'_{t-1}$. Because there may be concerns about incidental parameters with a fixed effect in a probit model given the low number of time periods, I also estimated an OLS regression with fixed effects. I ran the fractional probit and OLS models separately on delegated and nondelegated issues.

Table 6.2 shows the results of the fractional probit and OLS regressions on delegated and nondelegated issues. Models 1 and 2 show that public attention positively predicts legislative debate on delegated issues, while

TABLE 6.2.
Impact of interest in topics on oversight hearings.

	Delegated issues		Nondelegated issues	
	Fractional probit	OLS	Fractional probit	OLS
	Model 1	Model 2	Model 3	Model 4
Internet interest	0.130***	0.00462**	−0.0566	−0.00239
	(0.046)	(0.0022)	(0.109)	(0.00506)
Lagged VNA attention (1 session)	−0.773	−0.0445	−4.210**	−0.156***
	(1.346)	(0.0855)	(1.717)	(0.0423)
Fixed effects	Yes	Yes	Yes	Yes
Constant	−2.504***	0.0117***	−1.658***	0.0166*
	(0.0925)	(0.00247)	(0.413)	(0.00769)
Observations	348	348	108	108
R-squared/pseudo R-squared	0.0632	0.018	0.0385	0.024

Robust standard errors in parentheses.
* $p < 0.1$, ** $p < 0.05$, *** $p < 0.01$

models 3 and 4 show no effect on the nondelegated issues. The findings hold using fixed effects OLS. However, even within the delegated issues, the relationship is not particularly strong, and a lot of variance is unexplained. This is likely due to the infrequency of the oversight sessions, which cannot address all of the topics that accrued during the intervening periods. It is also likely that a number of issues raised were of local concern and thus did not appear in the national media. Finally, it is possible that some speeches were "planted" to serve regime goals that we cannot observe, such as advancing a particular policy agenda.

A final point to note is the lack of autoregressive effects, which are typical in these types of studies. In the context of this study, the lack of effects is quite understandable because the sessions were separated by more than five months and featured different ministers. As such, it is more likely that a given session would feature less relationship than would be the case in a setting where sessions occur regularly.

Case Studies

While the preceding analysis aligns with my predictions, does VNA attention result from intentional party agenda control? To address this in greater detail, I consider a few hot button issues generating public interest and the decision to debate or not debate them on the floor of the VNA. I consider first issues pertaining to ministries controlled by the party: the South China Sea and repression of dissidents. I then consider two issues—land use rights and management of Vinashin—relating to government-controlled ministries. I chose these cases because each was salient to the public, and therefore, according to the theory in this chapter, only those issues that the government controlled should have been discussed on the floor. Furthermore, the parameters of the debate should have clearly focused on components of the debate that challenged the government, not issues for which party policy was settled. These cases are also important because they are key in driving the empirical findings in the previous section and correspond to the illustrative graph in figure 6.2.

SOUTH CHINA SEA

Figure 6.3 shows the salience of the South China Sea issue in Vietnam since 2007. Using Google Trends, it compares searches for "South China Sea" (*Biển đông*) to "pho," Vietnam's national dish. This comparison is necessary because Google Trends is a relative index and not an absolute number of searches. Therefore, in the interest of comparability, I compared all the search terms to "pho."

The three major surges in interest in the South China Sea depicted on this graph occurred in June 2011, June 2012, and March 2014. In June 2011, protests erupted in Vietnam after a Chinese fishing vessel cut a seismic exploration cable towed by the *Viking II*, an oil exploration ship contracted by PetroVietnam. The vessel was not sailing in disputed territory near the Spratly Islands, but was actually within two hundred miles of Vietnam's coastline.[8] China justified its actions because the ship was sailing within China's U-shaped line, which the 2016 UNCLOS tribunal confirmed had no basis in international law.[9] Tensions flared again in 2012 when Chinese state oil company CNOOC opened bids for oil blocks within Vietnam's claimed exclusive economic zone (EEZ). Vietnam responded, once again, saying that the area, which overlapped China's nine-dash line but was not near the Spratlys, was not disputed territory. Both incidents led to protests.[10]

The most inflammatory provocation occurred in May 2014, when CNOOC moved the Haiyang Shiyou Oil Rig 981 (HYSY 981) within 120 miles of Vietnam's shore, once again in the zone overlapping Vietnam's EEZ

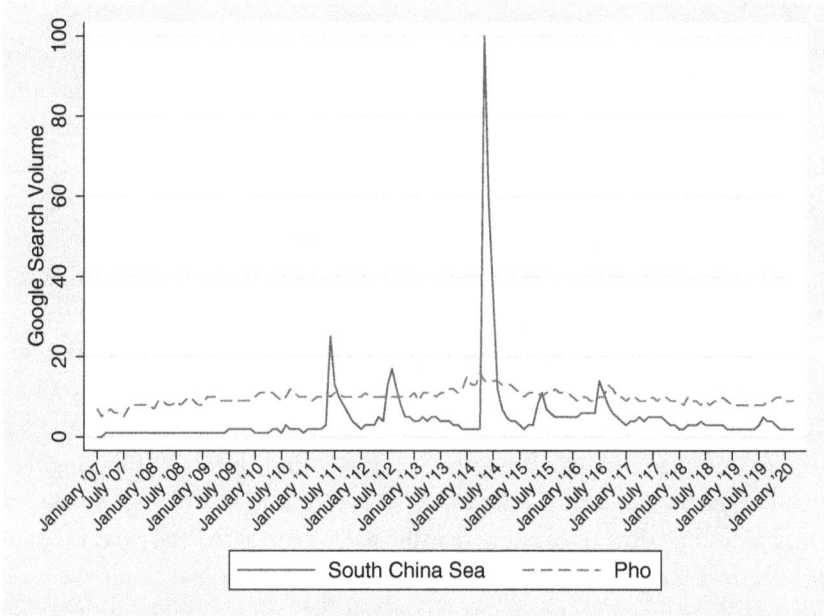

FIGURE 6.3. Google searches for the South China Sea. Note: Data are from Google Trends and compare searches for South China Sea (Biển đông) in Vietnam cto searches for pho (phở), Vietnam's national dish.

and China's nine-dash line.[11] Vietnam immediately called for China to remove the rig, which it finally did two months later, in July. In the intervening period, some of the largest protests in Vietnam since unification took place, causing the deaths of several workers and the evacuation of many Chinese nationals.[12]

In each of these incidents, but particularly after the HYSY 981 incident, the party faced the issue of how to respond. A particular issue of debate was whether to pursue legal action in either of these cases or to join a Philippines-led UNCLOS tribunal over the legal definition of the territories in the Spratly Islands. Several news articles suggest that former prime minister Nguyen Tan Dung was most strongly in support of such measures, and he did publicly raise the possibility shortly after the incident.[13] Ultimately, Vietnam did not take legal action. After meetings with China's state counselor, Jang Yiechi, Vietnam did not pursue legal action, and China withdrew the rig ahead of schedule. How was the course of action decided upon?

While there is disagreement about specifically who in the Politburo fa-vored more or less assertive actions vis-à-vis China, what is not in dispute is that ultimate authority to decide the issue rested with the Politburo and the Central Committee, not the government.[14] Indeed, Thayer suggests that China's decision to move the rig in July 2014 was driven by the desire to con-vince the VCP Central Committee not to take legal action.[15] Importantly, although foreign minister and Politburo member Pham Binh Minh was involved in key meetings, on the issue of foreign affairs party officials such as Nguyen Phu Trong have greater institutional capacity to make policy.

While taking a lower profile than the government-led Ministry of Foreign Affairs, the party's Central Committee on External Relations conducts for-eign affairs activities on a regular basis. Indeed, on several occasions the chair of the committee, Hoang Binh Quan, has met directly with Xi Jinping. In-terestingly, the state media refer to Minh as "Nguyen Phu Trong's envoy" in these accounts, thus confirming that the party general secretary has his own parallel foreign policy adviser.[16] While the articles are vague about the con-tents of these meetings (they simply discuss the desire to maintain friendly ties), the meetings underscore the degree to which Nguyen Phu Trong and the position of the general secretary have institutional capacity with regard to foreign policy. This capacity, both to gain information on the views of important foreign countries and to influence policy directly, provides Trong and others within the party institutions greater ability to engage actively in important policy decisions such as those pertaining to the South China Sea.

The theory presented in this chapter would suggest that the party would have less interest in having debate on the issue occur within the VNA. Having direct influence over the issue through party-led institutions, Trong and oth-ers within the party institutions should be more satisfied with the course of action chosen and therefore reluctant to have the VNA weigh in on the deci-sions. This is indeed what happened. In the VNA sessions following the crises in the South China Sea, Minister of Foreign Affairs Pham Binh Minh was never called before the legislature to discuss Vietnam's policy on the South China Sea or to debate the responses. In the sessions, while several ministers were questioned, the ministers of foreign affairs and defense were not.[17]

It is perhaps most striking that in the June 2014 session, while the stand-off against China remained ongoing, the delegates were not afforded the opportunity to discuss the issue publicly. In a concession to the legislature, a private meeting was scheduled at which the minister of foreign affairs provided a briefing.[18] However, some delegates were critical of this and suggested the legislature needed an opportunity to express the sentiments of the legislature publicly. Duong Trung Quoc, for example, said: "Last year, when China moved the Hai Duong 981 Oil Rig in Vietnamese waters, the Minister of Foreign Affairs reported on the situation to the legislature, but we need public information to provide to the public."[19]

On this issue, the party and the VNA leadership saw foreign affairs as an issue for the party and not the legislature. Deputy Chairman of the VNA Office Nguyen Sy Dung said: "All countries have two criteria for not holding public debate. . . . The first is whether not the issue is a difficult one. . . . The second is whether the issues are defense issues."[20] Therefore, he continued, the ministers of foreign affairs and defense should not appear before the VNA.

ARRESTS OF CU HUY HA VU AND LE CONG DINH

Another party-controlled issue is repression of political dissidents. Since 2007, dozens of dissidents have been arrested or expelled from the country.[21] Given their prominence, this section considers the cases of Cu Huy Ha Vu and Le Cong Dinh. As figure 6.4 shows, these two dissidents, described in the following paragraphs, received a great deal of public attention after their arrests. One of the major issues was the legality of the arrests, both made under Article 88 of the criminal code, which outlaws anti-state propaganda. Although the VNA may not necessarily have intervened to overturn these arrests, some within the legislature may have sought to raise the issue in relation to oversight over the police and the judiciary.

The theory in this chapter suggests that the degree of party control over the relevant portfolio will influence whether the VNA is invited to speak on the issue. In Vietnam, the repressive apparatus within the state is the Ministry of Public Security. However, despite the ostensible importance of this ministry, the party has institutional capacities that enable it to wield greater direct control over this institution than over other ministries. The military and the Ministry of Public Security are the only government bodies explicitly mentioned in the VCP's party regulations (*Điều lệ Đảng*).[22]

With regard to the police, the primary mechanisms that allow the party to exert control are the institutionalization of and membership in the ministry's party cell. While all ministries have a "party cell" (*Đảng uỷ*), in non-party-controlled ministries the minister is the highest-ranking party member in the

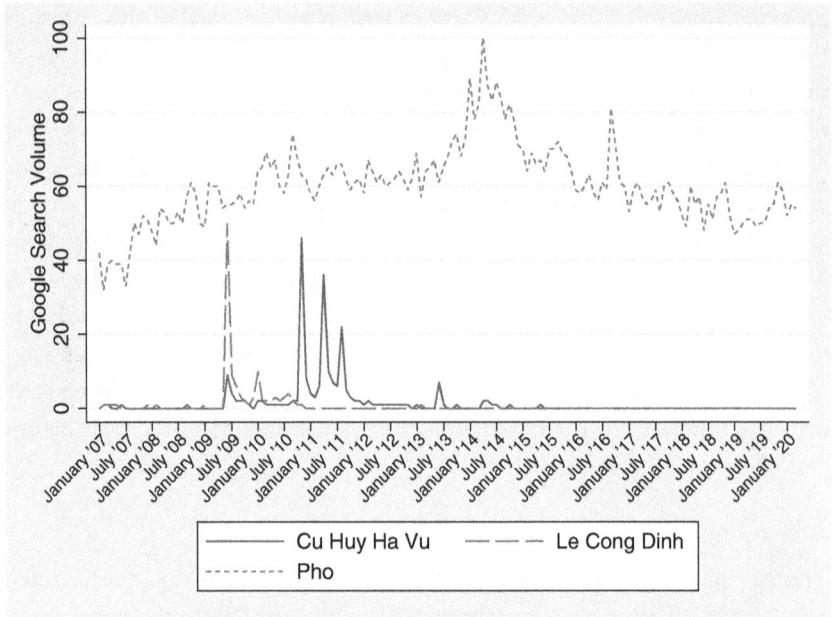

FIGURE 6.4. Google searches for Cu Huy Ha Vu and Le Cong Dinh. Note: Data are from Google Trends and compare searches for Cu Huy Ha Vu and Le Cong Dinh in Vietnam to searches for pho (phở), Vietnam's national dish.

ministry and ranks higher than any member of the ministry's party cell. Furthermore, members of the ministry party cell mostly come from the ministry itself. For example, the chair of the Ministry of Industry party cell is Minister Tran Tuan Anh, who is also a member of the VCP Central Committee. The deputy heads of the party cell are Dao Minh Hai and Dao Van Hai, who are not members of the VCP Central Committee. This gives the minister greater control over his ministry and its implementation of policy.[23]

In the Ministry of Public Security, the minister is both a Politburo member and chair of the ministry's party cell. However, to exert leverage over the minister, party regulations explicitly require that the ministry party cell include "some Central Committee members from the Ministry of Police and some Central Committee members from outside the Ministry of Police."[24] In practice, those members from "outside" the ministry historically have included two higher-ranking Politburo members, the president and the prime minister. This weakens the role of the minister to unilaterally make policy outside of the purview of the Politburo. Furthermore, with the addition of the president it means that the prime minister does not have sole authority to manage the position. It is noteworthy that perhaps sensing that having the president alone sit alongside the prime minister in the party cell was insufficient to control the independence of the police and the prime minister, Nguyen Phu Trong moved in 2016 to become the first general secretary to also take a seat in the ministry's party cell.[25] This gives the general secretary and the party greater ability to monitor the activities of the police, which means greater ability to direct its activities.

Turning to the specific cases of Cu Huy Ha Vu and Le Cong Dinh, the greater party control of the police should mean that the decision to arrest the two was not solely made by the government, and that therefore the party should have resisted any attempt by the VNA to intervene or discuss the issue. Vu is a lawyer and the son of a high-ranking party member involved in the revolution.[26] He achieved fame through several high-profile challenges to the government and party. In 2006, this son of revolutionary poet Cu Huy Can and nephew of famous poet Xuan Dieu nominated himself to the position of minister of culture. He then attracted more attention in 2009 when he filed a lawsuit against Prime Minister Nguyen Tan Dung over a controversial bauxite mine project in the Central Highlands.

After tolerating Vu's activism for several years, in November 2010 the police arrested him. As Human Rights Watch notes, his arrest attracted great public attention, in part because of his prominence, but also due to the public activism on his behalf by his wife and family.[27] Figure 6.4 provides empirical support for this claim. During the month of his arrest, nearly as many Vietnamese searched for "Cu Huy Ha Vu" as searched for "pho."

What was the role of the VNA in November 2010 or in May 2011 after he was arrested? At the time of his arrest, Nguyen Tan Dung, the target of Vu's criticism, and Truong Tan Sang were members of the party cell.[28] Unfortunately, we have no way of knowing how Vu's arrest was planned or who supported it. Vu himself explicitly laid the blame on Prime Minister Dung.[29]

Importantly for this chapter, aside from public opinion, several prominent figures, including Vu himself, publicly called for intervention from the party, state, and legislature. Former ambassador to China Nguyen Trong Vinh wrote a public letter on Vu's behalf urging clemency.[30] Vu himself reached out to then president Nguyen Minh Triet and former general secretary Nong Duc Manh after an incident in which a wall outside Vu's house was destroyed.[31] Finally, Vu's family members reached out to the National

Assembly, with his wife sending a letter to the National Assembly Justice Committee protesting the legality of his arrest.[32]

Similar entreaties were made on behalf of another prominent dissident, Le Cong Dinh, who was arrested in a sweep of several activists between May and July 2009 (Thayer 2009). Dinh, a lawyer who made his name defending foreign firms doing business in Vietnam, increasingly took cases defending dissident groups such as Bloc 8406. In 2009, he was arrested for plotting to overthrow the government due to his alleged contacts with foreign groups supporting multiparty democracy in Vietnam. Although Dinh challenged Dung specifically on the bauxite issue and thus may have been useful to some in the party who challenged Dung in the following party congress, Thayer suggests that it was conservatives and Dung alike who collectively acted to detain Dinh.

As figure 6.4 shows, there was clearly public interest in both Vu's and Dinh's cases. However, despite the public interest, in the sessions following their arrests, the National Assembly did not raise either issue. In the November 2009 session, the first since Dinh's arrest, his name did not come up. Similarly in the November 2010 session, the query sessions occurring between November 22 and November 24 made no mention of Vu's case. Vu's case is notable both because his family explicitly reached out to the VNA and because the November 2010 session was notably raucous. As noted previously, this was the same session at which Thuyet issued the call for a vote of no confidence in the prime minister! In short, while Thuyet was free to challenge the prime minister to a vote of no confidence over mismanagement of SOEs, neither he nor the rest of the delegates felt free or compelled to raise the issue of the recent arrest of a high-profile dissident.

Are these cases typical? While they are two of the more high-profile dissident cases in Vietnam, a word search of more than forty dissident names for all speeches between 2007 and 2013 reveals that no dissident's name was ever mentioned during this period. Anecdotal evidence from other periods suggests that this period was not special in that regard. To the best of my knowledge, no issue pertaining to a dissident has ever been discussed publicly within the VNA. The argument in this chapter suggests that because the party already controls this issue through its domination of the public security party cell, it has no need for public interference from the VNA. In short, while the VNA may be raucous, it is silent on the issue of dissident arrests.

LAND USE RIGHTS

Turning to a government-controlled issue, land use is a perennial hot button issue in Vietnam (Kerkvliet 2014).[33] However, it surged in importance in February 2012 when a shrimp farmer in Tien Lang district near Hai Phong took his concerns about land seizures into his own hands. Figure 6.5 shows the spike in national interest in the Tien Lang incident and another land incident in Van Giang district of Hung Yen province at roughly the same time. In the Tien Lang incident, protesting the seizure of his farms at a compensation rate that he felt did not match the improvements he had made to the land, Doan Van Vuon booby trapped his house and fired on several local police officers attempting to seize his land. According to this chapter's theory, because the central party leadership has fewer institutional controls over land issues, the VNA should have been able to engage in more robust oversight of this issue.

It should be noted that this should be a particularly *hard* case for the theory of this chapter. In particular, if *issue sensitivity* is the theoretical reason

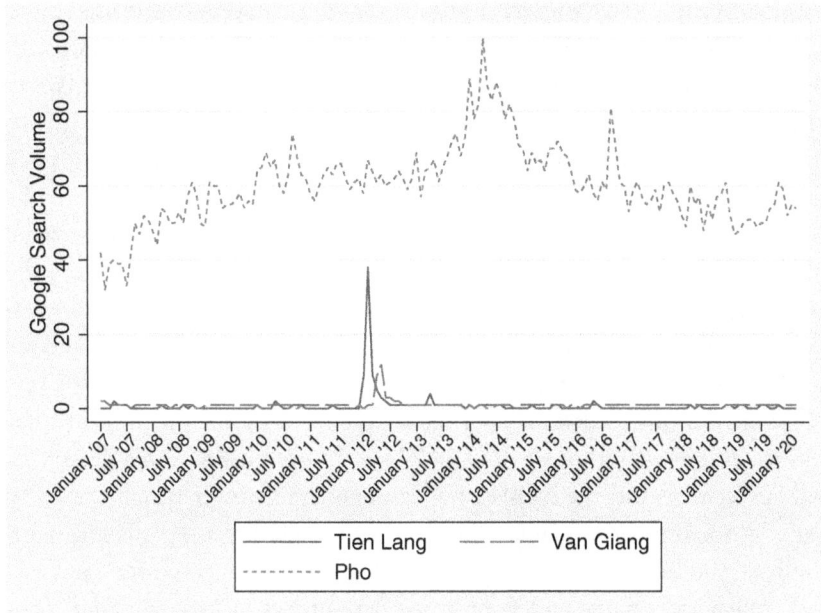

FIGURE 6.5. Google searches for Tien Lang, Van Giang land seizure cases. Note: Data are from Google Trends and compare searches for Tien Lang and Van Giang, two districts with land protests, in Vietnam to searches for pho (phở), Vietnam's national dish.

for not discussing the issue, land should be among the candidates for sensitive issues. Indeed, the Land Law was delayed several times because as Deputy VNA chair Uong Chu Luu suggested, it would have significant "political ramifications" (Le 2016, 302). Furthermore, as Le (2016) outlines, the central party leadership has historically taken special interest in the Land Law, particularly pertaining to the issue of state ownership of the land. More recently, General Secretary Nguyen Phu Trong was reportedly resistant to the idea of eliminating the public ownership of land, something that Minister of Planning and Investment Vo Van Phuc had advocated at the 2011 Party Congress (Le 2016, 294–295).[34] If the party finds an issue more sensitive, it should be more reluctant to allow the VNA to discuss it.

An additional reason that this should be a hard case is that at first glance it seems as though the VNA could potentially be on the same side as the government in pushing for greater reforms to the Land Law. Indeed, as Le (2016) notes, it was likely Minister of Planning and Investment Vo Van Phuc who was instrumental in putting the Land Law and the larger land debate on the agenda. On this issue, Phuc appeared to align with several members of the VNA who have pushed for consideration of a revised Land Law in hopes of removing state ownership of land. If the VNA sides with the government, then we should not see it acting at the behest of the party to challenge the state.

However, closer analysis of the response to the Doan Van Vuon issue shows that the VNA was actually quite silent on state ownership of the land. This makes sense, as Nguyen Phu Trong privately declared the issue of state ownership "closed off for public discussion" after February 2013 (Le 2016, 305). What role, then, might the VNA usefully play for the party with regard to land, particularly after Doan Van Vuon both raised the salience of the issue and became a kind of martyr in his own right?

To answer this, I first consider the party's institutional capacity with regard to implementation of the Land Law. In contrast to the Ministry of Public Security and the Ministry of Foreign Affairs, over which the party has additional institutional leverage either through direct representation on the party bodies or through policy-making organizations under the Central Committee, party leaders have fewer resources to manage the day-to-day operations of land policy. While the party may have concrete policy views on private ownership, it has less capacity to manage the ways in which government officials may write and implement laws to ease expropriation, the most common source of frustration for citizens.

To this end, while the legislature may be less necessary from the central party leaders' perspective in raising issues pertaining to private ownership, it might be useful in two ways. First, it might help shift blame to the government for not adhering to the laws as written. Second, the VNA might help tighten legislation aimed at tying the hands of government officials who want to seize land at below-market compensation rates. Indeed, Le (2016, 304) notes that the Central Committee issued a "strongly worded" decision in March 2012 instructing the government to draft laws to more clearly outline the discretion of lower-level officials in seizing land.

Seen in this light, the party's management of debate in the VNA in the sessions following Doan Van Vuon's attack on the Hai Phong police now makes more sense. During the first VNA session following Vuon's February 2012 attack, in contrast to how issues related to defense or foreign affairs were handled, on June 13, 2012, VNA chair Nguyen Sinh Hung called Minister of Natural Resources and Environment Nguyen Minh Quang to take the hot seat. In opening the debate, Hung included as part of the agenda for Quang's session "all issues pertaining to land management, compensation for land clearance, shortcomings in land management, and other issues of frustration in this area."[35]

In the subsequent debate, the VNA did just that. The questions leveled at Quang related to the management of the crisis, but not the state's ownership of the land. Delegate Bui Thi An asked about the minster's "feelings regarding the direction and progress in solving the issues related to land, specifically the issues concerning the public such as the case of Doan Van Vuon, Van Giang, Can Tho, Vu Ban, etc. . . . What is wrong, what is right, and when will they be resolved?"[36] More tellingly, Tran Thi Quoc Khanh followed up on An's question, raising the issue of public ownership of the land. However, in her case, she flipped the issue of public ownership into an attack on the government, particularly efforts to increase privatization:

[T]he Constitution and the 2003 Land Law decides that land, forests, rivers, houses, and natural resources are all owned by the people and the state represents the ownership of the people, according to the 2003 law, but the master plan for economic restructuring with the changed growth model that the government has introduced the National Assembly this session suggests that land and natural resources must be transferred to investors and projects that will use them more efficiently. I want to ask whether this plan moves past the 1992 constitution and whether this will continue to inflame issues that localities are already dealing with?[37]

The minister responded that there was "no conflict" between the people's ownership of the land and allocating land to efficient investors. Further emphasizing that the delegates were not acting out of line, VNA chair and Politburo member Nguyen Sinh Hung pressed the minister to answer the questions directly. In particular, he urged Quang to answer An's question of who was at fault for the Doan Van Vuon land dispute, saying, "I want the minister to answer directly, clearly" after An asked a follow-up question.

Therefore, the initial response to the Doan Van Vuon case in June 2012 was to use the VNA to challenge the government over its handling of the case. Interestingly, the delegates who raised the issue also did not challenge the party's position on state ownership of the land. Rather, they actually used state ownership of the land as a line of attack for a government restructuring plan to allow investors easier access to land. In this way, rather than *challenging* state ownership, the VNA responded to the Tien Lang crisis by *defending* it.[38]

This approach persisted through the first round of debates on the revisions to the law on November 19, 2012. It is telling that in her introduction to the debate, Nguyen Thi Kim Ngan did not raise the issue of state ownership of land as one of the issues she wanted debated.[39] In the following debate on the land law and the subsequent debate on the constitution, while a handful of delegates such as Duong Trung Quoc, Vu Tien Loc, and Do Van Ve challenged the logic of citizens and the state owning the land[40], most delegates who participated in the debate took as given that the state retained ownership of the land.

Huynh Van Tiep enunciated a typical view: "[R]egarding ownership of the land: During meetings to collect opinions on the law in the provinces voters were unified that the ownership of the land belongs to all the people; there were only a few opinions that ownership should be of the state and private. I align with the majority."[41] Indeed, deputy VNA chair Nguyen Thi Kim Ngan's assessment of the November 19 hearing was that "the majority of opinions were that the land is owned by the people, with the state as the representative of their ownership. However, there are some opinions that we should accept private ownership in some residential properties."[42] Again, this suggests that the purpose of the VNA, at least from the perspective of the party leadership, was not to challenge its established position on land ownership, which was ultimately retained. Rather, it was to invoke public ownership as a means to increase scrutiny of the government's management of land.

Perhaps highlighting how the issue was managed by the party, Nguyen Ba Thuyen noted in the final debate on the Land Law on June 6, 2013, that

the final report from the chair of the Economic Committee, which had jurisdiction over the law in the VNA, perhaps falsely noted that "the majority
of citizens agreed" that land should be owned by the public: "[A]ccording
to my perspective, this is not the case. Writing this is a little biased, because
the majority of citizens want recognition of private ownership of residential
land."[43] This highlights that despite some dissent on the floor, the goal of
the debate was not to gather information but to demonstrate the consensus
behind the law. The oversight was to redirect public anger over conflicts
raised by the law away from the party toward the state.

VINASHIN

Another issue pertaining to the state is the example discussed in the introduction: the VNA's oversight of Vinashin. As noted previously, this case
culminated in Nguyen Minh Thuyet's dramatic call on the VNA floor on
November 2, 2010, for a vote of no confidence in Prime Minister Nguyen
Tan Dung and an independent commission to investigate the affair. As figure
6.6 shows, the issue had been on the public's radar since June of that year. To
what degree did his speech represent an attempt by party members within
the Politburo to check the government? An informational or representational
account would suggest that grassroots pressure forced a reluctant party to allow the VNA to discuss the issue. The perspective offered in this chapter suggests that party leaders within the Politburo may have encouraged the VNA
to wade into the incident to deflect blame, damage Dung, and perhaps exert
influence in an issue area where party institutions are comparatively weak.

To provide some background on the Vinashin crisis, Vinashin was initially established as a shipbuilding SOE in 1996. However, using an experimental organizational structure initially designed, but never used, by Prime
Minister Vo Van Kiet, Prime Minister Phan Van Khai converted Vinashin
into a state-owned conglomerate in 2006 (Duc 2012; Nguyen and O'Donnell 2017). The Vinashin conversion was part of a wave of new conglomerates set up by the Vietnamese government in an attempt to follow South
Korean *chaebols*. Under this structure, conglomerates served as umbrellas
for subsidiary organizations to integrate different pieces of a larger production chain within a single organization (Vu 2009). In the case of Vinashin,
this would allow the shipbuilder to potentially integrate shipbuilding with
other related industries such as steel (Vu 2009). Others skeptically suggested
it was a way to allow Vinashin to set up financial instruments to raise short-
term capital quickly (Pincus 2009).

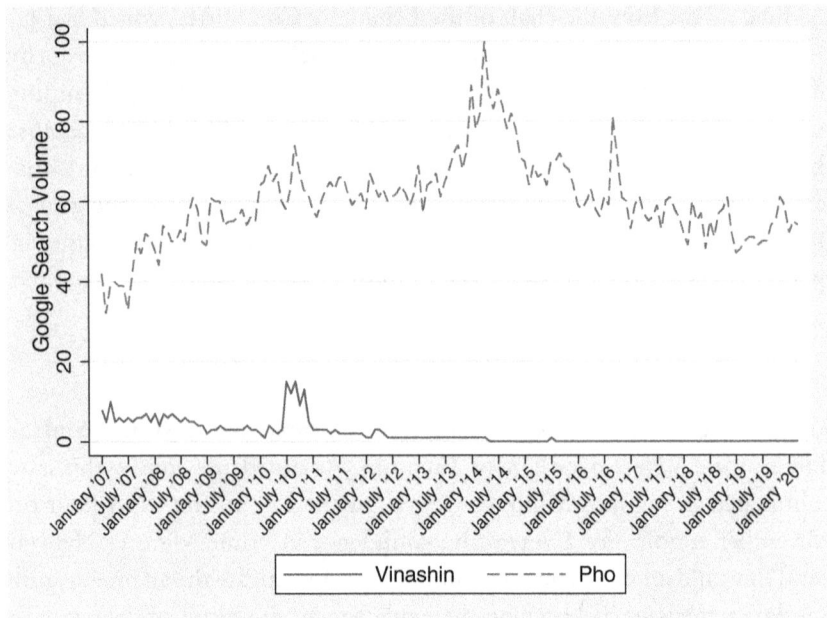

FIGURE 6.6. Google searches for Vinashin in Vietnam. Note: Data are from Google Trends and compare searches for Vinashin, a state-owned industry found to be billions in debt, in Vietnam to searches for pho (phở), Vietnam's national dish.

Although Khai initially approved Vinashin's reorganization, the overall policy was heavily associated with his successor, Nguyen Tan Dung. Khai created the first two such conglomerates, but Dung created an additional nine. Also, under Dung's tenure, these groups rapidly increased the number of subsidiaries under their operation and expanded into a wider range of business sectors unrelated to their core industries (Pincus 2009). The reorganization scheme also was implemented during a period when the government emphasized economic growth at all costs, which contributed to inflation. There were several potential logics for the decision to expand the use of these conglomerates. Duc (2012) attributes it to Dung's desire to make an immediate impact during his first term. Others have suggested that it was a way to win local political allies by setting up investments and subsidiaries in different regions (Pincus and Anh 2008).[44] Yet others have suggested it was a way to maintain the relevance of SOEs in Vietnam's economic development plan.[45]

Almost immediately after Dung began setting up these companies up, observers expressed concern about the rapid expansion generally and

Vinashin specifically. Pincus (2009) argued that the number of subsidiaries was expanding too rapidly. Vu Quang Viet (2009) argued that the expansion was taking place without sufficient economic logic or reporting requirements. The National Assembly also became increasingly involved, and a 2008 meeting of the National Assembly Economic Committee demanded greater reporting on the operation of the conglomerates (Vu 2009). The Politburo itself, revealing the divisions with the party leadership, issued a decision on October 4, 2009, cautioning that while the experiment with conglomerates had achieved some successes, there were issues with excessive investments in noncore industries. This report also required the party cell within the government, which the prime minister leads, to "report to the Politburo at the end of 2010 the results of the continuing experiment to set up the conglomerates."[46]

With that said, the government, with the tacit consent of the party, had bailed Vinashin out on previous occasions. It had taken out several million US dollars in loans in 2006 and 2007 from foreign and domestic sources in order to rapidly expand and sell ships internationally. However, the 2008 financial crisis led to the cancellation of many orders, exposing Vinashin's rapid expansion and putting it in a liquidity crunch. In 2009, the government put $158 million into the company to keep it afloat.[47]

However, until June 2010, while there were concerns, it appeared to be business as usual for Vinashin. In previous years, when the company had run short of cash it had been able to tap into the state budget. The situation changed on June 22, 2010, when news began to trickle out that the party was going to force Vinashin to restructure. Then, more dramatically, the Central Inspection Commission announced the results of an investigation into Vinashin, which as far as I can determine had not been previously acknowledged. The report found serious mismanagement at the hands of Dung's appointee, Pham Thanh Binh.

Then, more ominously, on August 5 the media reported on the results of a July 31 Politburo meeting, at which the Politburo issued conclusions stating that Vinashin had made many "mistakes." Although it suggested there were some factors such as the global financial crisis outside of Vinashin's control leading to the company's troubles, the majority of blame was placed on the company's management. The report said that although the company had been inspected eleven times and the media had reported on its excessive expansion, the company had done little to address the underlying problems.

In particular, it had not implemented the recommendations from the 2009 Politburo decision.

Therefore, by the time the November 2010 National Assembly session came up, Vinashin had already been thoroughly investigated by the party. Furthermore, the party leadership and the Politburo itself had already delivered stinging criticism of the management of Vinashin, and implicitly, of Nguyen Tan Dung himself. In this context, what role did the VNA play in raising the issue? Was it the representation of citizen concerns? Did the VNA provide information to the party leadership on Vinashin's management?

What is clear is that Thuyet's speech in 2010 was not in opposition to the party leadership, but should rather be seen as a gambit to use an alternative strategy to weaken Dung. Harkening back to Tanner's (1999, 289–290) insight that the Chinese NPC was a staging ground for those threatened by reformists in the government, Thuyet's speech was likely sanctioned by the party leadership. Indeed, the chair of the VNA in 2010 was none other than Nguyen Phu Trong, who would later lead the charge to oust Dung from the Politburo in October 2012. In opening the fall 2010 plenary session of the VNA, Trong explicitly raised Vinashin as a topic of debate for the upcoming session. In laying out issues on which the VNA should focus its oversight during that session, he specifically cited the "activities of Vinashin."[48] He once again raised the issue as a key part of the agenda for the query sessions, instructing delegates to challenge the ministers of finance and transportation on the issue.[49]

Two things are immediately clear from this timeline. First, prior to the VNA's challenge to Dung on Vinashin, the party was already thoroughly investigating the issue. Second, the Politburo, and the chair of the VNA himself, were manifestly opposed to Dung and his policies by this point. Therefore, challenges from the VNA likely represented a useful way to damage Dung ahead of the January 2011 Party Congress. This suggests that the VNA, at this juncture, was likely acting as a way to shift blame for Vinashin to the government and damage Dung in the process.

The theory in this chapter suggests that the VNA may also play a role in assisting the party in an issue area where it has weaker capacity. Here, it is revealing that in the July 31, 2010, Politburo meeting, when the Politburo first issued a decision blaming the mishandling of the enterprise on Vinashin's management, the VNA Economic Committee was included in the meeting. The media reports issued by the state said: "At the meeting on July 31, after hearing the Government party cell report regarding Vinashin's situation and opinions from the Office of the Central Committee, the Central Inspection Commission, the *VNA Economic Committee*, the Ministry of Police, and central offices; the Politburo debated and concluded."[50] Two things stand out. First, the party itself had no agency with expertise in economic affairs. Second, it appears that to make up for this deficiency, it relied on the VNA Economic Committee. This suggests that while the VNA was used in November 2010 as a cudgel to damage Dung, earlier in the process it may have played a role in providing the Politburo with key technical information the latter lacked, due to its delegation of economic decision making to the government.

As a coda to this story, it is noteworthy that since 2010 the party has moved to bolster its capacity in economic management. In 2010 the party's ability to make and manage economic policy was relatively weak. Indeed, after 1992 the party disbanded nearly half of its policy-making bodies (Thayer 1992), and perhaps more important, it disbanded the Central Committee's Central Economic Commission in 2007 as part of the party's greater devolution of economic responsibility to the government (Pham 2016, 277). This would suggest that as this body strengthens, the party should find less use for the VNA in managing the government's economic policies.

Conclusion

The VNA is at times surprisingly vocal, leading some to suggest that perhaps it does reflect citizens' interests and represent a possible venue for increasing political pluralism. The theory in this book, particularly outlined in this chapter and chapter 4, is that this assertiveness results from a desire by the party to challenge and check the government. I argue that seeing VNA debate as an example of citizen information or a check on the party misreads legislative debate in a single-party regime. Rather, the VNA is occasionally empowered to act when the party hopes to challenge the government. The quantitative and case study evidence in this chapter is consistent with that argument.

SEVEN

Intimidation or Legitimation?
The Signaling Value of the VNA

The previous chapters showed that the VNA serves to mobilize participation in regime rituals and provide a check by the party on the government. They have also shown that there is limited informational content in or meaningful engagement with elections. A final piece of the puzzle is the effect public displays of electoral support or legislative activity have on public perceptions of the regime. Indeed, one of the goals of signaling strength and unity is to generate support for the party and lower the likelihood that citizens will oppose the regime.

As noted in chapter 1, the signaling literature parallels a large literature on propaganda. Signaling, like propaganda, ultimately intends to send a message to a target that the regime is strong, powerful, or popular, and therefore resistance is futile. Like propaganda, signaling can work through two primary channels. First, under the hard propaganda mechanism (Huang 2015, 2018), it may signal strength and convince citizens, bureaucrats, or elite rivals that resistance will not work (Simpser 2013; Gehlbach and Simpser 2015; Wedeen 2015). Alternatively, under the soft propaganda mechanism (Huang 2015, 2018), signaling may directly convince citizens to support the regime. In this way, elections and legislative activity may have a direct effect of increasing support for the regime by demonstrating that the regime is working through legitimate, democratic channels.

To assess which of these two channels explains the signaling value of the VNA, this chapter examines an Internet survey of Vietnamese citizens in which they were provided with information typically made available through state-run media about elections and the VNA. The primes

included information about the number of non-party members in the legislature (a sign of competitiveness and/or strength of the party), the high vote
totals for legislation passed in the VNA (a sign of deliberation and/or unity
within the VNA), and the high levels of turnout in VNA elections (a sign of
public complicity with the elections procedures). To test the first signaling
channel, I assessed whether this information reduced people's estimation
of the competitiveness of elections and their willingness to participate in
antiregime activity. To test the second channel, I examined whether the information increased the assessment of the competitiveness of elections and
activity in the legislature. Furthermore, I assessed whether this improved
their estimation of the VNA and the regime.

The findings provide little evidence that information about the VNA
bolsters the regime through the hard propaganda mechanism. Instead, there
is some evidence that information about elections and the legislature increases perceptions of the competitiveness of the elections and the activity
of the VNA. Furthermore, through a mediation analysis, the results provide
suggestive evidence that the increased perception of competitiveness and
efficacy in the VNA increases satisfaction with the situation in Vietnam,
confidence in the VCP, and confidence in the VNA. More speculatively, it
may have some effect in reducing willingness to protest.

Of course, some caveats are in order, which are discussed in the conclusion to this chapter. In particular, given that Vietnamese citizens are
subjected to information about the strength and unity of the party on a
continual basis, it is unclear how much an Internet-based survey can meaningfully shift attitudes from the baseline. Furthermore, there are ever-
present concerns about preference falsification, even in Internet surveys.
The conclusion of the chapter discusses some of the implications of these
concerns for the results.

Theory and Hypotheses

When reading about VNA elections or results of legislative votes in the VNA,
what signals do citizens receive? Predictions vary by theory. One version of
the signaling story predicts that domination of the legislature should signal a
party's ability to secure compliance and win elections (Simpser 2013). Under
this view, which parallels the hard propaganda view, information about the
VNA and VNA elections should decrease the degree to which citizens feel

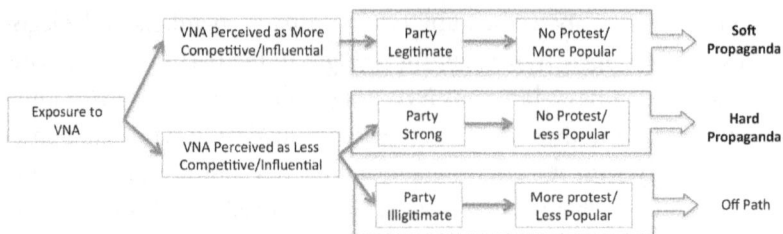

FIGURE 7.1. Possible effects of exposure to the VNA.

the legislative process is meaningful and elections are competitive (Huang 2015, 2018). Targets may be inclined to support the regime by virtue of the fact that their forced participation renders them complicit in the regime's behavior (Wedeen 2015; Mertha 2017). Therefore, they will be reluctant to oppose the regime by virtue of their past behavior. Furthermore, this domination may undermine the popularity of the regime. However, because of the signaling effect, it should also decrease the degree to which citizens are willing to protest against the regime about policies they disagree with.

In addition, the hard propaganda theory predicts a mediating relationship between perceptions about the competitiveness and effectiveness of the legislature and the willingness to protest against and popularity of the regime. If the hard propaganda theory holds, citizens should not believe the propaganda. Rather, it should reinforce their negative views toward the regime. Nonetheless, they are cowed by the propaganda into not resisting. Therefore, the decreased popularity of the regime and willingness to protest should be mediated by the effect of the information on reinforcing the lack of competition and independence of the VNA. This leads to the following set of hypotheses (see figure 7.1 for a summary of the theory and hypotheses):

Hypothesis 1a: Information about the VNA decreases perception of the competitiveness and representativeness of the VNA.

Hypothesis 1b: Information about the VNA decreases willingness to protest against the regime.

Hypothesis 1c: Information about the VNA decreases support for the party/overall satisfaction.

Hypothesis 1d: Information about the VNA decreases support for the party through the mediating effect of decreased perception of competitiveness/activity/representation in the VNA.

An alternative view of the signaling argument is that information about the electoral and legislative processes increases the perceived legitimacy of the system and therefore increases support for the regime. This would be in line with the legitimation view of authoritarian legislative and electoral institutions (Alagappa 1995; Thayer 2009a). In a related finding, and consistent with research on propaganda from Nazi Germany, China, and other contexts, some research shows that propaganda may be genuinely convincing for at least some citizens (Adena et al. 2015; Peisakhin and Rozenas 2018; Cantoni et al. 2017). In this way, elections and legislatures could operate closer to what Huang calls *soft propaganda*, which is propaganda that is meant to be believed or is genuinely convincing (Huang 2015, 2018). This leads to the following hypotheses:

> *Hypothesis 2a: Information about the VNA increases perception of the competitiveness of and activity in the VNA.*

> *Hypothesis 2b: Information about the VNA decreases the willingness to protest against the regime.*

> *Hypothesis 2c: Information about the VNA increases support for the party/overall satisfaction.*

> *Hypothesis 2d: Information about the VNA increases support for the party through the mediating effect of increased perception of competitiveness/activity/representation in the VNA.*

Before proceeding, it is important to note what predictions could be inconsistent with the theory in this book or *off path*. If the goal of the regime is to gain information or perhaps provide a constraint on itself, it may open up election procedures and legislative debate despite the costs it could incur with regard to public opinion. Therefore, if exposure to the VNA signaled that the VNA was less competitive *and* this undermined the legitimacy of the party, that result would not be consistent with the argument put forward in this book. In short, there must be some kind of benefit with regard to public opinion, through either intimidation or legitimation, for the theory to hold.

On another note, it is important to highlight reasons that we may observe weak or null findings even if they do not ultimately veer off path. The most important reason is that citizens may simply be saturated with information about the VNA and politics in general. Priming experiments, such as the one that I report on in this chapter, ultimately rely on the ability of the prime to increase the salience of a phenomenon relative to a control group, which presumably does not have the prime at the "top of their head" (Zaller and Feldman 1992). Where the respondents are saturated with the treatment prior to the survey, the experiment is likely to underestimate the effects of the treatment (Gaines, Kuklinski, and Quirk 2007).

Another final, ever-present concern about surveys in authoritarian regimes is preference falsification (Bischoping and Schuman 1992; Kalinin 2016). The questions contained in this survey could potentially have been sensitive to respondents. Despite assurances that the response would be confidential and that all the questions would pertain to legal behavior, respondents may nonetheless have wanted to err on the side of caution and may have provided the responses they thought the regime would want to hear. While that is certainly a concern in this survey, identification in this case relies on differences between those receiving information about the VNA and those who did not. For preference falsification to be a threat to validity, we should find that those receiving the prime regarding the VNA were more cautious in admitting to sensitive behaviors than those who did not receive the prime. I discuss the implications of possible preference falsification after the results.

Data and Research Design

The data come from an Internet-based survey conducted with 473 respondents through Qualtrics in May 2019. For cost reasons and because of skepticism that even a demographically "representative" sample would be genuinely representative, the survey was not representative based on descriptive statistics. It featured a higher number of younger respondents and included slightly more men than women. The participants were also more educated than the average level of education in Vietnam. Given the difficulty of conducting a survey of this nature in Vietnam, conducting an online survey was the best alternative, one used by others interested in similar questions (Pan and Xu 2017; Truex 2017).

To provide information about the VNA, I varied primes that are typical of information Vietnamese citizens receive about the VNA from the domestic media. I primed respondents with information about the degree of unity in votes for legislation in the VNA, how many party members were elected

TABLE 7.1.
Research design of an Internet survey experiment on signaling effect of VNA.

	Treatment	N
Group 1: Control	No prime	141
Group 2: Single dose treatment	One prime (from table 7.2)	175
Group 3: Double dose treatment	Two primes (from table 7.2)	82
Group 4: Triple dose treatment	Three primes (from table 7.2)	75

to the most recent VNA, and the extreme levels of reported turnout for the VNA. The information should have generated the signaling effect through either the hard or soft propaganda mechanisms. In terms of the research design, I randomized the treatment in two ways. I varied the type of prime, but then I also varied the *dose*. To some respondents I gave only one of the three primes. To others I provided two primes, and to others, all three (see table 7.1).

Table 7.2 details the specific primes used in the survey. The goals of the different primes as well as the dosage were twofold. First, with the different

TABLE 7.2.
Primes used in an Internet survey experiment on signaling effect of VNA.

	Prime
Prime 1	In the last VNA session, can you guess on average what percentage of the vote the eight laws passed received from the VNA? • 51% • 76% • 86% • **90% [correct answer]** • 94% • 100% If correct: "You are right! It is 90%" If incorrect: "Almost! The actual percentage was 90%"
Prime 2	How many party members do you think there are in the VNA? • 0% • 27% • 52% • **96% [correct answer]** • 100% If correct: "You are right! It is 96%" If incorrect: "Almost! The actual percent is 96%"

(continues)

TABLE 7.2.   (*Continued*)

	Prime
Prime 3	Respondents are presented with the following excerpt of a news story about turnout in the most recent election.
	"On May 22, 2016, across the country all election precincts conducted the 14th VNA election and election for the People's Councils at all level for the 2016–2021 period. In a peaceful, serious environment, *98.77 percent of the voters voted.*"
	About what percent of the population voted? • 55% • 80% • **99% [correct answer]** • 100%

primes, the goal was to make sure that the outcome was not dependent on a quirk of the specific prime used. This method of varying the prime has been used in other research on the effects of propaganda (Huang 2018). With regard to the dose treatment, the goal was to possibly counteract the concerns about a weak treatment. In terms of the analysis, for each I conducted two sets of analysis. For the first, I aggregated groups 2–4 into a single treatment group. For the second analysis I used the treatment as a continuous dose treatment, where 0 is the control, 1 is group 1, 2 is group 3, and 3 is group 4.

CONTROL VARIABLES

Although the treatment was randomized, to validate the randomization and allow for some heterogeneous treatment effect analyses, I also asked a series of pretreatment questions to assess the balance between the groups. The factors included ethnicity, gender, age, education, and income, among others. I also asked a series of questions related to respondents' satisfaction with the economic situation in Vietnam as well as their party status, risk tolerance, political awareness, nationalism, and desire for centralized authority. The balance table (table 7.3) shows no major concerns between the treatment and control groups. The entire sample was on average more likely to be male, younger, highly educated, and members of the ethnic majority Kinh than the average Vietnamese. However, the treatment and controls show balance across nearly all the variables, with the exception of the minority variable.

TABLE 7.3.
Assessment of balance between groups in survey.

Variable	Control mean	Treatment mean	P-value (2-sided)
Male (0 female; 1 male)	0.52	0.55	0.69
Age	26.10	25.68	0.37
Education (0–10)	8.28	8.22	0.70
Minority	1.08	1.05	0.15
Income (1–20 scale)	14.62	14.02	0.33
Risk taking (1–10 scale)	6.60	6.58	0.94
Watch news	1.88	1.87	0.79
Watch politics	4.12	4.13	0.79
Pocketbook economy bad	3.41	3.51	0.23
Sociotropic economy bad	3.28	3.39	0.24
Party member	0.22	0.23	0.72
Proud of Vietnam	8.28	8.50	0.35
Proud of Vietnamese anthem	4.30	4.22	0.41
Proponent of strong Vietnam	3.74	3.77	0.77

DEPENDENT AND MEDIATING VARIABLES

To measure the outcomes of interest, I included a number of variables to assess the degree to which respondents felt good about the situation in Vietnam, how they felt toward the regime, their perception of the level of satisfaction among others, and whether they would be willing to protest against the government in the event they disagreed with a policy. In addition, the moderating variable was the effect of the treatment on their perception of the competitiveness of VNA elections and the representativeness of VNA delegates.

The soft propaganda effect should operate through convincing citizens that the legislature and its elections are *more* competitive and *more* representative of citizens. This in turn should improve evaluations of the situation in Vietnam and reduce the willingness to protest. The hard propaganda effect should operate through information about the VNA priming people to think the VNA is less competitive and less representative than the control group. In turn, this should reduce satisfaction with the situation in Vietnam, satisfaction with the party, and willingness to protest.

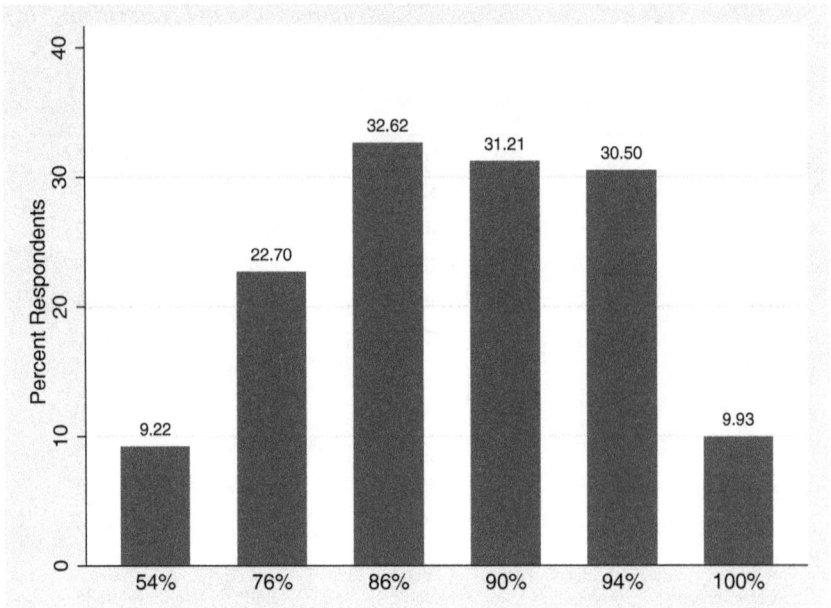

FIGURE 7.2. Respondents' estimates of average percentage vote share for VNA laws. The response to the first prime in table 7.2 is included.

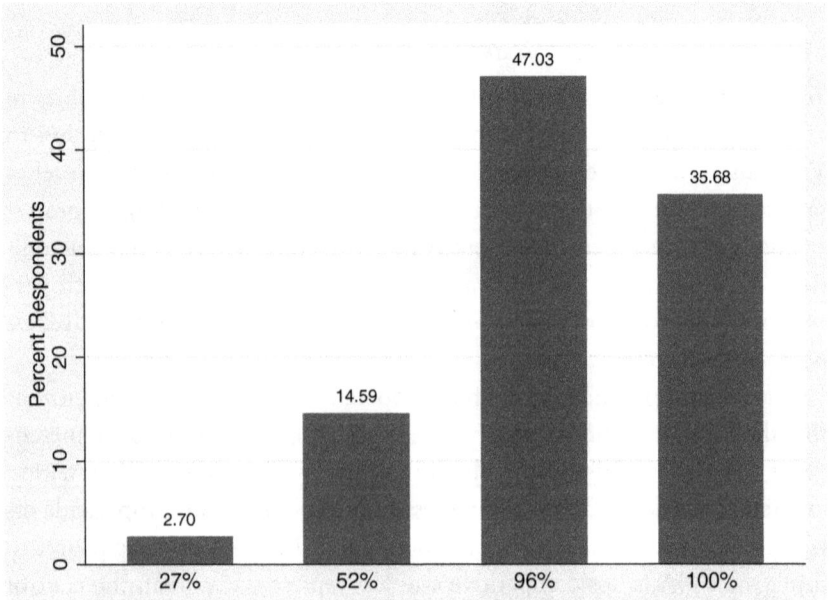

FIGURE 7.3. Respondents' estimates of average percentage seat share for VCP members. The response to the second prime in table 7.2 is included. No respondents estimated there were 0% party members in the VNA.

Before proceeding, it is worth examining how competitive respondents felt the legislature was in aggregate. With regard to the first question, people in general thought that the VNA passes bills with about 90 percent of the vote (see figure 7.2). With regard to the second question, more than 80 percent of the respondents thought there were either 96 or 100 percent party members in the VNA (see figure 7.3). Taken together, this indicates that citizens in the sample generally perceived the VNA to have high degrees of unity and party dominance. This also suggests that the treatment may be weak, given the high level of knowledge about the VNA and penetration of state information among the sample.

Moving to the outcome variables, in terms of perspectives on the VNA, I asked whether respondents thought the VNA was competitive, the degree to which it represented citizens, and the degree to which it has influence over policy. Figures 7.4–7.6 show that on each of these dimensions, citizens had a relatively positive view of the VNA's competitiveness, representativeness, and efficacy. Consistent with the soft propaganda, this suggests that the saturation with information about the VNA has convinced citizens of the

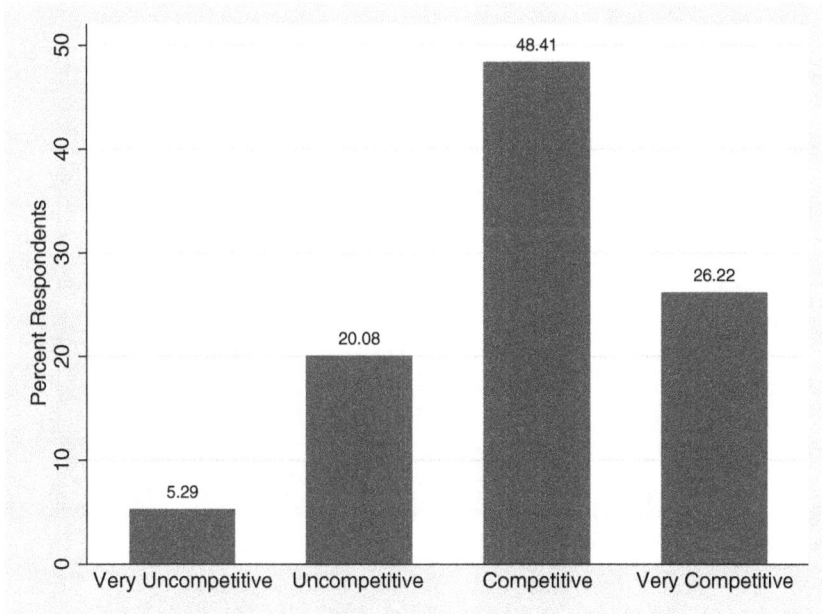

FIGURE 7.4. Respondents views of competitiveness of VNA elections.

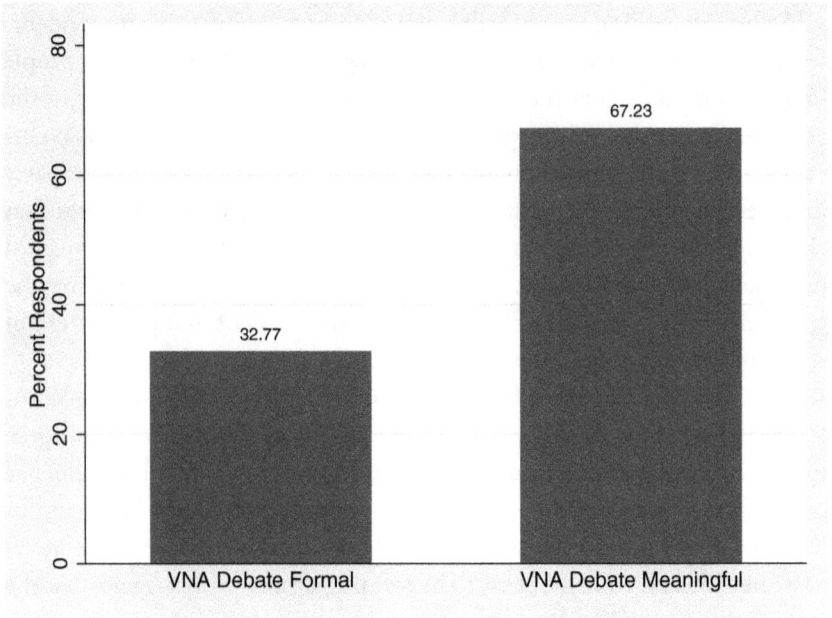

FIGURE 7.5. Respondents' views of VNA debates as formal or meaningful.

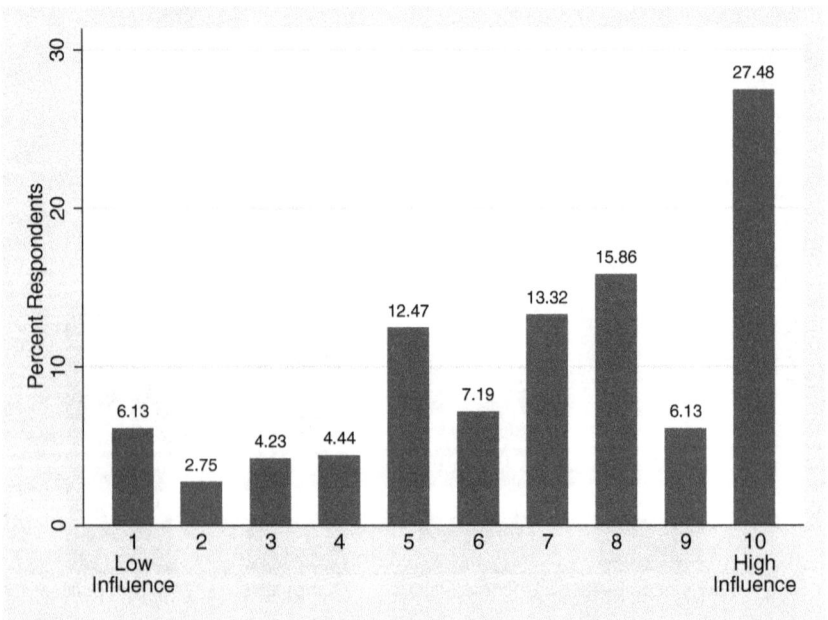

FIGURE 7.6. Respondents' assessment of VNA's influence over policy.

legitimacy of the VNA, even if they are not moved to participate meaning-fully in its rituals.

Results

This section looks at the direct effects of exposure to the VNA on the out-comes of interest. First, it examines the impact of exposure to the VNA on perceptions of the VNA's competitiveness and efficacy itself. It then looks at the direct effects on support for satisfaction with the overall situation in Viet-nam, assessment of others' satisfaction with the situation in Vietnam, satis-faction with the party, and willingness to protest. The following section then looks at the mediating effects of the impact of the treatment of perceptions of the VNA's competitiveness and efficacy on those downstream outcomes.

The results depicted in table 7.4 and figure 7.7 show that the impact of the treatment of perceptions of competitiveness and efficacy was modest. However, where it had an impact it was in the direction of the soft propa-ganda theory. In terms of the competitiveness of the VNA, the treatment increased the perception that elections were competitive, though not at stan-dard levels of significance. The treatment had no impact on whether or not debate in the VNA was meaningful. However, the treatment did have a sig-nificant effect on the perception that the VNA could influence legislation. While the effect was modest (less than a standard deviation in the dependent variable), it was significant at the 95 percent level. What this suggests is that while perceptions of the VNA were already relatively closely in line with the soft propaganda theory before the survey experiment, information about the VNA appeared to *increase* the perceived importance of the VNA.

TABLE 7.4.
Impact of treatment on perceptions of VNA efficacy and competitiveness.

	VNA competitive	VNA debate meaningful	VNA influential
Treatment	0.129	−0.002	0.614*
	(0.082)	(0.047)	(0.273)
Constant	2.865**	1.674**	6.546**
	(0.069)	(0.04)	(0.229)
Observations	473	473	473
R-squared	0.005	0	0.011

NOTE: Standard errors in parentheses.

* $p < 0.05$, ** $p < 0.01$

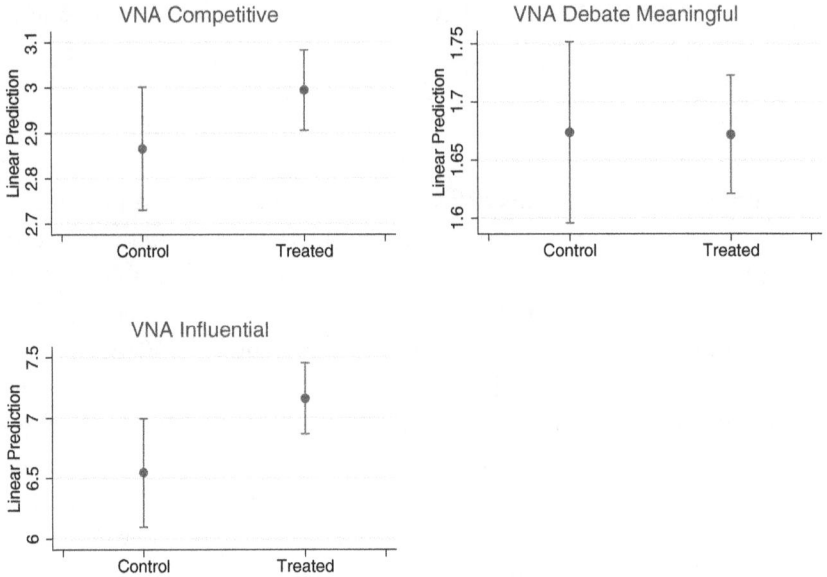

FIGURE 7.7. Impact of treatment on perceptions of VNA.

Looking at the dosage, the effects of the treatment are broadly consistent. It appears that more information about the VNA generally cumulates on itself. Table 7.5 and figure 7.8 show that cumulating the primes increased the degree of competitiveness citizens perceived in the VNA. Surprisingly, however, increasing the number of primes to three decreased the degree to which citizens thought the VNA was competitive from what would have been the case if they had received only two primes. There was little impact of the primes on whether or not citizens thought debate in the VNA was

TABLE 7.5.
Impact of treatment dosage on perceptions of VNA.

	VNA elections competitive	VNA debate meaningful
Treatment	0.044	0.013
	(0.036)	(0.021)
Constant	2.904*	1.656*
	(0.058)	(0.033)
Observations	473	473
R-squared	0.003	0.001

Standard errors in parentheses.
* p < 0.01

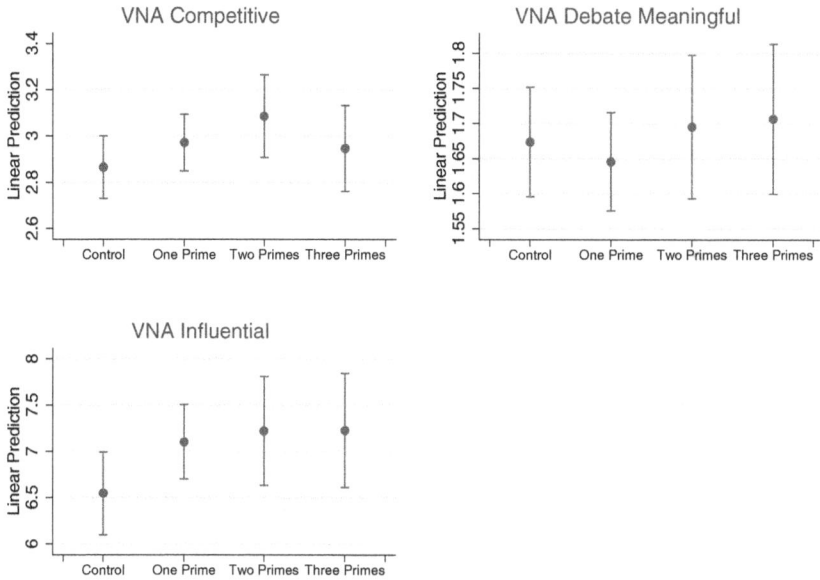

FIGURE 7.8. Impact of treatment dosage on perceptions of VNA.

meaningful. The primes had a more consistent cumulative effect on whether or not the VNA was influential (figure 7.8).

DOWNSTREAM VARIABLES

Moving to the downstream variables, table 7.6 and figure 7.9 show the impact of exposure to the VNA on one's own satisfaction with the situation in Vietnam, willingness to protest, and one's own evaluation of the party. While the results are also consistent with the soft propaganda theory, the

TABLE 7.6.
Impact of treatment on general support, support for regime, and willingness to protest.

	Overall satisfaction	I believe in VNA	I believe in party	Willing to protest
Treatment	0.064	0.114	0.112	−0.054
	(0.07)	(0.101)	(0.109)	(0.323)
Constant	2.936*	3.801*	3.794*	4.177*
	(0.058)	(0.085)	(0.092)	(0.271)
Observations	473	473	473	473
R-squared	0.002	0.003	0.002	0

Standard errors in parentheses.

* $p < 0.01$

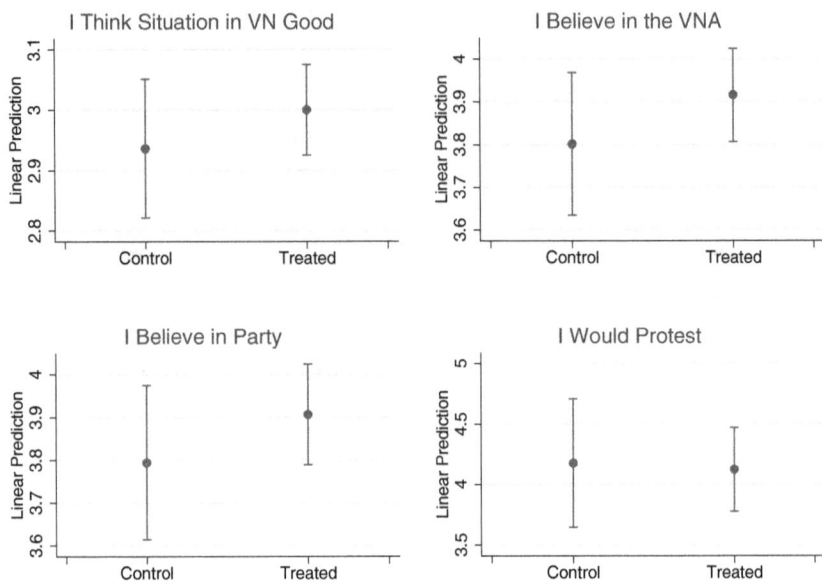

FIGURE 7.9. Impact of treatment on general support, support for regime, and willingness to protest.

results here are weak. There was a weak but positive effect in belief in the party and the VNA, but not at standard levels of significance.

Finally, looking at the dosage, the effects are consistent with the findings from the aggregated treatment. Some of the variables show slightly stronger effects, such as the direct effect of the evaluation of the situation in Vietnam and belief in the party. Figure 7.10 and table 7.7 show that the

TABLE 7.7.
Impact of treatment dosage on general support, support for regime, and willingness to protest.

	I think situation in Vietnam is good	I believe in VNA	I believe in party	I would protest
Treatment dosage	0.041	0.055	0.056	−0.061
	(0.031)	(0.045)	(0.048)	(0.14)3
Constant	2.932*	3.816*	3.806*	4.212*
	(0.049)	(0.071)	(0.076)	(0.226)
Observations	473	473	473	473
R-squared	0.004	0.003	0.003	0.000

Standard errors in parentheses.

* $p < 0.01$

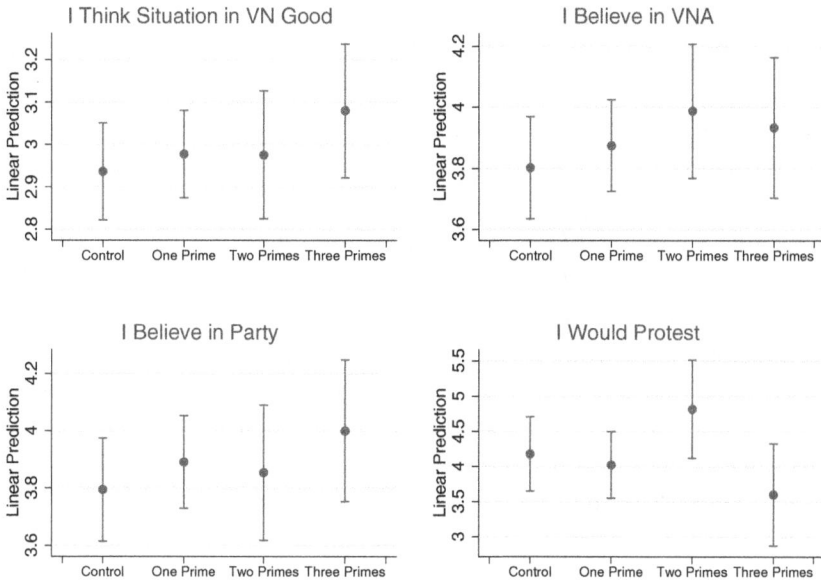

FIGURE 7.10. Impact of treatment dosage on general support, support for regime, and willingness to protest.

dosage generally seemed to amplify the effect of the treatment on those two outcomes.

Mediation Analysis

While the findings are not strong in terms of direct effects on the downstream variables, possibly due to the strong pretreatment saturation of information about the VNA, the results are in line with the soft propaganda explanation and against the hard propaganda explanation in the context of the VNA. To assess whether information about the VNA influenced support for the regime and a more positive attitude toward the situation in Vietnam in general by increasing the perceptions of VNA influence, I conducted a mediation analysis (Imai, Keele, and Yamamoto 2010). While there is debate as to whether the assumptions underlying mediation analysis hold (Green, Ha, and Bullock 2010), with a sensitivity analysis I can at least assess the conditions under which it is plausible that the outcomes of interest—in this case confidence in the party and perceptions of the general situation in Vietnam—operate through the increased perception that the VNA is a meaningfully influential body.

To conduct the mediation analysis, I used the mediating variable most strongly impacted by the treatment, the increase in the perceived efficacy of the VNA. As figure 7.7 shows, the treatment had a significant impact on the degree to which respondents thought the VNA was influential. To estimate the mediating effect on general satisfaction and attitude toward the party, I used the "mediation" package in Stata (Hicks and Tingley 2011). The results show that the treatment impacted general satisfaction and views toward the party (see table 7.8) nearly entirely through convincing respondents that the VNA was more influential. The ACME of .07 on attitude toward the situation in Vietnam (1 standard deviation = .69) is small at just over .1 standard deviation of the dependent variable. Once I accounted for the impact on the views toward the VNA, the treatment had nearly no direct effect on thinking the situation in Vietnam was good or on views toward the party. The substantive effects were broadly similar for believing in the VNA and believing in the party. The effects were not significant for willingness to protest.

I also looked at whether views on competitiveness of the VNA mediated outcomes, with broadly similar results. I conducted the same analysis with the dose treatment, showing broadly similar results. In terms of the sensitivity analysis, figure 7.11 shows that a high degree of correlation between a potential confounder and the mediator would be required to nullify the effects of the mediator for all except the case where the dependent variable is willingness to protest. In all, the results show that exposure to the VNA seems to increase the degree to which citizens think it is active and

TABLE 7.8.
Mediated effects of treatment through feelings toward VNA.

	I think situation in Vietnam is good			I believe in VNA		
	Mean	95% CI		Mean	95% CI	
ACME	0.07	0.01	0.13	0.1	0.01	0.19
Direct effect	0	−0.13	0.12	0.01	−0.17	0.2

	I believe in party			I would protest		
	Mean	95% CI		Mean	95% CI	
ACME	0.106	0.01	0.21	0.03	−0.03	0.13
Direct effect	0.008	−0.19	0.2	−0.08	−0.73	0.56

Mediator = VNA influential

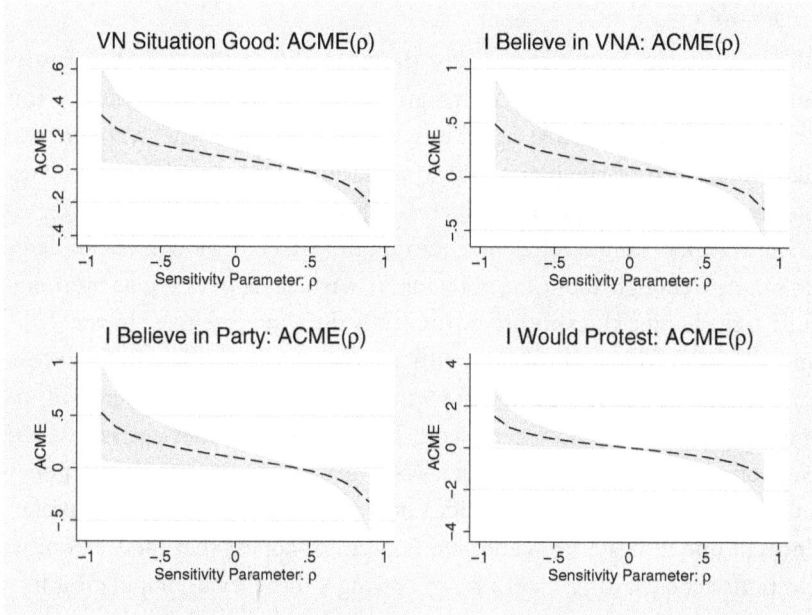

FIGURE 7.11. Sensitivity analysis of mediated effects of treatment through feelings toward VNA.

legitimate. Furthermore, this effect mediates an overall increase in support for the party and general satisfaction with the overall situation in Vietnam. The effects on protests are in the direction predicted by the soft propaganda theory, though weaker than expected, perhaps due to pretreatment saturation of exposure to the VNA.

A WORD ON PREFERENCE FALSIFICATION

One can never rule out preference falsification in surveys. One concern in this survey is that the results may have been driven by preference falsification. That is, mention of the VNA may have primed respondents to be more cautious in how they responded to questions. For this to have impacted the results reported here, respondents would have to have been more willing to express positive attitudes about the party when the VNA was mentioned than when it was not. While this is possible, in some sense it is consistent with the theory. When the VNA is discussed or mentioned, citizens are more on their guard and express preferences in line with what the regime wants. This is a form of intimidation that cows the behavior of respondents.

Conclusion

The overall argument of the book is that national elections and legislatures under authoritarian rule signal strength at the expense of information. This chapter examines how that signal was received. Although the treatment was likely weakened by the pretreatment saturation of the signal, in general exposure to the VNA appears to increase the view that the VNA is a legitimate, competitively elected, and meaningful body. Although respondents do not care enough about the outcomes to participate in elections meaningfully (see chapter 5), exposure to the VNA does increase trust in the VNA and the VCP. This is consistent with a soft propaganda signaling effect of authoritarian institutions, whereby exposure convinces the audience of the message the regime intends to send. In this case, the message is that the elections are competitive and the VNA is a meaningful player in policy making even if citizens have no idea how to differentiate the policy preferences of one delegate from another. It does not appear that the VNA or its elections act as hard propaganda, by cowing a disbelieving population into not protesting while increasing their dissatisfaction with the regime.

Conclusion
Curbing Our Expectations for the VNA, Single-Party Legislatures

The evidence and theory in this book focus squarely on how elections and legislatures evolve in single-party regimes and the role they play in politics. As highlighted in the introduction, while interest in these questions persists (Bonvecchi and Simison 2017; Manion 2016; Woo and Conrad 2019; Rivera 2016), some are skeptical of the importance of literature on this topic. In particular, some question the seemingly inordinate focus on quasi-democratic institutions in distinctly nondemocratic systems (Art 2012; Pepinsky 2014; Greitens 2016). This critique is echoed, albeit in slightly different ways, by some scholars of Vietnamese politics (Gainsborough 2018; Fforde 2016). The criticism is that such institutions have a minimal impact on important outcomes of concern to scholars and policy makers, such as regime longevity, citizen welfare, policy outcomes, and democratization.

Despite writing about a specific single-party legislature and its elections in great detail, I share some of the concerns of the skeptics. In particular, I argue that while elections and legislatures are useful in generating regime stability by projecting an image of strength, their impact on improving policy outcomes and citizen welfare in single-party systems is minimal. While this finding is consistent with some work on authoritarian institutions highlighting the importance of signaling (Little 2017; Simpser 2013; Wedeen 2015; Mertha 2017), the argument also has much in common with classic views of authoritarian institutions. Indeed, the classic rubber-stamp view is not that authoritarian institutions serve no purpose. The difference between the signaling view and the rubber-stamp view, however, is that cloaking decisions made by the autocracy in a democratic veneer increases legitimacy (Fainsod 1963; Friedrich and Brzezinski 1961). The signaling argument suggests that the legislature may or may not increase the legitimacy of the regime in the eyes of some, but instead serves to change beliefs about the strength of the regime and the perception of support for the regime in society.

This raises the question of why this book should have been written in the first place. If the VNA is peripheral, why focus on it at all? While the VNA is peripheral to policy making, I argue that the apparent activity in the VNA can nonetheless be misinterpreted as genuine representation or bottom-up information. By showing the logic of institutionalization, the role of the VNA and elections, and the impact on public opinion, I have provided an alternative interpretation that explains these outcomes while still cohering with more classic views of authoritarian institutions. In short, it is perhaps more important to understand the proceedings of the VNA if we think they ultimately do not impact policy in order to avoid falsely attributing to them a role that does not exist.

With that said, a number of questions remain that the book has not yet fully addressed. I take up some of these questions here. First, I discuss the generalizability of the theory and findings. Many of the theories discussed in this book apply to hybrid and single-party systems. The first section of this chapter revisits this important distinction to discuss which aspects of my argument apply solely to single-party systems and which aspects have broader implications for hybrid regimes. I argue that while elections may be more informative in hybrid regimes, the difference in the importance of the elected legislature itself for policy outcomes is minimal in most cases. Following this, I offer some thoughts about why, if such legislatures ultimately have little effect on policy, they are associated with positive economic outcomes.[1]

The third part of this chapter discusses the implications of the findings for democratization. In particular, do more robust single-party legislative institutions matter at all for the prospects that a country will democratize? Here I suggest that while the VNA is not likely to hasten a transition, it could possibly play a role in a posttransition environment. Using a brief comparison between Vietnam and other single-party regimes with less active legislatures, I argue that it is plausible any transition in Vietnam could be smoother given the presence of a more active, visible legislature. That section focuses in particular on the inability of regimes to roll back institutional changes when the temporary logic of institutional design is gone.

The final section focuses more closely on the case of Vietnam, considering what the theory and findings suggest for the future of political development there. Here I suggest that my findings point to anything but a preordained "increased assertiveness" of the VNA. Rather, it is quite possible that if the VCP moves to more directly control the government, as has occurred since 2016, the party will see less reason for keeping a vociferous VNA. Rather, the party may, where possible, seek to scale back some of the VNA's roles as it moves to more directly control policy. Indeed, Nguyen Phu Trong's consolidation of the general secretary and presidency positions is a sign that this process is already underway.

Single-Party Legislatures and Elections versus Hybrid Legislatures and Elections

The arguments in this book are specifically tailored to single-party systems as opposed to hybrid regimes. The fundamental distinction between the two types of systems is that single-party regimes, whether they allow nominal opposition or not, have the ability to vet all candidates for the legislature, whereas hybrid regimes do not.[2] This distinction is important not simply because single-party elections "cannot be lost" (Hyde and Marinov 2011), but also because such elections and legislatures ultimately provide little information on the strength of the opposition or of the regime (Malesky and Schuler 2011). In short, while single-party elections *project strength*, they *do not provide information about strength*. This is because the variation in the fortunes of the non-party candidates across time—the key source of information in authoritarian elections—will depend more on variation in party-controlled vetting procedures than on the genuine popularity of the regime or the candidates.

Hybrid regimes, however, are different, at least with regard to elections. Where opposition parties are allowed to form, select their own candidates, and win seats, some of the dynamics theorized by the existing literature may occur. A poor showing in an election with competition may indeed signal waning popularity, thus inducing the regime to provide more policy concessions (Miller 2015). It may also signal that the time is right to "transition from strength" (Slater and Wong 2013). Therefore, while welfare benefits to the regime and citizens may flow from hybrid elections (Little 2017), these outcomes will not result from single-party elections.

However, with regard to legislative procedures, we should see less differ-ence between single-party regimes and hybrid regimes. This is because even in hybrid regimes, it is unlikely that legislatures will impact policy in the manner suggested by existing research (Gandhi 2008; Gehlbach and Keefer 2012; Wright 2008). Indeed, while legislatures do challenge the autocrat or government on occasion (Loidolt and Mecham 2013), ultimately the op-position's minority status means it is unlikely to have the power to mean-ingfully change policy. If opposition parties in democratic settings without divided government have little ability to shape policy (Tsebelis 2002), why would we expect any difference in an autocracy?

With this in mind, it is interesting to note that the one paper that does find effects of hybrid legislatures in an authoritarian system on micro-level outcomes is about subnational legislatures in Russia, where evidence shows that protests decline in regions where opposition parties control the legis-latures (Reuter and Robertson 2015). This paper highlights an important difference from most national-level legislatures in hybrid regimes, that op-position parties do not control the agenda. In some subnational legislatures, however, the opposition *controls the legislature*. With actual legislative con-trol, which almost never exists in hybrid regimes at the national level, the opposition is likely to have an impact.

In contrast to hybrid regimes, in some monarchies, military regimes, and unconsolidated civilian autocracies (sometimes coded as personalist), dif-ferent organizations sometimes do control the legislature. In these cases, it is possible that the party or group controlling the executive may not be the same as the party or group controlling the legislature. Some examples are monarchies such as Morocco or Kuwait, where the ruling family may dom-inate the executive but not the legislature. In some military regimes, such as Brazil in the 1970s and 1980s, or unconsolidated party-based regimes such as Yeltsin's Russia in the 1990s, this may also be the case. In these cases, much as in a divided government within a democracy, the legislature may aggressively challenge the autocrat on key policy issues. Indeed, most case studies of aggressive legislatures come from monarchies or military regimes (North and Weingast 1989; Gandhi 2008; Herb 2014),[3] not party-based re-gimes, where legislatures are purported to have a stronger constraining ef-fect (Wilson and Wright 2015; Wright 2008)

Therefore, the critical factor determining whether authoritarian leg-islatures play a meaningful role will be the degree to which separate organizations control the legislature and the executive. Where they do not, which is almost always the case in single-party regimes and party-based hybrid regimes, one is not likely to see the legislature impact outcomes. Where they do not, consistent with logic from democratic systems, the legislature may be a more important player.

Explaining Better Outcomes under Toothless Legislatures

If parties dominate legislatures in single-party regimes and hybrid regimes, why then do we only see the macro-level salutary effects of legislatures such as economic growth and investment in these settings and not in personalist regimes? A number of seminal studies show that investment and growth improve in autocracies with legislatures (Gandhi 2008, Wright 2008). Furthermore, this effect is most pronounced in party-based regimes, precisely the type of regime that I argue is least likely to impact outcomes. Why, then, is there a correlation between legislative institutions and outcomes in these cases?

A possible reason for the robust correlation between outcomes could be the rare conditions under which party-based regimes (whether single-party or hybrid) *do not* have legislatures. As Wright (2008) notes, more than 92 percent of single-party regime years feature a legislature. The argument in this book provides a possible explanation of why there is so little variation, which is that such legislatures are relatively costless in terms of the degree to which they will challenge the autocrat on key policy questions. The puzzle, from this perspective, is not why a party-based regime would have a legislature, but rather why a party-based regime *would not* have a legislature. Indeed, because of cross-national findings indicating a positive effect of legislatures on outcomes, theorizing the rare cases in which party-based regimes do not have legislatures is just as important for outcomes as theorizing the cases in which the regime does have a legislature.

Seen from this perspective, it seems possible that the reason for the correlation between single-party legislatures and outcomes has something to do with the peculiar 8 percent of party-based regime years without legislatures. One explanation is that legislatures in party-based regimes are closed in order to purge enemies of the regime, which could signal broader instability. If this is the case, the autocrat closes the legislature when it does not yet have full control of the ruling coalition. That is, the regime closes the legislature when it is trying to *consolidate power.* Therefore, we might expect to see legislative closures, when they occur, take place early in a regime's life cycle.

To assess the plausibility of this conjecture, I used two standard datasets of regime type and legislative institutions to measure legislative closures. To measure the existence of a legislature I used the Cheibub, Gandhi, and Vreeland (CGV) measure of whether or not there was an elected legislature during that year (Wilson and Wright 2015, 10). To measure regime type, I used the Geddes, Wright, and Frantz (GWF) dataset of authoritarian regimes (2014). This dataset codes all authoritarian regime years since 1945 and distinguishes them based on whether the ruler is a civilian party, a military regime, a personalistic dictator, or a monarch.

Using these datasets, which cover the years 1945–2010, figure C.1 shows the number of regime years by regime type that do not have legislatures.[4] As the figure shows, single-party regimes are much more likely to have legislatures closed early in their life cycles, with 36 percent of the regime years in the first five years of the regime not having a legislature, compared to 32 and 24 percent in the next two five-year periods. After 15 years, the number drops below 10 percent. Figure C.2 also shows that the relationship between regime duration and the probability of not having a legislature in single-party regimes is substantively strong and significant even after controlling for other factors that might impact the decision to seat a legislature, such as oil rents, GDP per capita, region, and decade fixed effects. After controlling for a range of covariates, single-party regimes have an estimated .43 probability of having no legislature in their first year in power, compared to only a .3 probability in their thirtieth year in power.

Military and personal regimes also have the same negative relationship between duration and legislative closures. Only monarchies show no relationship during the period observed (see figure C.2, bottom right). The figures clearly show that legislatures are more likely to close early in a regime's tenure. Indeed, in no case did a legislature close in a party-based regime that lasted more than thirty years. Furthermore, the bulk of the closures occurred within the first decade of a regime's life cycle, which are particularly volatile years for an authoritarian regime (Haber 2006; Albertus and Menaldo 2014). In short, the evidence seems to suggest that factors endogenous to the timing of legislative closures may explain outcomes just as well as the constraining nature of the legislatures themselves.

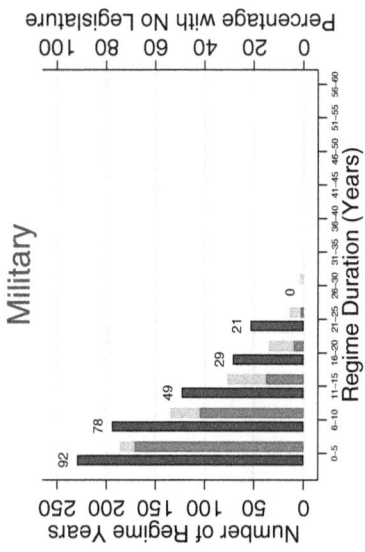

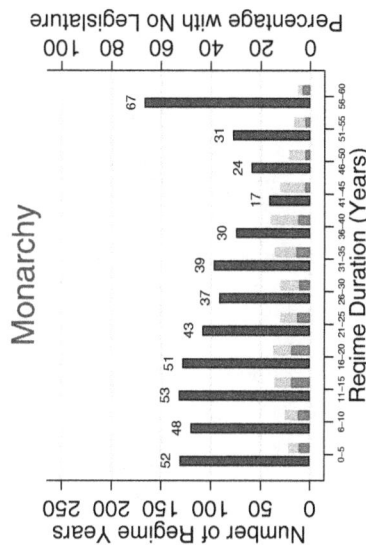

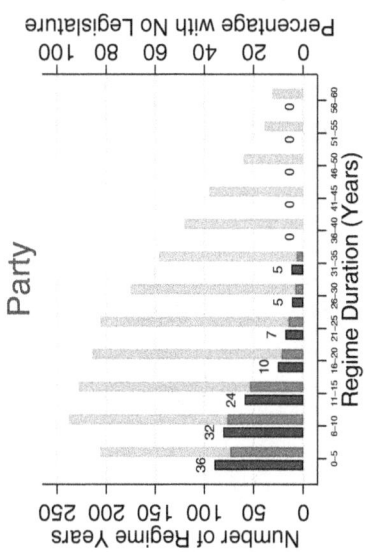

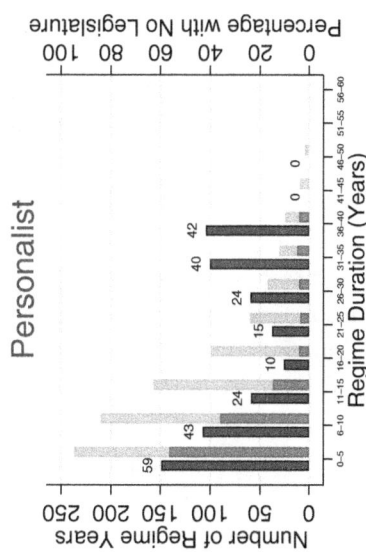

FIGURE C.1. Autocracies, legislative closures, and regime age, 1945–2010.

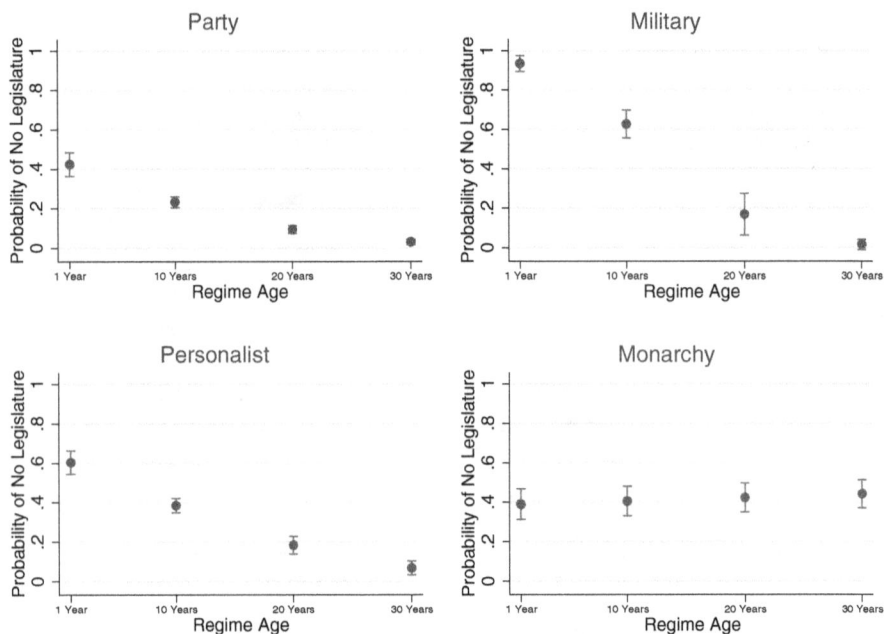

FIGURE C.2. Impact of regime age on legislative closures by regime type.

Of course, existing research does use regime duration as a proxy to control for the possibility that authoritarian consolidation drives legislative closures and lower economic growth, investment, and private property protections (Wright 2008; Wilson and Wright 2015). In theory, this should purge the effect of consolidation from the legislative closure measure. The problem lies in the possibility that legislative closures are a better measure of the consolidation process than regime duration. If this is the case, then regime duration will not capture the full effect of consolidation, thus leading some of the effect to still operate through the proxy of legislative closures. This might be the case if consolidation takes varying amounts of time across cases *and* if autocrats routinely reopen legislatures once they have eliminated rivals.

Qualitative evidence, which I systematically assess in other work, suggests that this is possible (Schuler and Westerland 2018). Iraq, for example, which was ruled by the Ba'ath Party from 1968 to 2003, did not seat a legislature from 1968 until 1979. After this eleven-year period, Saddam Hussein finally instituted the legislature in 1979 once he had defeated his rivals within the regime and the Iraqi Communist Party outside the legislature. By contrast, Hungary's legislature was closed from 1947 to 1949, during which time the Hungarian Communist Party was able to eliminate the rival Social Democrat Party and the Smallholder Party (Kovrig 1979). Once its rivals had been eliminated, the regime held a single-party election and reopened the legislature. In Hungary's case, the process took two years, while in Iraq's the consolidation process took eleven years. If the legislative opening marks the ending point for consolidation, then using a regime duration proxy in these cases will not fully control for the relationship between legislative closures and consolidation.

Turning to Vietnam and China, although they have never witnessed an official legislative closure—their legislatures simply failed to meet for a number of years—even these cases provide some evidence that conditions correlated with the legislative closures potentially drove the negative outcomes associated with legislative inactivity, rather than the salutary effects of the newly constituted legislatures themselves. In Vietnam, the VNA was effectively shut down during the country's conflicts with France and the United States. Indeed, once the country was unified in 1975, the VNA began to meet more regularly. The reopening likely had to do with the normalization of political life in Vietnam, a fact that also undoubtedly impacted the investment environment in North Vietnam and unified Vietnam.

Similarly, in China the National People's Congress met regularly during the early years of the regime. From 1954 to 1964, the NPC met roughly the same number of days per year as it does today. However, it became dormant during the Cultural Revolution, which was Mao's great purge of all perceived opponents within the party and bureaucracy. Indeed, consistent with the consolidation logic, the legislature was closed to purge enemies and reshuffle the ruling coalition. Legislative activity and positive outcomes in Vietnam and China correlate not so much because the legislatures became bastions of effective policy making, but rather because the closure periods were associated with consolidation crises.[5] While this requires further research, it seems plausible that consolidation explains both legislative closures and negative outcomes under single-party rule.

This does raise one final question: Why is there a lack of relationship between closures and outcomes in non-party-based regimes? This is even more surprising given that legislatures in such regimes appear more constraining than in party-based regimes. The lack of a positive relationship in these cases may result from the fact that legislatures, regardless of regime, may not have a positive impact on policy outcomes such as growth or investment. Indeed, research suggests that in democracies more active legislatures lead to higher budget deficits due to the common pool resource problem (Wehner 2009). The theory of legislative institutions and outcomes under authoritarian rule rests on the premise that legislatures are more inclined to protect property rights or citizen interests than autocrat is. While I do not argue that autocrats are benevolent or altruistic, the idea that legislators in single-party settings have purer motives also seems debatable. Indeed, one important theory of authoritarian elections and legislatures is that representatives hope to receive rents (Blaydes 2011; Truex 2014; Lust-Okar 2006). If this is the case, it is possible that a more powerful legislature simply signals a regime more reliant on patronage and corruption to stay in power. Therefore, a legislature could have ambiguous or even possibly negative effects on growth and investment.

Do Single-Party Elections and Legislatures Matter for Democratization?

Another important question is how legislatures and elections impact authoritarian stability, particularly the prospects for democratic transition. Does the VNA or other single-party legislatures or elections ultimately matter for democratization or democratic transition? The short answer from this book is that single-party legislatures certainly do not hasten democratic transitions and may in fact forestall them through their soft propaganda effects. Because the party remains in control of the legislative institutions and guarantees itself victories at the ballot box, the party is at little risk of losing control of the public transcript. As chapter 6 shows, once the party wants to shut down an issue, it can use control over the legislative agenda to do so. With regard to elections, despite attention to the short-term risks of "elections that can be lost" (Hyde and Marinov 2011; Huntington 1993; Harish and Little 2017; Tucker 2007), as Schuler, Gueorguiev, and Cantu (2013) show, these risks do not transfer to single-party regimes. This is because the risks associated with authoritarian elections—miscalculation or focal point effects—do not apply in situations where the regime is guaranteed to win.

Other work on partial liberalization under authoritarian rule has stressed the importance of learning (Lindberg 2006; Hadenius and Teorell

2007). Under this theory, experience with more open elections and legislatures acclimatizes citizens to democracy, thus increasing both the prospect of a transition and the stability of a transition should it occur. Empirically, cross-national evidence seems to suggest that quasi-democratic procedures do little to hasten a democratic transition (McCoy and Hartlyn 2009; Kaya and Bernhard 2013). However, should a transition occur, an active legislature makes it more likely that such a transition would be to a democracy (Brownlee 2009; Schuler, Gueorguiev, and Cantu 2013). This book provides additional insights into why that might be the case. As the book shows, the legislature itself is not going to push for transition, as it is under the thumb of the party. However, should a transition occur, a more active, institutionalized legislature might facilitate a more stable transition to democratic rule.

Consider, for example, the case of Indonesia. While President Suharto had a nominally multiparty legislature, in practice the Indonesian legislature operated more like a single-party regime than a multiparty regime, given the control he had in vetting the opposition candidates (Eklof 1997, 1183). As Ziegenhain (2008) nicely describes in his book on the role of the parliament in Indonesia's transition, even as protesters spilled into the streets, parliament was reluctant to push Suharto out the door. This is not surprising given that its members were selected for their subservience. However, once the transition occurred, due to Suharto's decision to step down, parliament did play an important role in stabilizing the regime while a new constitution was debated. Without a viable legislature, Indonesia would have had to hold an election for a constituent assembly before considering a new constitution, thus potentially adding more complicating factors to the transition. Iraq, for example, after the fall of Saddam Hussein and the disintegration of his parliament, had to hold a constituent assembly election in order to create an election law.

China provides another example of a regime in which the parliament failed to provide a push for democratization, even when the regime was close to the brink of collapse. One of the more famous episodes of the Tiananmen Crisis in China, for example, was the "signature incident," in which a delegate rallied a number of delegates to sign a petition to call on the National People's Congress Standing Committee to convene a special legislative session to address the crisis. After the imposition of martial law and before the military moved into the square, Hu Jiwei submitted the petition to Wan Li, the chair of the Standing Committee, to convene the session, presumably acting in support of the protesters (Truex 2016, 166; Hu 1993). Ultimately, Wan Li rejected the petition, possibly after pressure by the party.

While one could see this as an act of assertiveness or representation in the NPC (Hu 1993), an alternative interpretation is that it demonstrated how unlikely it would be for the legislature to provide the impetus for a transition. Much like in Indonesia, even with massive protests in the square for more than a month, the NPC failed to act to deal with the crisis. The evidence from this book suggests that even the VNA, which is potentially more active than China's NPC, is not likely to lead a push for democratic transition, though it may facilitate one that has already occurred.

Implications for Political Liberalization in Vietnam

While the VNA is not likely to be the leading edge of democratization in Vietnam, its role in *political liberalization* is somewhat more complex. Political liberalization, unlike democratization, does not require regime change. It can involve allowing greater choice for candidates and more opportunities for public officials to voice differing views. Regimes can politically liberalize or deliberalize without fundamentally transitioning to a different regime (Pop-Eleches and Robertson 2015).

In terms of cross-national measures, Vietnam's scores exhibit little variation with regard to political liberalization. Indeed, Freedom House has given Vietnam the lowest score for political liberties every year since the inception of its index. However, much as O'Brien observed subtle shifts in the degree of openness of the NPC in China in the 1980s, Vietnam also varies in the degree of openness in the VNA over the years.

During some legislative sessions, like the November 2010 session wherein Nguyen Minh Thuyet made his speech, there is robust debate that captures the attention of the media. Other sessions come and go with little fanfare. Again, this is consistent with the overall argument of the book that when there is division within the party, there might be greater room for debate. However, when the party is unified, the VNA is less likely to voice its concerns. Indeed, while there have been a number of notable speeches in the VNA since Prime Minister Nguyen Tan Dung failed to win the general secretary position,[6] none have risen to the level of Nguyen Minh Thuyet's speech in 2010 or Duong Trung Quoc's urging him to resign in 2012.[7]

This suggests that the regime can modulate the temperature of the debate in the VNA like a faucet. When the general secretary is more concerned about the independence of the government, he may dial up the heat in the VNA. When the general secretary is more firmly in control, he may attempt to cool the rhetoric. While the degree to which this occurs is difficult to measure, this dynamic does help explain some of the more explosive episodes in the VNA. However, it also overstates the ability of the regime to scale back some of the institutional reforms it has passed. Much like putting toothpaste back in the tube, it may be difficult to undo institutional reforms intended to provide a check on the prime minister even after the short-term logic of the institutional design is gone. Just as demonstrating unity signals strength, once an institution is created, removing a highly visible democratic reform could be perceived as a sign of weakness.

The institution of the public vote of no confidence in ministers is an example. As chapter 4 indicates, this was agreed to by the general secretary as a way to check the prime minister. However, when the logic of its creation faded, the institution remained. This is because the visibility of the institution made it difficult to remove. Furthermore, as long as the party remains in control of the legislature, it likely feels more confident in retaining and controlling the institution rather than rolling it back and suffering the costs in terms of public opinion. Indeed, there is some evidence the party did hope to scale back this reform, without completely doing away with it. In the 13th VNA (2011–2016), the votes were held twice. Since 2016, however, the VNA has reduced the number of votes to one per five-year legislative session, suggesting that the regime did desire to scale back the reform once the target of the reform—Prime Minister Dung—was no longer a threat.

With regard to liberalization, this book also provides some insights into where future legislative reforms are likely to come from. It shows that past reforms to the VNA did not come from Vietnamese officials typically identified with political reforms. In particular, Vo Van Kiet and his protégés were not most responsible for the legislative institutionalization of the VNA, as has been suggested (Vasavakul 2019). Rather, it was the party secretaries who did the most to increase the power of the VNA. The expansion of the VNA's influence was due to the increased independence of the government vis-à-vis the party.

This suggests that going forward, if the VCP does centralize power more tightly in the hands of the general secretary, as some observers have suggested is occurring, the role of the VNA should decline. If the general secretary more directly controls policy making through more centralized control of the party and an increased number of party committees, this should reduce that individual's incentive to agree to any expansion of power in the VNA. While this may or may not have an impact on the prospects of regime change in Vietnam, it suggests that if a chance does come, it could be a rockier transition from the current system to whatever comes next.

Notes

Introduction

1. The Associated Press, "Moody's Cuts Vietnam Rating Amid Vinashin Crisis," *San Diego Union Tribune*, December 15, 2010, http://www .sandiegouniontribune.com/sdut-moodys-cuts-vietnam-rating-amid-vinashin -crisis-2010dec15-story,amp.html.

2. Nguyen Minh Thuyet, speech delivered to the Vietnam National Assembly, November 1, 2010 (VNA online archives, http://quochoi.vn).

3. For example, see James Hookway, "Vietnamese Premier Faces Fallout on Vinashin," *Wall Street Journal*, November 2, 2010, https://www.wsj.com/articles /SB10001424052748703778304575589980974179868.

4. David Schenker, "Silencing the Opposition," *Weekly Standard*, February 12, 2008, https://www.weeklystandard.com/david-schenker/silencing-the-opposition.

5. There are a number of other explanations, discussed in chapter 1.

6. One possible rebuttal is that legislators could provide feedback to the regime in private. Unfortunately, without the ability to monitor legislators' comments, citizens will be unable to verify that their activity reflects the citizens' interests. Therefore, comments generated through these private channels should not differ from bottom-up feedback the regime receives through other private channels such as state-linked journalists (Schoenhals 1985; Dimitrov 2017) or internal polls, which many single-party regimes past and present rely or have relied on.

7. This argument also bears similarities to other research demonstrating the importance of elections (Simpser 2013; Magaloni 2006; Blaydes 2011) and parties (Geddes 2005) signaling strength to deter support for the opposition. At the same time, as chapter 1 discusses, there are important differences between this book and the existing work, particularly with regard to the role played by legislative institutions and rent distribution. In addition, the theory in this book pays closer

attention to potential contradictions in achieving divergent outcomes through the same institution.

8. A possible criticism of this argument is that citizens may not be able to distinguish between the party and the government broadly, even when there is a formal separation. As I discuss in chapter 1 and the other empirical chapters, while citizens may not distinguish between the two in the abstract, the separation does allow for the possibility that the autocrat can blame the head of the government without undermining confidence in the autocrat and the autocratic institutions.

9. As I discuss in the conclusion, regime age does not adequately control for consolidation because the length of time the consolidation process takes varies from case to case. In fact, the opening of the legislature may be a more consistent measure than regime age of the end of consolidation across cases. Other forms of instability such as coups and violence may be picked up, but at present other forms of instability, such as purges, are not consistently measured.

10. Remaining major single-party regimes include China, Vietnam, Cuba, Laos, Eritrea, and North Korea. Other post–Cold War single-party regimes that have subsequently allowed additional parties include Turkmenistan (1991–2014), Kazakhstan (1991–2012), and Iraq under Saddam Hussein.

11. See Bonnie Girard, "Is There Really a 'China Model?,'" *Diplomat*, July 13, 2018, https://thediplomat.com/2018/07/is-there-really-a-china-model/.

12. Interestingly, an opponent of studying the legislature also offers a view that fits in this perspective. Gainsborough (2005), arguing that researchers should take the VNA "on its own terms," examines communication between the party and voters to discuss the messages that the former attempts to transmit to the latter. Similar to old institutionalist work, this perspective takes the form of communication as given without accounting for how the communication style has evolved or whether it achieves its aims.

13. One important exception is Huy Duc's (2012) journalistic account of post-war politics. Although it does not provide a "theory" of Vietnamese politics, it does provide rare insight into the personal and institutional logic of institutional change in Vietnam. Chapter 4 in this book owes a great deal to Duc's work.

Chapter 1

1. For a discussion, see Malesky and Schuler (2011).

2. This theory is consistent with Simper's (2013) "separating equilibrium" solution to the signaling theory, in which electoral manipulation can reveal information on the strength of the regime. Under this theory, the election (the level of information rather than the result) provides information about the strength of the regime.

3. See similar points made in Doring's (2001) edited volume on parliaments in Western Europe.

4. Hou (2019) raises the possibility that perhaps provincial legislatures could provide a more suitable venue for businesspeople to defend their interests.

5. Unlike rent-based co-optation, in which the silence of potential opponents is bought, under the signaling argument, silence is induced through the threat of punishment, the fear that others will not join in opposition, or the view that resistance is futile. Silence is induced rather than purchased.

6. Some accounts mention the VNA introducing Vo Van Kiet to compete with Do Muoi, the Politburo's nominee for prime minister, in 1988. However, in its announcement of Muoi's eventual selection, no mention was made in *Nhan Dan*, the party's official mouthpiece, of the competition (see "Ngày 22-6, Kỳ Họp Thứ Ba Quốc Hội Khoá VIII," *Nhan Dan*, June 23, 1988)

7. Michael Meyer, "Gunter Schabowski, the Man Who Opened the Wall," *New York Times*, November 6, 2015, https://www.nytimes.com/2015/11/07/opinion/gnter-schabowski-the-man-who-opened-the-wall.html.

8. For example, Truex shows that those reselected to the Chinese NPC offer more proposals than those not reselected. This could also be consistent with the rationalizing argument that delegates are rewarded for providing technocratic advice on policy. Truex also shows compelling evidence that delegate proposals are consistent with the policy preferences of citizens in their districts. He carefully addresses the alternative explanation that the delegates are reflecting the interests of local elites rather than local citizens, with mixed evidence of delegates following elites and delegates also reflecting the interests of citizens (Truex 2016, 95–97). For Vietnam, interviews and research suggest that provincial leaders have a strong influence over the types of comments delivered by delegates. So perhaps here the Vietnam case could operate differently than China's, or perhaps more research could uncover a similar dynamic in China.

9. Although see Letsa (2020) and Frantz (2018).

Chapter 2

1. "Đại biểu quốc hội không lệ thuộc vào nhân dân mà lệ thuộc vào những người chọn mình ra ứng cử để trở thành đại biểu quốc hội. Cho nên những người đại biểu quốc hội làm theo ý chí và quyền lực của người chọn ra họ thì làm sao là đại biểu là cao nhất, đại diện nguyện vọng ý chí của nhân dân được? Họ được chọn ra là theo ý chí của người cầm quyền, chứ không theo ý chí của nhân dân." Radio Free Asia, "Những vấn đề lớn trong tổ chức Quốc hội," May 1, 2014, https://www.rfa.org/vietnamese/in_depth/org-nat-ass-big-iss-05012014062153.htm,

2. See Article 7 of the 2015 Election Law. This was the case in each of the election laws since 1992. The 1980 Election Law stipulated a minimum of two per province.

3. For a discussion of province splitting in Vietnam, see Malesky (2009).

4. This restriction was added in the 1992 Election Law. The 1980 Election Law allowed the State Council (akin to the VNASC) to choose the number of election districts in a province and the number of seats in each district.

5. See paragraph 6 of Article 57 of the 2015 Election Law.

6. For critiques of this system, see especially Nguyen Sy Dung (2017) and Nguyen Minh Quang (2005).

7. Quý Châu, "Con số 50 người tự ứng cử ĐBQH thể hiện tính dân chủ," VTVnews.vn, March 4, 2016, https://vtv.vn/trong-nuoc/con-so-50-nguoi-tu-ung-cu-dbqh-the-hien-tinh-dan-chu-20160304091720309.htm.

8. The characterization of Vietnamese elections as "Đảng cử, dân bầu" is mentioned by delegate Huynh Nghia and lawyer Tran Quoc Thuan. Radio Free Asia, "Những vấn đề lớn trong tổ chức Quốc hội," May 1, 2014, https://www.rfa.org/vietnamese/in_depth/org-nat-ass-big-iss-05012014062153.html; and Lê Kiên, "Cần xoá cơ chế 'Đảng cử dân bầu,'" Tuổi Trẻ Online, June 16, 2014, https://tuoitre.vn/can-xoa-co-che-dang-cu-dan-bau-613128.htm.

9. The 1980 Election Law mentions that the Fatherland Front should organize negotiation meetings (*hiệp thương*) with voters in order to provide input on the candidates nominated by the party or state organizations (see Article 26). The 1959 Election Law merely states that the Election Board will come up with the final list of candidates after they are introduced by the party groups or people's groups (see Articles 24, 28, 29).

10. See Article 26 of the 1992 Election Law.

11. Kim Anh, "Tự ứng cử Đại biểu Quốc hội của ta dễ dài quá," VOV.vn, April 22, 2016, https://vov.vn/chinh-tri/tu-ung-cu-dai-bieu-quoc-hoi-cua-ta-de-dai-qua-502280.vov.

12. Quốc Phương, "Lập lưỡng viện hay để nguyên Quốc hội?," BBC Vietnam, April 4, 2014, https://www.bbc.com/vietnamese/vietnam/2014/04/140401_vn_party_and_congress.

13. M. Huy, "Cơ cấu QH không còn chỗ cho Đại biểu tự ứng cử?," Vietnam-Net, February 23, 2007, http://vietnamnet.vn/chinhtri/2007/02/666452/: "Cử người theo cơ cấu định trước là không nên. Muốn có cơ cấu thì phải tìm giải pháp (solution) hiệp thương, tuyên truyền bầu cử để có được cơ cấu như mong muốn."

14. See Nam Nguyên, "Người tự ứng cử và cạm bẫy hiệp thương," RFA, March 18, 2016, https://www.rfa.org/vietnamese/news/programs/the-so-called-2-negotiation-of-election-process-nn-03182016092405.html.

15. See Article 45 of the 2015 Election Law.

16. See "Hội nghị Cử tri: chấp nhận hay không?" BBC Vietnam, April 10, 2016, https://www.bbc.com/vietnamese/vietnam/2016/04/160410_quang_a_xuan_dien_voter_conference: "Đại biểu cử tri ở đây thì đều là những người có lẽ là ngoài báo Nhân Dân, bên ti vi và các con đường, mặt trận của Đảng thì họ không có nguồn tin nào khác cả. Mà đối với tôi thì họ được cung cấp thông tin rất là xấu."

17. These numbers show a higher number of mass organization members and party members than are actually in the population, because the survey only surveys those age eighteen and older.

18. Matt Spetalnick and Martin Petty, "Obama Prods Vietnam on Rights after Activists Stopped from Meeting Him," Reuters, May 25, 2016, http://www.reuters.com/article/us-vietnam-obama-idUSKCN0YE2RX.

19. Pham Chi Dung, "'Hiệp thương dân phố': Giới tự ứng cử có bị chính quyền 'đấu tố,'" Voice of America, March 27, 2016, https://www.voatiengviet.com/a/hiep-thuong-to-dan-pho/3256862.html.

20. See Ngoc Thanh, "Quốc hội bỏ phiếu bầu Hội đồng Bầu cử Quốc gia gồm 21 thành viên," VOV.com, November 25, 2016, https://vov.vn/chinh-tri/quoc-hoi/quoc-hoi-bo-phieu-bau-hoi-dong-bau-cu-quoc-gia-gom-21-thanh-vien-453396.vov.

21. In previous iterations of the electoral law, the legislature did not even need to approve the board. It was simply handpicked by the Standing Committee. (See Article 14 of the 1997 Election Law and Article 12 of the 1992 Election Law. This wording lasted through the 2010 revision to the Electoral Law.) The 2013 Constitution, however, adds that the National Assembly (not the Standing Committee) has the power to "vote" (bầu) the Central Election Commission chair and "approve" (phê chuẩn) the rest of the commission (Article 70, paragraph 7).

22. See speech by delegate Huynh Van Ti on the floor of the VNA during a debate on the 2013 Constitution, June 4, 2013.

23. "Chúng ta đã có 13 cuộc bầu cử Quốc hội, Hội đồng nhân dân các cấp thì rất nhiều cuộc. Tất cả các cuộc bầu cử Quốc hội và Hội đồng nhân dân vừa qua trên thực tế cho thấy dân chủ được đảm bảo và phát huy rất tốt, bảo đảm khách quan rất tốt thì có lý do gì chúng ta lại nêu lý do đó để tiến tới chúng ta lập Hội đồng bầu cử quốc gia?"

24. See speech by delegate Danh Ut on the floor of the VNA during a debate on the 2013 Constitution, June 3, 2013. Pham Xuan Thuong, Nguyen Van Tuyet, Pham Duc Chau, and Tran Van Tu echoed similar sentiments.

25. He suggests that local election officials may ensure that there are not many strong candidates running against a central nominee.

26. For the 2007 election, the candidate list was released by Central Election Board resolution 373/2007; for the 2011 election the candidate list was accessed from Central Election Board resolution 351/2011; and for the 2011 election the candidate list was accessed from Central Election Board resolution 270/2016.

27. This measure was used in Malesky and Schuler (2011).

28. One potential objection to these models could be that there is mechanical correlation between the measures. However, given that there are multiple members of the provincial party secretariat, multiple central committee members, and multiple central committee nominees, it is feasible for these candidates to run against each other. Indeed, if the goal was to ensure tournament competition they

should be *more* likely to run against each other. Furthermore, other coefficients demonstrate the lack of mechanical correlation between the candidate's traits and similar traits in the district. As the party variable shows, being a party member actually increases the likelihood that other candidates in the district are also party members. Similarly, the district official variable is also positively associated with the sacrificial lamb variable, even though it is the basis of that measure. This suggests that district members are more likely to face other district members.

29. See speeches by several delegates in the VNA plenary session on June 3, 2015. Most of them raised the issue, such as Nong Thi Lam, Danh Ut, and Au Thi Mai.

30. See Article 65 of the 2015 Election Law.

31. See speech by delegate Bui Ngoc Chuong on the VNA floor, June 3, 2015: "về công tác vận động tuyên truyền. Trong dự thảo ở chương VI thiết kế một chương với 7 điều về công tác tuyên truyền vận động bầu cử. Nhưng chủ yếu tập trung vào các quy định về vận động bầu cử đối với các ứng cử viên, mà chưa có điều khoản nào nêu quy định về công tác tuyên truyền vận động với cử tri. Theo tôi, đây là vấn đề cần đặc biệt quan tâm, vì kết quả bầu cử hay chất lượng của bầu cử còn phụ thuộc nhiều vào nhận thức cũng như là ý thức vừa quyền, vừa trách nhiệm của cử tri trong việc thực hiện quyền cũng như trách nhiệm tham gia bầu cử. Đề nghị trong chương này nên thiết kế một điều khoản nào đó về công tác tuyên truyền, vận động để cử tri hiểu rõ và thực hiện tốt quyền cũng như trách nhiệm của mình trong tham gia bầu cử Quốc hội, Hội đồng nhân dân."

32. See speech by delegate Au Thi Mai on VNA floor, June 3, 2015.

Chapter 3

1. Author's calculation from the VNA website, Đại biểu Quốc hội các khoá [National Assembly delegates from each session], http://dbqh.na.gov.vn.

2. See Article 23 of the Law on the Organization of the National Assembly.

3. Officially, per Article 66 of the Law on the Organization of the National Assembly, it includes nine committees (Law; Justice; Economic; Finance and Budget; Military and Security; Culture, Education, and Youth; Social Affairs; Science, Technology, and Environment; and Foreign Affairs). The other committee is the Council on Ethnic Affairs.

4. See Article 33 of the 1960 Law on the Organization of the National Assembly.

5. See Article 45 of the 1981 Law on the Organization of the National Assembly.

6. See 2007 Amendment to the 1992 Law on the Organization of the National Assembly.

7. Interview 13, VNA official, August 8, 2013.

8. See Xuan Tuyen, "Ông Dương Quốc Anh được bổ nhiệm làm Phó Chủ tịch Uỷ ban Giám sát Tài chính Quốc gia," Cafevn.com, July 9, 2012, http://cafef.vn/vi -mo-dau-tu/ong-duong-quoc-anh-duoc-bo-nhiem-lam-pho-chu-tich-uy-ban-giam -sat-tai-chinh-quoc-gia-20120709050735624.chn.

9. Vuong Dieu Quan and Hoang Ly, "Ông nghị nói ngược," CafeBiz, September 1, 2017, http://cafebiz.vn/ong-nghi-noi-nguoc-toi-chua-bao-gio-nghi-minh-la -mot-nha-chinh-tri-20170901161913104.chn.

10. Article 5: "Quốc hội quyết định chương trình xây dựng luật, phap lệnh theo đề nghị của Uỷ ban thường vụ Quốc hội."; Article 48 also specifies that the VNASC has the power to set the schedule for the laws that will be debated, subject to the VNA's approval.

11. The meetings are called "Phiên trù bị." Interview 11, June 2013, Hanoi.

12. "Luật Biểu tình và 'ranh giới mỏng manh,'" BBC Vietnam, May 9, 2016, https://www.bbc.com/vietnamese/vietnam/2016/05/160509_duong_trung_quoc _bieu_tinh_legislation.

13. "Luật Biểu tình và 'ranh giới mỏng manh.'"

14. Article 29 of the 2013 Law on the Organization of the National Assembly.

15. Trong Phu, "ĐBQH Trần Thị Quốc Khánh trình dự Luật Hành Chính Công," Pháp Luật, August 18, 2017, http://plo.vn/thoi-su/dbqh-tran-thi-quoc -khanh-trinh-du-luat-hanh-chinh-cong-722167.html.

16. Interview 25, former government official, September 2017, Hanoi.

17. See Article 31 of the Law on the Promulgation of Legal Documents.

18. See Article 35 of the Law on the Promulgation of Legal Documents.

19. See Article 52 of the Law on the Promulgation of Legal Documents.

20. Interview 14, VNA official, June 30, 2013, Hanoi.

21. Interview 14, VNA official, June 30, 2013, Hanoi.

22. David Koh, "Vietnam: The Party Will Not Be Railroaded," *Straits Times*, June 30, 2010.

23. Mai Nguyen and Matthew Tostevin, "Vietnam Plans to Open 'Outstanding' Special Economic Zones," Reuters, May 24, 2017, https://www.reuters .com/article/us-vietnam-investment/vietnam-plans-to-open-outstanding-special -economic-zones-idUSKBN18K1BH.

24. Nguyen Minh Quang, "SEZs in Vietnam: What's in a Name?," *Diplomat*, September 14, 2018, https://thediplomat.com/2018/09/sezs-in-vietnam-whats-in-a-name/.

25. See Dien Luong and Vu Vi, "Top Vietnamese Lawmaker Calls for Setting Up 'Red Light Areas' in Special Economic Zones," *VNExpress International*, September 12, 2017, https://e.vnexpress.net/news/news/top-vietnamese-lawmaker-calls -for-setting-up-red-light-areas-in-special-economic-zones-3640492.html.

26. The Dung, "Đặc khu kinh tế Vân Đồn, Bắc Vân Phong, Phú Quốc văn có HĐND, UBND?," *Người Lao Động*, April 4, 2018, https://nld.com.vn/chinh

-tri/dac-khu-kinh-te-van-don-bac-van-phong-phu-quoc-van-co-hdnd-ubnd
-20180404111659795.htm.

27. Duy Anh, "Exclusive Incentives for Economic Zones Recommended," *Vietnam Economic Times*, September 12, 2017, http://vneconomictimes.com/article /vietnam-today/exclusive-incentives-for-special-economic-zones-recommended.

28. See https://www.facebook.com/danlambaovn/posts/1596887773699868/.

29. Nguyen Tuyen, "Xây Đặc khu: Không được để công ty nước ngoài xây 'lãnh địa riêng,'" *Dân Trí*, September 20, 2017, https://dantri.com.vn/kinh -doanh/xay-dac-khu-khong-duoc-de-cong-ty-nuoc-ngoai-xay-lanh-dia-rieng -20170920100546375.htm.

30. Article 32 of the 2015 Law on the Organization of the National Assembly gives VNA delegates the authority to question officials directly.

31. Article 13 of the 2015 Law on the Organization of the National Assembly. It should be noted that the votes of confidence, which require ministers to resign if two-thirds vote against them, differ from the regular votes of approval, which are held once every five years. Those votes of approval, discussed in chapter 7, require delegates to simultaneously assess the performance of all top government and national assembly officials.

32. Paragraph 1 of Article 70 of the 2013 Constitution grants the legislature the power to "pass and amend the constitution, pass and amend laws."

33. "Ủy ban thường vụ Quốc hội trình Quốc hội quyết định nhóm vấn đề chất vấn và người bị chất vấn."

34. See Article 12 of the Law on National Assembly Oversight Activities.

35. The distance of two hundred miles is pertinent because this is within the Exclusive Economic Zone granted to countries under the United Nations Convention on the Law of the Seas (UNCLOS).

36. Chi Hieu, "Đại biểu muốn Thủ tướng trả lời chất vấn vấn đề về Biển Đông," *VnExpress,* June 6, 2014, https://vnexpress.net/tin-tuc/thoi-su/dai-bieu-muon-thu -tuong-tra-loi-chat-van-ve-bien-dong-3000888.html.

37. "Những vấn đề lớn trong tổ chức Quốc hội," Radio Free Asia, May 1, 2014. https://www.rfa.org/vietnamese/in_depth/org-nat-ass-big-iss-05012014062153.htm; and Viên Sự, "Vì sao y tế và BOT không được chọn để chất vấn?," Tuổi trẻ, November 9, 2017, https://tuoitre.vn/vi-sao-y-te-va-bot-khong-duoc-chon-de-chat-van -20171109103325785.htm.

38. Some former VNA officials suggest that the decision about who to question results from a negotiation between the VNASC and the government ("Những vấn đề lớn trong tổ chức Quốc hội").

39. Interview 22, VNA delegate, September 2017, Hanoi.

40. The 2015 Law on National Assembly Oversight Activities lays out the steps for a confidence vote, which includes allowing the official to explain his or her

performance, followed by meetings within the provincial delegations. Afterward, the VNASC makes a report on the discussions within the delegation before a secret vote is cast.

41. According to this list (from Voice of Vietnam, https://vov.vn/chinh-tri /quoc-hoi/danh-sach-bo-may-lanh-dao-quoc-hoi-khoa-xiv-vua-duoc-bau-532973 .vov#p13), Vu Hong Thanh, chair of the VNA Economic Committee, and Phan Thanh Binh, chair of the Culture, Education, Youth and Children Committee, are not Central Committee members and thus not on the VNA Party Committee. It is not clear why only these two officials are not members of the party committee. This list also only shows the members of the VNASC on the party committee. It does not provide information about whether any other members might be part of the committee.

42. Interview 28, VNA official, September 2017, Hanoi.

Chapter 4

1. Other recent work challenges the notion that foreign aid inhibits growth because aid, in comparison to oil, is less fungible, less constant over time, and features greater conditionality on its use (Altincekic and Bearce 2014). However, this argument suggests that if aid does come without such strings, as may be the case for Chinese or Soviet aid (Dreher et al. 2015), then it should indeed have the same theorized effects as oil.

2. Such reforms are often referred to as "fence breaking" (*pha rao*) in the Vietnam context.

3. See Keyfacts Energy, "Vietnam," https://www.keyfactsenergy.com/country _review/country/85/view/.

4. Fforde and de Vylder (1996) reject the common assertion that reform started with the 6th Party Congress in 1986, although they do acknowledge that it was a turning point at which the party more fulsomely supported the legitimacy of the individual economy in rhetoric.

5. Fforde and de Vylder (1996, 148), Beresford and Dang (2000), and Dang (2008) concur with the assessment that 1989 constituted a major cut point.

6. "By 1989, with the imminent breakdown of the Soviet economy, a steep reduction in the aid program was occurring. Between 1989 and 1990, the recorded trade deficit had been cut back substantially. . . . [T]he expectation of this shift almost certainly had a major effect upon the 1989 Vietnamese decision to abolish central planning entirely" (Fforde and de Vylder, 1996, 148).

7. Vietnam, like other countries in the region, does have a significant number of minorities living in its mountainous areas, which Scott (2010) calls "Zomia." While Vietnam's ethnic minorities constitute an important 14 percent of the population, some of whom cooperated with Vietnam's foreign adversaries against the

regime, their fragmentation renders them relatively weak as a potential organized challenger for power in the country.

8. As Unger (1988) notes, the Republic of Vietnam also imposed harsh restrictions on the ethnic Chinese population in Saigon, who were more numerous and wealthier in the South than in the North.

9. Duc (2012) uses the terms "decoration" and "forum."

10. For literature on the economic reforms see Fforde and de Vylder (1996), Beresford (2008), Beresford and Dang (2000), Dang (2008), Riedel and Turley (1999), and Vasavakul (2019).

11. See Presidential Order 51, October 17, 1945 (Sắc lệnh Của Chủ tịch Nước Số 51 Ngày 17 Tháng 10 Năm 1945).

12. For example, Article 28 of the 1959 Election Law gave the Election Board the power to create the final list of candidates. Perhaps more important, the Election Board is handpicked by the VNA Standing Committee (VNASC), which is a small subset of the legislature (typically fifteen to twenty members) voted on by the VNA at the beginning of each term.

13. For a description of the "five gates" system, see Malesky and Schuler (2009) and Koh (2006).

14. Article 43 of the 1959 Constitution.

15. The meetings would be divided into two weeklong sessions, one in the spring or summer and another in the fall or winter.

16. See Duc (2012) and Abuza (2001) for a discussion of this.

17. This analysis comes from a review of *Nhan Dan* news reports on VNA sessions from 1988 to 1998.

18. See "Ngày 22-6 Kỳ họp thứ ba Quốc hội Khoá VIII," *Nhan Dan*, June 23, 1988.

19. See Abuza (2001, 168–169) for a good discussion of this.

20. "Nguyen Van Linh anticipated the reaction from the south when he decided to choose Do Muoi." [Nguyễn Văn Linh cũng tiên liệu được sự phản ứng khi quyết định chọn Đỗ Mười] (Duc 2012, 83).

21. Nguyen Van Linh, "Speech Opening the 8th National Assembly," June 22, 1987, http://quochoi.vn/tulieuquochoi/anpham/Pages/anpham.aspx?AnPhamItemID=237#_ftnref3.

22. Nguyen, "Speech Opening the 8th National Assembly."

23. See State Council decisions 109, December 10,1988; 158, June 16, 1989; 265, May 24, 1990; and 510, December 2, 1991.

24. See State Council decisions 53, January 16, 1988; and 76, June 6, 1988.

25. "Về lâu dài, Quốc hội sẽ chuyển dần sang hoạt động thường xuyên và thăng thêm đại biểu chuyên trách" (M. Vu 2004).

26. "The revised points [in the constitutional revision] that have drawn the most public attention are probably those revolving around the state apparatus.

Here are some examples. . . . The first draft stipulated that the chairman, vice chairmen, secretary and at least one-third of the members of the Nationalities council [permanent committees] should work under a system of specialized responsibilities [be fulltime delegates]. The chairmen, vice chairmen, secretaries, and at least one-half of the members of the permanent committees of the National Assembly should work under a system of specialized responsibilities. The third draft leaves the number of members of the National Assembly Nationalities Council and permanent committees who should work under the specialized committees to be determined by law." Nguyen Huy Thuc (lawyer), interview in *Tuoi Tre*, January 11, 1992; republished in translated form in Joint Publications Research Service-Southeast Asia (JPRS-SEA-92-005).

27. While the 1960 Law did not specify any permanent committees, the 1981 Law included a law committee; an economic, planning, and budget committee; a culture and education committee; a science and technology committee; a health and social affairs committee; a committee on youth; a foreign affairs committee; and the Council on Ethnic Affairs, which acts as a committee.

28. Examples include the Foreign Investment Law (1988), Law on Import and Export Taxation (1988), Labor Union Law (1990), Law on Business Tax (1990), and the Enterprise Law (1991).

29. Duc (2012, 235) writes: "Người nhận được nhiều lợi ích chính trị nhất từ hoạt động này không phải là ông Vũ Mão mà chính là Chủ tịch Quốc hội Nông Đức Mạnh. . . . Hình ảnh ông Mạnh, tóc tai chải chuốt, ăn nói mềm mỏng và đôi khi đột nhiên loé sáng trước ống kính truyền hình dần dần được công chúng thừa nhận như là một nhà lãnh đạo." ["The person who received the greatest political benefit from this was not Vu Mao, but primarily VNA Chair Nong Duc Manh. . . . As the image of Manh, with his groomed hair, and soft spoken nature periodically flashed across the television, gradually the public saw him as a leader."]

30. "Thay vì dùng những bản tin công thức cua Thông tấn xã hoặc của báo Nhân Dân, các báo—đặc biệt là báo chí Sài Gòn—bắt đầu gửi phóng viên về Thủ đô. Chính trị không còn là một đề tài tẻ nhạt, số lượng phát hành của những tờ báo như Tuổi Trẻ, Thanh Niên, Người Lao Động . . . đã tăng rõ rệt mỗi kỳ Quốc hội học."

31. Almen (2013) makes a similar argument.

32. Geddes, Wright, and Frantz's (2018) measure of personalization increases during the Le Duan era.

33. Fforde and de Vylder (1996) challenge the notion that the central party and state controlled policy. Instead, they argue that the regime reacted to challenges from citizens and provincial leaders. However, while there was certainly bottom-up pressure to change policy, the decision to recognize this pressure and formalize these changes at the national level was ultimately made by a more centralized party-state apparatus.

34. The concept of rule of law in China and Vietnam is conceived in a narrower sense than the common definition holding that party leaders must be accountable to the law (Holmes 2003).

35. See Nayan Chanda, "VIETNAM: The South Leads the Country Away from Subsidised Socialism; The New Revolution," *Far Eastern Economic Review*, April 10, 1986 (CD-ROM).

36. Nguyen, "Speech Opening the 8th National Assembly."

37. Nguyen, "Speech Opening the 8th National Assembly."

38. Le Quang Dao (former VNA chair), interview by Minh Duc, *Tuoi Tre*, April 18, 1992; translated by Joint Publications Research Service (JPRS-92-012) in June 1992.

39. "'Đại diện' ở đây cần là đại diện cho cái 'tâm', cái 'trí', cái 'dũng' hơn là đại diện bởi chon người cụ thể. Một nhà khoa học có cái 'tâm' vì người nông dân, có cái 'trí' để hiểu cuộc sống của người nông dân, có cái 'dũng' để mạnh dạn nói lên tiếng nói vì người nông dân tại diễn đàn Quốc hội tại sao không thể coi là người đại diện chân chính cho giai cấp nông dân?"

40. "Với cách phân bố nguồn lực như hiện nay, nếu gay gắt với Trung ương, thì chắc chắn sẽ làm ảnh hưởng tiêu cực tới địa phương. Mà như vậy thì đến kỳ bầu cử Quốc hội khoá sau, lãnh đạo địa phương chắc gì đã để đại biểu đó trúng cử nữa."

41. The decision was made ahead of the midyear session. See Quoc Dung and Bui Phu, "Quốc hội chất vấn cần đi đến cùng trong việc quy trách nhiệm" [National Assembly query sessions need to meet their responsibility], *Viet Times*, June 12, 2017, https://viettimes.vn/quoc-hoi-chat-van-can-di-den-cung-trong-viec-quy-trach-nhiem-125846.html.

42. This account draws largely on a personal document provided to me by a direct observer of many of the events. Many of the details are corroborated in Huy Duc's (2012) account of the events.

43. See Phuong Yen, "Phải nghe dân nói" [Must listen to the people speak], *Lao Dong*, April 21, 1998.

44. See T.V–B.T, "Các Thành viên Chính phủ Trả lời Chất vấn," *Lao Dong*, May 15, 1998.

45. See Vu Duy, "Tiếp xúc cử tri quận Ba Đình: Tổng Bí thư; Lấy phiếu tín nhiệm là để cảnh tỉnh." [Meeting with voters in Ba Dinh: General Secretary; vote of confidence serves as warning], VOV.vn, June 6, 2013, https://vov.vn/chinh-tri/dang/tong-bi-thu-lay-phieu-tin-nhiem-la-de-canh-tinh-268543.vov (emphasis added).

46. Nghị quyết của Hội đồng Nhà Nước về Quy chế xây dựng luật và pháp lệnh ngày 6 tháng 8 năm, 1988; and Luật Ban Hành Văn Bản Quy Phạm Pháp Luật, 1996.

47. Luật Hoạt động giám sát của Quốc hội, 2003.

Chapter 5

1. Hoang Long, "Dân Việt làm gì có quyền bầu cử," BBC Vietnam, November 7, 2014, https://www.bbc.com/vietnamese/culture_social/2014/11/141107 _nguyenminhthuyet_hoanglong_views: "Người ta sẽ thấy không phải dân Việt Nam 'không quan tâm đến chính trị' đâu, họ không được phép quan tâm thì đúng hơn."

2. While strategic voting is only possible with information, a lack of strategic voting does not necessarily mean uninformed voting. Strategic voting may fail because of low information about the state of the race but not about the actual qualities of the individual candidates.

3. The data on Thailand were collected from the Constituency-Level Election Archives (Kollman et al. 2016). The years 1996 and 1995 were chosen because the electoral system was changed after 1997 to a mixed system with single-member districts.

4. The index includes a point for a Central Committee member, a Politburo member, a provincial party committee member, and a provincial party committee chair or deputy chair. Because the district rather than the candidate is the unit of analysis, this index measures the whole district rather than the district features minus a specific candidate as in Malesky and Schuler (2011).

5. In Vietnam, these organizations include the Women's Union, the Farmer's Union, and the General Confederation of Labor, among others.

6. Results are robust to dropping this dummy variable.

7. The intent of the survey question was to assess whether voters would vote for such a candidate if one were actually on the ballot.

Chapter 6

1. Duong Trung Quoc, speech on the floor of the VNA, June 7, 2012, http://quochoi.vn/hoatdongcuaquochoi/cackyhopquochoi/quochoikhoaXIII /kyhopthuba/Pages/bien-ban-ghi-am.aspx?ItemID=23562. "Vì sao khi xảy ra những vụ việc như Tiên Lãng—Hải Phòng, Văn Giang—Hưng Yên chẳng thấy Quốc hội sớm vào cuộc. Tại sao xảy ra hiện tượng người Trung Quốc nuôi cá ngay địa bàn quân sự Cam Ranh, người phát hiện chỉ là báo chí. Tất cả các bản Báo cáo ngân sách Chính phủ trình Quốc hội đều cho qua thì sự thất thoát ngân sách lớn như thế có trách nhiệm của Quốc hội không?"

2. Discussion of the 1992 Land Law is from Duc (2012), as quoted in Le (2016, 291).

3. Quoted in an interview with Stein Tonneson, "Phỏng vấn Phan Đình Diệu Ứng dụng toán học và dân chủ," Diendan.org, https://www.diendan.org/tai-lieu

216

/bao-cu/so-020/phong-van-pdd: "Tôi không mấy tin tưởng vào Quốc hội mới được bầu [tháng 7.1992]. Cuộc bầu cử quốc hội vừa rồi là chọn giữa vài ứng cử viên đã được đảng và Mặt trận Tổ quốc lựa ra từ trước. Khoảng 40 người ra ứng cử độc lập, nhưng người ta chỉ chấp nhận cho 2 người ứng cử, và cả hai đều thất cử. Trình độ học vấn của các đại biểu khoá này cao hơn khoá trước, nhưng tôi không thấy ai có thể đóng một vai trò độc lập. Các cuộc thảo luận ở Quốc hội vẫn diễn ra trong lằn ranh do đảng vạch ra."

4. One caveat is that in 2012 the party created the Central Economic Commission, with subcommittees covering five of the ministries. Given that the commission was created only before the last two sessions analyzed in this chapter, these ministries are considered independent for the analysis.

5. I used the LDA model as opposed to a dictionary approach because constructing a dictionary that would connect language used in the media and public to the VNA, which may use different vocabulary, would have been unwieldy. However, I have conducted a number of validity checks, described later in the chapter, to ensure that the LDA substantively captures the topics of interest.

6. See Blei, Ng, and Jordan (2003) for a description.

7. Google is the most popular search engine in Vietnam. Because the Google Trends scores are a relative index, all scores are benchmarked against the term "East Sea." Also, Internet penetration in Vietnam is substantial, with recent estimates suggesting that about 50 percent of the population has online access (see http://www.internetlivestats.com/internet-users/viet-nam/).

8. See Phan Le, "Trung Quốc phá cáp tàu thăm dò của Việt Nam" [China cuts Vietnamese boat exploration cable," VNExpress, June 9, 2011.

9. It is important to note that the U-shaped line could be interpreted as demarcating the islands claimed by China or Taiwan (see https://amti.csis.org/phantom-u-shaped-line/). However, cutting the cable where Vietnam's claimed exclusive economic zone overlaps with the U-shaped line implies that China's actions were defending the interpretation of the line as demarcating marine territory, which the tribunal rejected.

10. See "Vietnam Decries 'Illegal' South China Sea Oil Bid," BBC News, June 27, 2012, https://www.bbc.com/news/world-asia-18610886.

11. For a good analysis of the territorial implications of the placement of the oil rig, see Michael Green, Kathleen Hicks, Zack Cooper, John Schaus, and Jake Douglas, "Counter-Coercion Series: China-Vietnam Oil Rig Standoff," Asia Maritime Transparency Initiative, June 12, 2017, https://amti.csis.org/counter-co-oil-rig-standoff/.

12. See "At Least 21 Dead in Vietnam Anti-China Protests over Oil Rig," *Guardian*, May 15, 2014, https://www.theguardian.com/world/2014/may/15/vietnam-anti-china-protests-oil-rig-dead-injured.

13. "Vietnam Considering Legal Action against China," Voice of America, May 22, 2014, https://www.voanews.com/a/vietnam-considering-legal-action-against-china-reu/1920048.html.

14. See Carl Thayer, "Vietnam, China, and the Oil Rig Crisis: Who Blinked?," *Diplomat*, August 4, 2014, https://thediplomat.com/2014/08/vietnam-china-and-the-oil-rig-crisis-who-blinked/; Zachary Abuza, "Vietnam Buckles under Chinese Pressure," *Asia Times Online*, https://defence.pk/pdf/threads/vietnam-buckles-under-chinese-pressure.336526/; and Alexander Vuving, "Did China Blink in the South China Sea?," *National Interest*, July 27, 2014, https://nationalinterest.org/feature/did-china-blink-the-south-china-sea-10956?page-show.

15. See Carlyle Thayer, "4 Reasons Why China Moved Oil Rig HYSY-981 Sooner Than Planned," *Diplomat*, July 22, 2014, https://thediplomat.com/2014/07/4-reasons-china-removed-oil-rig-hysy-981-sooner-than-planned/

16. On at least two visits with Xi Jinping, Quan was referred to as "Đặc phái viên của Tổng bí thư Nguyễn Phú Trọng [Trong's envoy]." See "Ông Tập Cận Bình tiếp đặc phái viên của Tổng Bí thư Nguyễn Phú Trọng," Voice of Vietnam, October 30, 2017, https://vov.vn/chinh-tri/ong-tap-can-binh-tiep-dac-phai-vien-cua-tong-bi-thu-nguyen-phu-trong-689367.vov; "Đặc phái viên Tổng Bí thư Nguyễn Phú Trọng gặp Chủ tịch Trung Quốc" [Nguyen Phu Trong's envoy meets president of China], *Lao Dong*, March 1, 2016, https://laodong.vn/the-gioi/dac-phai-vien-tong-bi-thu-nguyen-phu-trong-gap-chu-tich-trung-quoc-523107.bld.

17. The ministers questioned were in the November 2011 session on transportation, agriculture, education, finance, and the state bank; the June 2012 session on natural resources and environment, planning and investment, industry, and police; and the June 2014 session on finance, education, justice, and the state inspectorate.

18. See "Quốc hội họp kín về Biển Đông," BBC News Tiếng Việt, May 20, 2014, https://www.bbc.com/vietnamese/vietnam/2014/05/140520_vn_na_scs.

19. See "Đại biểu Quốc hội đề nghị có biện pháp bảo vệ chủ quyền biển đảo," *VNExpress*, June 5, 2015, https://vnexpress.net/tin-tuc/thoi-su/dai-bieu-quoc-hoi-de-nghi-co-bien-phap-bao-ve-chu-quyen-bien-dao-3229203.html.

20. See "Những vấn đề cơ mật không chất vấn công khai," Baophapluat.vn [Legal news], June 4, 2015, http://baophapluat.vn/thoi-su/nhung-van-de-co-mat-khong-chat-van-cong-khai-220506.html.

21. Kerkvliet (2014) traces the repression of more than fifty dissidents. Since then, Human Rights Watch has tracked the arrest of twenty-seven dissidents in 2018 alone; see Human Rights Watch, "Vietnam: Clean Up Abysmal Rights Record," July 23, 2018, https://www.hrw.org/news/2018/07/23/vietnam-clean-abysmal-rights-record.

22. See Articles 25–29.

23. See "Đại hội Đảng bộ Bộ Công Thương lần thứ II thành công tốt đẹp!," Công Thuong, August 20, 2015, https://congthuong.vn/dai-hoi-dang-bo-bo-cong -thuong-lan-thu-ii-thanh-cong-tot-dep.html.

24. See Điều lệ Đảng [Party regulations], Article 28.

25. See "TBT Trọng lần đầu vào Đảng uỷ Công an." BBC Vietnam, September 21 2016, https://www.bbc.com/vietnamese/vietnam/2016/09/160921 _nguyenphutrong_police.

26. For a summary of his case, see Human Rights Watch, "Vietnam: The Party vs. Legal Activist Cu Huy Ha Vu," May 26, 2011, https://www.hrw.org/report/2011 /05/26/vietnam-party-vs-legal-activist-cu-huy-ha-vu.

27. Human Rights Watch, "Vietnam: The Party vs. Legal Activist."

28. See "Thủ tướng Nguyễn Tấn Dũng tham dự Hội nghị thứ nhất của Đảng uỷ Công an Trung ương," nguyentandung, August 31, 2011, http://nguyentandung.org /thu-tuong-nguyen-tan-dung-tham-du-hoi-nghi-thu-nhat-cua-dang-uy-cong-an -trung-uong.html.

29. See "Công an đập phá tường rào nhà LS. Cù Huy Hà Vũ" [Police destroy house wall of lawyer Cu Huy Ha Vu], RFA, January 27, 2010, https://www.rfa .org/vietnamese/in_depth/Police-pulled-down-laywer-cu-huy-ha-vu-house-fense -01272010112735.html.

30. See "Tướng Vĩnh gửi thư về TS Cù Huy Hà Vũ," BBC Vietnam, June 14, 2013, https://www.bbc.com/vietnamese/vietnam/2013/06/130614_nguyentrongvinh_chhv.

31. See "Công an đập phá tường rào nhà LS. Cù Huy Hà Vũ."

32. Human Rights Watch, "Vietnam: The Party vs. Legal Activist."

33. "Losing the Plot," *Economist*, March 16, 2013, https://www.economist.com /asia/2013/03/16/losing-the-plot.

34. Le's account is based on a 2011 article in *Pháp Luật*. Nghĩa Nhân, "Đại biểu Võ Hồng Phúc nói lời tâm huyết" [Delegate Vo Hong Phuc speaks from the heart], *Pháp Luật*, January 14, 2011, http://plo.vn/thoi-su/theo-dong/dai-bieu-vo-hong -phuc-noi-loi-tam-huyet-385498.html.

35. The transcript of the June 13, 2012, session, which was collected from the National Assembly website, is no longer in the archives. "[Đ]ồng chí Bộ trưởng Bộ tài nguyên và môi trường Nguyễn Minh Quang sẽ trả lời những vấn đề liên quan đến quản lý đất đai, đền bù giải phóng mặt bằng, những vấn đề tiêu cực trong quản lý đất đai, những vấn đề bức xúc trong lĩnh vực này."

36. "Câu hỏi thứ nhất, đề nghị đồng chí cho biết một cách cụ thể thái độ của Bộ về phương hướng và tiến độ để giải quyết các vấn đề liên quan đến đất đai nhưng tôi tập trung vào những vụ mà dư luận cả nước quan tâm như vụ ông Đoàn Văn Vươn, Văn Giang, Cần Thơ, Vụ Bản, v.v . . . đúng sai thế nào và bao giờ thì xong."

37. "Vấn đề thứ hai là trong Hiến pháp và Luật đất đai năm 2003 quy định đất đai, rừng núi, sông, hồ, tài nguyên đều thuộc sở hữu toàn dân và Nhà nước là đại diện chủ sở hữu là luật 2003 quy định, nhưng Đề án tổng thể tái cơ cấu kinh tế với

chuyển đổi mô hình tăng trưởng của Chính phủ trình ra Quốc hội trong kỳ họp này có nêu là đất đai, tài nguyên cũng phải được phân bổ cho những nhà đầu tư, những dự án sử dụng hiệu quả cao hơn. Chúng tôi muốn hỏi quy định trong đề án tổng thể đó có vượt xa hơn Hiến pháp 1992 hay không, từ đó liệu có thể tiếp tục tạo ra những điểm nóng như những địa phương vừa rồi nêu hay không?"

38.   Other delegates raised the issue during the June 7, 2012, debate on the implementation of the socioeconomic plan. Delegates Duong Trung Quoc and Bui Manh Hung discussed the issue as an example of the failure of the government to manage local administrative units.

39.   She raised the following issues as issues for discussion: land use plans, the power of the state and citizens to use land, mechanisms to seize land, compensation and relocation when the state seizes land, land prices, and solutions to petitions and denunciations related to land.

40.   Do Van Ve, for instance, suggested that people using land should have ownership of the land (VNA, November 19, 2012).

41.   Huynh Van Tiep (VNA, November 19, 2012): "[V]ề sở hữu đất đai. Qua hội nghị đóng góp ý kiến sửa đổi luật tại địa phương và ý kiến đóng góp của cử tri thống nhất đất đai là sở hữu của toàn dân, chỉ có một vài ý kên đất đai là sở hữu của nhà nước và của tư nhân. Tôi thông nhất theo đại đa số."

42.   Nguyen Thi Kim Ngan (VNA, November 19, 2012).

43.   Nguyen Ba Thuyen (VNA, June 17, 2013).

44.   See "Thủ tướng và cái giá sự 'ngạo mạn'" [The prime minister and arrogance], BBC Vietnamese, October 2017, https://www.bbc.com/vietnamese/mobile/business/2012/10/121017_nguyen_tan_dung_impact.shtml.

45.   See James Hookway and Alison Tudor, "Behind Firm's Default: Vietnam's Growth Mania," *Wall Street Journal*, December 25, 2010, https://www.wsj.com/articles/SB10001424052970203568004576043180815719282.

46.   See Politburo Decision 45, "Về thí điểm mô hình tập đoàn kinh tế và cơ chế, chính sách ngăn ngừa thất thoát tài sản nhà nước; cơ chế, chính sách bán cổ phần cho người lao động," October 4, 2009, https://thuvienphapluat.vn/van-ban/Doanh-nghiep/Ket-luan-45-KL-TW-thi-diem-mo-hinh-tap-doan-kinh-te-va-co-che-146618.aspx.

47.   See James Hookway and Patrick Barta, "A Troubled State Flagship Makes Waves in Vietnam," *Wall Street Journal*, September 22, 2010, https://www.wsj.com/articles/SB10001424052748704652104575493520176041784.

48.   See Nguyen Phu Trong's opening speech to the VNA, October 20, 2018, http://quochoi.vn/hoatdongcuaquochoi/cackyhopquochoi/quochoikhoaXII/kyhopthutam/Pages/van-kien-tai-lieu.aspx?ItemID=1599.

49.   See the transcript from the morning session of the November 22, 2010, query session, http://quochoi.vn/hoatdongcuaquochoi/cackyhopquochoi/quochoikhoaXII/kyhopthutam/Pages/tra-loi-chat-van.aspx?ItemID=22580.

50. See "Bộ Chính trị kết luận về Vinashin," *VnEconomy,* August 8, 2010, http://vneconomy.vn/doanh-nhan/bo-chinh-tri-ket-luan-ve-vinashin-201008090 25955314.htm.

Conclusion

1. By "salutary effects," I mean primarily economic growth and better policy. Consistent with Little (2017), one could argue that citizen welfare is better in regimes with elections than in those without due to increased information about the utility or futility of protests. I do not take a stand as to whether mobilizational elections inform or misinform both the regime and the public with regard to the futility of protest. However, I take a stronger stand that such elections and legislatures provide little additional information on citizen policy preferences.

2. There is a massive literature on this distinction, with various ways of distinguishing the competitiveness of electoral systems. For a review, see Gandhi and Lust-Okar (2009) or Hyde and Marinov (2012).

3. The cases in these studies include the Stuart monarchy in England, Kuwait, the UAE, Ecuador, and Morocco.

4. There are more single-party regime years lasting 0–5 years than 6–10 years because of the left-censoring of the data. Because the data start in 1945, a number of regimes enter the dataset already having existed for a number of years.

5. One could argue that in China, the inactivity of the legislature also coincided with the personalization of the regime, which would be consistent with the argument that legislatures under personalized systems are less effective (Wright 2008; Wilson and Wright 2015). However, in Vietnam the legislature was also relatively inactive under Ho Chi Minh, which most observers suggest was not heavily personalistic, at least not until Le Duan emerged as the dominant player after Ho Chi Minh's death in 1969 (Thai 1985).

6. For example, in November 2018, delegate Luu Binh Luong made news by suggesting that the Ministry of Police had not followed up on a number of denunciations and public reports of wrongdoing, numbers that the ministry publicly refuted (see "Bà Kim Ngân cần kết luận về ý kiến của ông Lưu Bình Nhưỡng?," BBC Vietnamese, November 8, 2018, https://www.bbc.com/vietnamese/vietnam -46134147.

7. See "Vietnam Prime Minister Nguyen Tan Dung Urged to Resign," BBC News, November 14, 2012, https://www.bbc.com/news/world-asia-20322830.

References

Abrami, Regina, Edmund Malesky, and Yu Zheng. 2013. "Vietnam through Chinese Eyes: Divergent Accountability in Single Party Regimes." In *Why Communism Did Not Collapse*, edited by Martin Dimitrov, 237–275. New York: Cambridge University Press.

Abuza, Zachary. 2001. *Renovating Politics in Contemporary Vietnam*. Boulder, CO: Lynne Rienner.

Achen, Christopher, and Larry Bartels. 2016. *Democracy for Realists: Why Elections Do Not Produce Responsive Government*. Princeton, NJ: Princeton University Press.

Adena, Maja, Ruben Enikolopov, Maria Petrova, Veronica Santarosa, and Ekaterina Zhuravskaya. 2015. "Radio and the Rise of Nazis in Prewar Germany." *Quarterly Journal of Economics* 4, no. 1: 1885–1939.

Adler, E. Scott, and John Lapinski. 1997. "Demand-Side Theory and Congressional Committee Composition: A Constituency Characteristics Approach." *American Journal of Political Science* 41, no. 3: 895–918.

Alagappa, Mutiah. 1995. *Political Legitimacy in Southeast Asia: The Quest for Moral Authority*. Stanford, CA: Stanford University Press.

Albertus, Michael, and Victor Menaldo. 2014. "The Political Economy of Autocratic Constitutions." In *Constitutions in Authoritarian Regimes*, edited by Thomas Ginsburg and Alberto Simpser, 53–82. New York: Cambridge University Press.

Aldrich, John. 1995. *Why Parties?* Chicago: University of Chicago Press.

Alesina, Alberto, Reza Baqir, and William Easterly. 1999. "Public Goods and Ethnic Divisions." *Quarterly Journal of Economics* 114, no. 4: 1243–1284.

Allmark, Liam. 2012. "More Than Rubber-Stamps: The Consequences Produced by Legislatures in Non-Democratic States beyond Latent Legitimation." *Journal of Legislative Studies* 18, no. 2: 184–202.

Almen, Oscar. 2013. "Only the Party Manages Cadres: Limits of Local People's Congress Supervision and Reform in China." *Journal of Contemporary China* 20, no. 80: 237–254.

Altincekic, Ceren, and David Bearce. 2014. "Why There Should Be No Political Foreign Aid Curse." *World Development* 64: 18–32.

Art, David. 2012. "What Do We Know about Authoritarianism after 10 Years?" *Comparative Politics* 44, no. 3: 351–373.

Aytac, S. Erdem, and Susan C. Stokes. 2019. *Why Bother? Rethinking Participation in Elections and Protests*. New York: Cambridge University Press.

Beazer, Quintin, and Ora John Reuter. 2019. "Who Is to Blame? Political Centralization and Electoral Punishment under Authoritarianism." *Journal of Politics* 81, no. 2: 648–662.

Beissinger, Mark. 2002. *Nationalist Mobilization and the Collapse of the Soviet State*. New York: Cambridge University Press.

Bell, Daniel. 2015. *The China Model*. Princeton, NJ: Princeton University Press.

Beresford, Melanie. 2008. "Doi Moi in Review: The Challenges of Building Market Socialism in Vietnam." *Journal of Contemporary Asia* 38, no. 2: 221–243.

Beresford, Melanie, and Phong Dang. 2000. *Economic Transition in Vietnam*. Cheltenham, UK: Edward Elgar.

Bischoping, Katherine, and Howard Schuman. 1992. "Pens and Polls in Nicaragua: An Analysis of the 1990 Preelection Surveys." *American Journal of Political Science* 36, no. 2: 331–350.

Blaydes, Lisa. 2011. *Elections and Distributive Politics in Mubarak's Egypt*. Cambridge, UK: Cambridge University Press.

Blei, David, Andrew Ng, and Michael Jordan. 2003. "Latent Dirichlet Allocation." *Journal of Machine Learning Research* 3: 993–1022.

Bonvecchi, Alejandro, and Emilia Simison. 2017. "Legislative Institutions and Performance in Authoritarian Regimes." *Comparative Politics* 49, no. 4: 521–544.

Brownlee, Jason. 2009. "Portents of Pluralism: How Hybrid Regimes Affect Democratic Transitions." *American Journal of Political Science* 53, no. 3: 515–532.

Bueno de Mesquita, Bruce, Alastair Smith, Ralph Siverson, and James Morrow. 2004. *The Logic of Political Survival*. Cambridge, MA: MIT University Press.

Bui, Son Ngoc. 2007. "Quốc hội Nước Công hoà Xã hội Chủ nghĩa Việt Nam Hiện Nay." In *Quốc hội Việt Nam Trong Nhà Nước Pháp Quyền*, edited by Dung Dang Nguyen. Hanoi: Nhà Xuất bản Đại học Quốc gia Hà Nội.

Bunce, Valerie, and Sharon Wolchik. 2011. *Defeating Authoritarian Leaders in Postcommunist Countries*. New York: Cambridge University Press.

Campbell, Angus, Phillip Converse, Warren Miller, and Donald Stokes. 1960. *The American Voter*. Chicago: University of Chicago Press.

Cancela, Joao, and Benny Geys. 2016. "Explaining Voter Turnout: A Meta-Analysis of National and Subnational Elections." *Electoral Studies* 42: 264–275.

Cantoni, Davide, Yuyu Chen, David Yang, Noah Yuchtman, and Y. Jane Zhang. 2017. "Curriculum and Ideology." *Journal of Political Economy* 125, no. 2: 338–392.

Chen, Jidong, and Yiqing Xu. 2017. "Why Do Authoritarian Regimes Allow Citizens to Voice Opinions Publicly." *Journal of Politics* 79, no. 3: 792–803.

Chen, Jie, and Yang Zhong. 2002. "Why Do People Vote in Semicompetitive Elections in China?" *Journal of Politics* 64, no. 1: 178–197.

Cotton, James. 1989. "Vietnam: Reform and Resistance." *Pacific Affairs* 2, no. 3: 256–258.

Cox, Gary. 1995. *Making Votes Count: Strategic Coordination in the World's Electoral Systems*. New York: Cambridge University Press.

———. 2006, "The Organization of Democratic Legislatures." In *Oxford Handbook of Political Economy*, edited by Barry Weingast and Donald Wittman, 141–161. New York: Oxford University Press.

Cox, Gary, and Mathew McCubbins. 1993. *Legislative Leviathan: Party Government in the House*. Cambridge, UK: Cambridge University Press.

Cox, Gary, and Matthew Shugart. 1996. "Strategic Voting Under Proportional Representation." *Journal of Law, Economics, and Organization* 12, no. 2: 299–324.

Dang, Phong. 2008. *Tư duy Kinh tế: Việt Nam 1975–1989*. Hanoi: Nhà Xuất bản Trí thức.

Dang, Phong, and Melanie Beresford. 1998. *Authority Relations and Economic Decisionmaking in Vietnam*. Singapore: NIAS.

Dassonneville, Ruth, Fernanda Feitosa, Marc Hooghe, Richard Lau, and Dieter Stiers. 2018. "Compulsory Voting Rules, Reluctant Voters and Ideological Proximity Voting." *Political Behavior* FirstView: 1–22.

De Paola, Maria, and Vincenzo Scoppa. 2014. "The Impact of Closeness on Electoral Participation Exploiting the Italian Double Ballot System." *Public Choice* 160, nos. 3–4: 467–479.

Delli Carpini, Michael, and Scott Keeter. 1996. *What Americans Know About Politics and Why It Matters*. New Haven, CT: Yale University Press.

Desposato, Scott. 2007. "How Does Vote Buying Shape the Legislative Arena?" In *Elections for Sale: The Causes and Consequences of Vote Buying*, edited by Frederic Shaffeer, 101–122. Boulder, CO: Lynne Rienner.

Diamond, Larry. 2002. "Thinking About Hybrid Regimes." *Journal of Democracy* 13, no. 2: 21–35.

Dickson, Bruce. 2016. *The Dictator's Dilemma: The Chinese Communist Party's Strategy for Survival*. Oxford: Oxford University Press.

Dimitrov, Martin. 2017. "The Political Logic of Media Control in China." *Problems of Post-Communism* 64, nos. 3–4: 121–127.

Djankov, Simon, Jose Montalvo, and Marta Reynal-Querol. 2008. "The Curse of Aid." *Journal of Economic Growth* 13: 169–154.

Doner, Richard, Bryan Ritchie, and Dan Slater. 2005. "Systemic Vulnerability and the Origin of Developmental States: Northeast and Southeast Asia in Comparative Perspective." *International Organization* 57: 327–361.

Doring, Herbert. 2001. "Parliamentary Agenda Control and Legislative Outcomes in Western Europe." *Legislative Studies Quarterly* 26, no. 1: 145–165.

Dowdle, Michael. 1997. "The Constitutional Development and Operations of the National People's Congress." *Columbia Journal of Asian Law* 11, no. 1: 1–125.

Dreher, Axel, Andreas Fuchs, Roland Hodler, Bradley Parks, Paul Raschky, and Michael Tierney. 2016. "Aid on Demand: African Leaders and the Geography of China's Foreign Assistance." Centro Studi Luca D'Agliano Working Paper 400.

Duc, Huy. 2012. *Bên Thắng Cuộc: II Quyền Bính*. New York: Osin Books.

Easterly, William, and Ross Levine. 1997. "Africa's Growth Tragedy: Policies and Ethnic Divisions." *Quarterly Journal of Economics* 112, no. 4: 1203–1250.

Eckstein, Harry. 1975. *Case Studies and Theory in Political Science*. Vol. 7 of *Handbook of Political Science: Scope and Theory*, edited by F.I. Greenstein and Nelson Polsby. Reading, MA: Addison-Wesley.

Egorov, Georgy, Sergei Guriev, and Konstantin Sonin. 2009. "Why Resource-Poor Dictators Allow Freer Media: A Theory and Evidence from Panel Data." *American Political Science Review* 103, no. 4: 645–668.

Eklof, Stefan. 1997. "The 1997 General Election in Indonesia." *Asian Survey* 37, no. 12: 1181–1196.

England, Sarah, and Daniel Kammen. 1993. "Energy in Vietnam." *Annual Review of Energy and the Environment* 18: 137–167.

Eulau, Heinz, and Paul D. Karps. 1977. "The Puzzle of Representation: Specifying Components of Responsiveness." *Legislative Studies Quarterly* 2, no. 3: 233–254.

Fainsod, Merle. 1963. *How Russia Is Ruled*. Cambridge, MA: Harvard University Press.

Fall, Bernard. 1960. "Constitution-Writing in a Communist State." *Howard Law Journal* 6: 157–168.

Fforde, Adam. 2009. "Luck, Policy or Something Else Entirely? Vietnam's Economic Performance in 2009 and Prospects for 2010." *Journal of Current Southeast Asian Affairs* 28, no. 4: 71–94.

———. 2016. "Review: Politics in Contemporary Vietnam: Party, State, and Authority Relations by Jonathan London, ed." *Journal of Vietnamese Studies* 11, nos. 3/4: 365–372.

Fforde, Adam, and Stefan de Vylder. 1996. *From Plan to Market: The Economic Transition in Vietnam.* Boulder, CO: Westview Press.

Frantz, Erica. 2018. "Voter Turnout and Opposition Performance in Competitive Authoritarian Elections." *Electoral Studies* 54: 218–225.

Friedrich, Carl, and Zbigniew Brzezinski. 1961. *Totalitarian Dictatorship and Autocracy.* New York: Praeger.

Gailmard, Sean, and Jeffery Jenkins. 2007. "Negative Agenda Power in the Senate and the House: Fingerprints of Majority Party Power." *Journal of Politics* 69, no. 3: 689–700.

Gaines, Brian, James Kuklinski, and Paul Quirk. 2007. "The Logic of the Survey Experiment Reexamined." *Political Analysis* 15, no. 1: 1–20.

Gainsborough, Martin. 2005. "Party Control: Electoral Campaigning in Vietnam in the Run-up to the May 2002 National Assembly Elections." *Pacific Affairs* 78, no. 1: 57–75.

———. 2007. "From Patronage to 'Outcomes': Vietnam's Communist Party Congresses Reconsidered." *Journal of Vietnamese Studies* 2, no. 1: 3–26.

———. 2010. *Vietnam: Rethinking the State.* London: Zed Books, 2010.

———. 2018. "Malesky vs. Fforde: How Best to Analyze Vietnamese Politics?" *Journal of Vietnamese Studies* 3, no. 12: 1–26.

Galston, William. 2001. "Political Knowledge, Political Engagement, and Civic Education." *Annual Review of Political Science* 4: 217–234.

Gandhi, Jennifer. 2008. *Political Institutions under Dictatorship.* New York: Cambridge University Press.

Gandhi, Jennifer, and Ellen Lust-Okar. 2009. "Elections Under Authoritarianism." *Annual Review of Political Science* 12: 403–422.

Gandhi, Jennifer, and Adam Przeworski. 2006. "Cooperation, Cooptation and Rebellion under Dictatorships." *Economics and Politics* 18, no. 1: 1–26.

———. 2007. "Authoritarian Institutions and the Survival of Autocrats." *Comparative Political Studies* 40, no. 11: 1279–1301.

Geddes, Barbara. 2005. "Why Parties and Elections in Authoritarian Regimes." Paper presented at Annual Meeting of the American Political Science Association, September 1–4, Washington, DC.

Geddes, Barbara, Joseph Wright, and Erica Frantz. 2014. "Autocratic Breakdown and Regime Transition: A New Dataset." *Perspectives on Politics* 12, no. 2: 313–331.

———. 2018. *How Dictatorships Work*. Cambridge, UK: Cambridge University Press.

Gehlbach, Scott, and Philip Keefer. 2011. "Investment without Democracy: Ruling-Party Institutionalization and Credible Commitment in Autocracies." *Journal of Comparative Economics* 39, no. 2: 123–139.

———. 2012. "Private Investment and the Institutionalization of Collective Action in Autocracies: Ruling Parties and Legislatures." *Journal of Politics* 74, no. 2: 621–635.

Gehlbach, Scott, and Alberto Simpser. 2015. "Electoral Manipulation as Bureaucratic Control." *American Journal of Political Science* 59, no. 1: 212–224.

Gerber, Alan, and Donald Green. 2000. "The Effects of Canvassing, Telephone Calls, and Direct Mail on Voter Turnout: A Field Experiment." *American Political Science Review* 94, no. 3: 653–663.

Gerber, Alan, Donald Green, and Christopher Larimer. 2008. "Social Pressure and Voter Turnout: Evidence from a Large-Scale Field Experiment." *American Political Science Review* 102, no. 1: 33–48.

Gerring, John. 2007. "Is There a (Viable) Crucial Case Method?" *Comparative Political Studies* 40, no. 3: 231–253.

Geys, Benny. 2006. "Explaining Voter Turnout: A Review of Aggregate-Level Research ." *Electoral Studies* 25: 637–663.

Gilligan, Thomas, and Keith Krehbiel. 1989. "Asymmetric Information and Legislative Rules with a Heterogenous Committee." *American Journal of Political Science* 33, no. 2: 459–490.

———. 1990. "Organization of Informative Committees by a Rational Legislature." *American Journal of Political Science* 34, no. 2: 531–564.

Golder, Matt, and Jacek Stramski. 2010. "Ideological Congruence and Electoral Institutions." *American Journal of Political Science* 54, no. 1: 90–106.

Green, Donald, Shang Ha, and John Bullock. 2010. "Enough Already about 'Black Box' Experiments: Studying Mediation Is More Difficult Than Most Scholars Suppose." *ANNALS of the American Academy of Political and Social Science* 628: 200–208.

Greene, Kenneth. 2011. "Campaign Persuasion and Nascent Partisanship in Mexico's New Democracy." *American Journal of Political Science* 55, no. 2: 398–416.

Greitens, Sheena Chestnut. 2016. *Dictators and their Secret Police: Coercive Institutions and State Violence*. Cambridge, UK: Cambridge University Press.

Grimmer, Justin, and Brandon Stewart. 2013. "Text as Data: Promise and Pitfalls of Automated Content Analysis for Political Texts." *Political Analysis* 21, no.3: 267-297.

Gueorguiev, Dimitar. 2014. "Retrofitting Communism: Consultative Autocracy in China." PhD diss., University of California–San Diego.

Guilbert, Francois. 1990. "Vietnam and Perestroika." *Pacific Review* 3, no. 3: 272–274.

Haber, Stephen. 2006. "Authoritarian Government." In *Oxford Handbook of Political Economy*, edited by Barry Weingast and Donald Wittman, 693–707. Oxford: Oxford University Press.

Hadenius, Axel, and Jan Teorell. 2007. "Pathways from Authoritarianism." *Journal of Democracy* 18, no. 1: 143–157.

Harbaugh, W. T. 1996. "If People Vote Because They Like to, Then Why Do Fo Many of Them Lie?" *Public Choice* 89: 63–76.

Harish, S. P., and Andrew T. Little. 2017. "The Political Violence Cycle." *American Political Science Review* 111, no. 2: 237–255.

Harrington, Joanna, Ted McDorman, and William Nielson. 1998. "The 1992 Vietnamese Constitution: Economic Reform, Political Continuity." In *Asia-Pacific Legal Development*, edited by Douglas Johnston, 243–266. Vancouver: University of British Columbia Press.

Hasson, Victoria. 2010. "Rules and Rituals: The Case of South Africa's New Committee System." *Journal of Legislative Studies* 16, no. 3: 366–379.

He, Baogang, and Mark Warren. 2011. "Authoritarian Deliberation: The Deliberative Turn in Chinese Political Development." *Perspectives on Politics* 9, no. 2: 269–289.

———. 2017. "Authoritarian Deliberation in China." *Daedalus* 146, no. 3: 155–166.

He, Baogang, and Stig Thogersen. 2010. "Giving the People a Voice? Experiments with Consultative Authoritarian Institutions in China." *Journal of Contemporary China* 19, no. 66: 675–692.

Hedru, Debessay. 2003. "Eritrea: Transition to Dictatorship, 1991–2003." *Review of African Political Economy* 30, no. 97: 435–444.

Herb, Michael. 2014. *Wages of Oil: Parliaments and Economic Development in Kuwait and the UAE*. Ithaca, NY: Cornell University Press.

Heurlin, Christopher. 2016. *Responsive Authoritarianism in China: Land, Protests, and Policy Making*. New York: Cambridge University Press.

Hicken, Allen. 2011. "Clientelism." *Annual Review of Political Science* 14: 289–310.

Hicks, Raymond, and Dustin Tingley. 2011. "Causal Mediation Analysis." *Stata Journal* 11, no. 4: 605–619.

Hill, Ronald. 1976. "The CPSU in a Soviet Election Campaign." *Soviet Studies* 28, no. 4: 590–598.

Holmes, Stephen. 2003. "Lineages of the Rule of Law." In *Democracy and the Rule of Law*, edited by Jose Maria Maravall and Adam Przeworski, 19–61. New York: Cambridge University Press.

Holmstrom, Bengt, and Paul Milgrom. 1991. "Multitask Principal-Agent Analyses." *Journal of Law, Economics, & Organization* 7: 24–52.

Hopkins, Raymond. 1970. "The Role of the M.P. in Tanzania." *American Political Science Review* 64, no. 3: 754–771.

Hou, Yue. 2019. *The Private Sector in Public Office.* New York: Cambridge University Press.

Hu, Shikai. 1993. "Representation without Democratization: The 'Signature Incident' and China's National People's Congress." *Journal of Contemporary China* 2, no. 2: 3–34.

Huang, Dongya, and Quanling He. 2018. "Striking a Balance between Contradictory Roles: The Overlapping Role Perceptions of the Deputies in China's Local People's Congresses." *Modern China* 44, no. 1: 103–134.

Huang, Haifeng. 2015. "Propaganda as Signaling." *Comparative Politics* 47, no. 4: 419–437.

———. 2018. "The Pathology of Hard Propaganda." *Journal of Politics* 80, no. 3: 1034–1038.

Huntington, Samuel. 1993. *The Third Wave: Democratization in the Late 20th Century.* Norman: University of Oklahoma Press.

Hyde, Susan, and Nikolay Marinov. 2012. "Which Elections Can Be Lost?" *Political Analysis* 20, no. 2: 191–210.

Imai, Kosuke, Luke Keele, and Teppei Yamamoto. 2010. "Identification, Inference and Sensitivity Analysis for Causal Mediation Effects." *Statistical Science* 25, no. 1: 57–71.

Jackee, Keith, and Guang-Zhen Sun. 2006. "Is Compulsory Voting More Democratic?" *Public Choice* 129, no. 1: 61–75.

Kalinin, Kirill. 2016. "A Study of Social Desirability Bias at the Russian Presidential Elections 2012." *Journal of Elections, Public Opinion, and Parties* 26, no. 2: 191-211.

Kalyvas, Stathis. 1999. "The Decay and Breakdown of Communist One-Party Systems." *Annual Review of Political Science* 2: 323–343.

Kam, Cindy, and Elizabeth Zechmeister. 2013. "Name Recognition and Candidate Support." *American Journal of Political Science* 57, no. 4: 971–986.

Kaminsky, Marek. 1999. "How Communist Could Have Been Saved: Formal Analysis of Electoral Bargaining in Poland in 1989." *Public Choice* 98, nos. 1/2: 83–109.

Kaya, Ruchan, and Michael Bernhard. 2013. "Are Elections Mechanisms of Authoritarian Stability or Democratization? Evidence from Postcommunist Eurasia." *Perspectives on Politics* 11, no. 3: 734–752.

Kerkvliet, Benedict J. Tria. 1995. "Village-State Relations in Vietnam: The Effect of Everyday Politics on Decollectivization." *Journal of Asian Studies* 54: 396–418.

———. 2005. *The Power of Everyday Politics: How Vietnamese Peasants Transformed National Policy.* Ithaca, NY: Cornell University Press.

———. 2014. "Protests over Land in Vietnam: Rightful Resistance and More." *Journal of Vietnamese Studies* 9, no. 3: 19–54.

Khng, Russell Heng Hiang. 1993. "Vietnam 1992: Economic Growth and Political Caution." *Southeast Asian Affairs,* 353–363. https://www.jstor.org/stable /27912084?casa_token=GaoU-uKjYXEAAAAA%3AY_ei1KfBpVx1J5H Dx8bN3ndHec0uP3qCxowiBXS91_sDKHNjEcQ0mwxuo7p4NWnb UWUOgAOhDDkxaTCuedOJqvZSoHvxH9vfJXyOMEsN6HPVVlMlTto &seq=1#metadata_info_tab_contents.

King, Anthony, and Ivor Crewe. 2014. *The Blunders of our Government.* London: OneWorld.

Knack, Stephen. 1992. "Civic Norms, Social Sanctions, and Voter Turnout." *Rationality and Society* 4, no. 2: 133–156.

———. 2001. "Aid Dependence and the Quality of Governance: A Cross-Country Empirical Analysis." World Bank Policy Research Working Paper.

Koh, David. 2006. *Wards of Hanoi.* Singapore: ISEAS Publications.

Kollman, Ken, Allen Hicken, Daniele Caramani, David Backer, and David Lublin. 2016. *Constituency-Level Elections Archive [Data File and Codebook].* Ann Arbor: Center for Political Studies, University of Michigan.

Kovrig, Bennet. 1979. *Communism in Hungary: From Kun to Kadar.* Stanford, CA: Hoover Institution Press.

Krehbiel, Keith. 1991. *Information and Legislative Organization.* Ann Arbor: University of Michigan Press.

Kuran, Timur. 1991. "Now Out of Never: The Element of Surprise in the East European Revolution." *World Politics* 44, no. 1: 7–48.

Landry, Pierre, Deborah Davis, and Shiru Wang. 2010. "Elections in Rural China: Competition without Parties." *Comparative Political Studies* 43, no. 6: 1–28.

Larcinese, Valentino. 2007. "Does Political Knowledge Increase Turnout? Evidence from the 1997 British General Election." *Public Choice* 131: 387–411.

Larreguy, Horacio, John Marshall, and James Snyder. 2016. "Leveling the Playing Field: How Campaign Advertising can Help Non-Dominant Parties." National Bureau of Economic Research Working Paper Series, December.

Lassen, David Dreyer. 2005. "The Effect of Information on Voter Turnout: Evidence from a Natural Experiment." *American Journal of Political Science* 49, no. 1: 103–118.

Le, Hong Hiep. 2012. "Performance-Based Legitimacy: The Case of the Communist Party of Vietnam and 'Doi Moi.'" *Contemporary Southeast Asia* 34, no. 2: 145–172.

Le, Toan. 2016. "Interpreting the Constitutional Debate over Land Ownership in the Socialist Republic of Vietnam (2012–2013)." *Asian Journal of Comparative Law* 11: 287–307.

Letsa, Natalie Wenzell. 2020. "Expressive Voting in Autocracies: A Theory of Non-Economic Participation with Evidence from Cameroon." *Perspectives on Politics* 18, no. 2: 439–453.

Levy, Dena, and Peverill Squire. 2000. "Television Markets and the Competitiveness of U.S. House Elections." *Legislative Studies Quarterly* 25, no. 2: 313–325.

Lieberthal, Kenneth, and David Lampton. 1992. *Bureaucracy, Politics, and Decision Making in Post-Mao China*. Berkeley: University of California Press.

Light, Margot. 1991. "Soviet Policy in the Third World." *International Affairs* 67, no. 2: 263–280.

Lindberg, Staffan. 2006. *Democracy and Elections in Africa*. Baltimore. MD: Johns Hopkins University Press.

Little, Andrew. 2012. "Elections, Fraud, and Election Monitoring in the Shadow of Revolution." *Quarterly Journal of Political Science* 7: 249–283.

———. 2017. "Are Non-Competitive Elections Good for Citizens?" *Journal of Theoretical Politics* 29, no. 2: 214–242.

Little, Andrew, Joshua Tucker, and Tom LaGatta. 2015. "Elections, Protest, and Alternation of Power." *Journal of Politics* 77, no. 4: 1142–1156.

Lockhart, Greg. 1997. "Mass Mobilization in Contemporary Vietnam." *Asian Studies Review* 21, nos. 2–3: 174–179.

Lohmann, Susan. 1994. "The Dynamics of Informational Cascades: The Monday Demonstrations in Leipzig, East Germany, 1989–91." *World Politics* 47: 42–101.

Loidolt, Bryce, and Quinn Mecham. 2013. "Parliamentary Opposition Under Hybrid Regimes: Evidence from Egypt." Paper presented at the Annual Meeting of the American Political Science Association, August 29–September 1, Chicago.

London, Jonathan. 2014. "Toward a New Politics?" In *Politics in Contemporary Vietnam: Party, State, and Authority Relations*, edited by Jonathan London, 1–20. London: Palgrave Macmillan.

Lorentzen, Peter. 2013. "Regularlizing Rioting: Permitting Public Protest in an Authoritarian Regime." *Quarterly Journal of Political Science* 8, no. 2: 127–158.

———. 2014. "China's Strategic Censorship." *American Journal of Political Science* 58, no. 2: 402–414.

Lu, Xiaobo, Mingxing Liu, and Feiyue Li. 2019. "Policy Coalition Building in an Authoritarian Legislature: Evidence from China's National Assemblies (1983–2007)." *Comparative Political Studies* OnlineFirst.

Lust-Okar, Ellen. 2006. "Elections under Authoritarianism: Preliminary Lessons from Jordan." *Democratization* 13, no. 3: 456–471.

Magaloni, Beatriz. 2006. *Voting for Autocracy: Hegemonic Party Survival and Its Demise in Mexico*. New York: Cambridge University Press.

Magaloni, Beatriz, and Ruth Kricheli. 2010. "Political Order and One-Party Rule." *Annual Review of Political Science* 13: 123–143.

Malesky, Edmund. 2009. "Gerrymandering—Vietnamese Style: Escaping Partial Reform Equilibrium in a Nondemocratic Regime." *Journal of Politics* 71, no. 1: 132–159.

———. 2014. "An Update on 'Adverse Effects of Sunshine.'" In *Politics in Contemporary Vietnam: Party, State, and Authority Relations*, edited by Jonathan London, 84–99. London: Palgrave Macmillan.

Malesky, Edmund, Regina Abrami, and Yu Zheng. 2011. "Institutions and Inequality in Single-Party Regimes: A Comparative Analysis of Vietnam and China." *Comparative Politics* 43, no. 4: 409–427.

Malesky, Edmund, and Paul Schuler. 2009. "Paint-by-Numbers Democracy: The Stakes, Structure, and Results of the 2007 Vietnamese National Assembly Election." *Journal of Vietnamese Studies*, no. 4: 1–48.

———. 2010. "Nodding or Needling: Analyzing Delegate Responsiveness in an Authoritarian Parliament." *American Political Science Review* 104, no. 3: 482–502.

———. 2011. "The Single-Party Dictator's Dilemma: Information in Elections Without Opposition." *Legislative Studies Quarterly* 36, no. 4: 491–530.

———. 2013. "Star Search: Do Elections Help Nondemocratic Regimes Identify New Leaders?" *Journal of East Asian Studies* 13, no. 1: 35–68.

Malesky, Edmund, Paul Schuler, and Anh Tran. 2011. "Vietnam: Familiar Patterns and New Development Ahead of the 11th Party Congress." *Southeast Asian Affairs*, 337–363. https://doi.org/10.1355/9789814345040.

Malesky, Edmund, Cuong Viet Nguyen, and Anh Tran. 2014. "The Impact of Recentralization on Public Services: A Difference-in-Difference Analysis of the Abolition of Elected Councils in Vietnam." *American Political Science Review* 108, no. 1: 144–168.

Maltzman, Forrest, and Lee Sigelman. 1996. "The Politics of Talk: Unconstrained Floor Time in the US House of Representatives." *Journal of Politics* 58, no. 3: 819–830.

Manion, Melanie. 2016. *Information for Autocrats: Representation in Chinese Local Congresses*. Cambridge, UK: Cambridge University Press.

Mann, Thomas, and Raymond Wolfinger. 1980. "Candidates and Parties in Congressional Elections." *American Political Science Review* 74, no. 3: 617–632.

March, James, and Johan Olsen. 1984. "The New Institutionalism: Organizational Factors in Political Life." *American Political Science Review* 78, no. 3: 734–749.

Markussen, Thomas, and Quang-Thanh Ngo. 2019. "Economic and Non-Economic Returns to Communist Party Membership in Vietnam." *World Development* 122: 370–384.

Marples, David. 2015. *The Collapse of the Soviet Union: 1985–1991*. London: Routledge.

Mayhew, David. 1974. *Congress: The Electoral Connection*. New Haven, CT: Yale University Press.

McCormick, Barrett. 1996. "China's Leninist Parliament and Public Sphere." In *China After Socialism: In the Footsteps of Eastern Europe or East Asia?*, edited by Barrett McCormick and Jonathan Unger, 29–53. London: M. E. Sharpe.

McCoy, Jennifer, and Jonathan Hartlyn. 2009. "The Relative Powerlessness of Elections in Latin America." In *Democratization by Elections: A New Mode of Transition*, edited by Staffan Lindberg, 47–56. Baltimore. MD: Johns Hopkins University Press.

Mellon, Jonathan. 2014. "Internet Search Data and Issue Salience: The Properties of Google Trends as a Measure of Issue Salience." *Journal of Elections, Public Opinion, and Political Parties* 24, no. 1: 45–72.

Mertha, Andrew. 2017. "'Stressing Out': Cadre Calibration and Affective Proximity to the CCP in Reform-era China." *China Quarterly* 229: 64–85.

Miguel, Edward, and Mary Kay Gugerty. 2005. "Ethnic Diversity, Social Sanctions, and Public Goods in Kenya." *Journal of Public Economics* 89, nos. 11–12: 2325–2368.

Miller, Michael. 2013. "Electoral Authoritarianism and Democracy: A Formal Model of Regime Transitions." *Journal of Theoretical Politics* 25, no. 2: 153–181.

———. 2015. "Elections, Information, and Policy Responsiveness in Autocratic Regimes." *Comparative Political Studies* 48, no. 6: 691–727.

———. 2017. "The Strategic Origins of Electoral Authoritarianism." *British Journal of Political Science* 51, no. 1: 17–44.

Milligan, Kevin, Enrico Moretti, and Philip Oreopoulos. 2004. "Does Education Improve Citizenship? Evidence from the United States and the United Kingdom." *Journal of Public Economics* 88: 1667–1695.

Morgenbesser, Lee. 2016. *Behind the Facade: Elections and Authoritarianism in Southeast Asia*. Albany: State University of New York Press.

Morrison, Kevin. 2010. "What Can We Learn about the 'Resource Curse' from Foreign Aid?" *World Bank Research Observer* 27, no. 1: 52–73.

Moser, Robert, and Ethan Scheiner. 2009. "Strategic Voting in Established and New Democracies: Ticket Splitting in Mixed Electoral Systems." *Electoral Studies* 28, no. 1: 51–61.

Myagkov, Mikhail, Peter Ordeshook, and Dimitri Shakin. 2009. *The Forensics of Electoral Fraud*. Cambridge, UK: Cambridge University Press.

Nalepa, Monika, and Grigore Pop-Eleches. 2014. "Explaining Authoritarian Collapse Through Public Opinion Surveys: Evidence from Poland (1985–1989)." Unpublished manuscript.

Ngo, Manh Duc. 2005. "Đại Biểu Quốc hội Chuyên Trách: Một Số Suy Nghĩ về Tăng Cường Năng Lực Hoạt Động." In *Quốc hội Việt Nam: Những Vấn đề Lý luận và Thực tiễn*, edited by Son Ngoc Bui. Hanoi: Nhà Xuất bản Tư Pháp.

Nguyen, Dang Dung. 1992. *Quốc hội nước cộng hòa xã hội chủ nghĩa Việt Nam: Những khía cạnh pháp lý theo hiến pháp và luật tổ chức Quốc hội năm 1992*. Hanoi: Phap Ly.

———. 2007. *Quốc hội Việt Nam trong nhà nước pháp quyền: Chuyên khảo dành cho đại học*. Hanoi: Nhà xuất bản Đại học quốc gia Hà Nộ.

Nguyen, Du Nhu. 2005. "Đồng chí Nguyễn Văn Linh Với Đổi Mới Hoạt Động Của Quốc Hội." In *Quốc hội: Những Vấn đề Lý luận và Thực tiễn*, edited by Thanh Ngoc Bui. Hanoi: Nhà Xuất bản Tú pháp.

Nguyen, Sy Dung. 2017. *Bàn Về Quốc hội*. Hanoi: Nhà Xuất Bản Chính trị.

Nguyen, Hai Hong. 2016. *Political Dynamics of Grassroots Democracy in Vietnam*. London: Palgrave Macmillan.

Nguyen, Hai Manh, and Michael O'Donnell. 2017. "Reforming State-Owned Enterprises in Vietnam: The Contrasting Cases of Vinashin and Viettel." *Asian Perspective* 42: 215–237.

Nguyen, Hung Manh. 2016. "Continuity and Change under Vietnam's New Leadership." *ISEAS Perspective*, no. 50: 1–7.

Nguyen, Minh Quang. 2005. "Bàn Về Tính Đại Diện Nhân Dân Của Quốc Hội." In *Quốc Hội: Những Vấn đề về Lý Luận và Thực Tiễn*, edited by Bui Ngoc Thanh. Hanoi: Nhà Xuất Bản Tư Pháp.

Niemi, Richard, Guy Whitten, and Mark Franklin. 1992. "Constituency Characteristics, Individual Characteristics and Tactical Voting in the 1987 British General Election." *British Journal of Political Science* 22, no. 2: 229–240.

Ninh, Kim. 1989. "In the Era of Renovation: Leadership and Security in Vietnam." *Contemporary Southeast Asia* 11, no. 2: 213–235.

Noble, Ben. 2014. "Executive Bill Failure under Authoritarianism: Evidence from the Russian Federation." Paper presented at the Annual Meeting of the American Political Science Association, August 28–August 31. Washington, DC.

North, Douglass, and Barry Weingast. 1989. "Constitutions and Commitment: The Evolution of Institutions Governing Public Choice in

Seventeenth-Century England." *Journal of Economic History* 4, no. 49: 803–832.

Nyland, Chris. 1981. "Vietnam: The Plan/Market Contradition and the Transition to Socialism." *Journal of Contemporary Asia* 11, no. 4: 426–448.

O'Brien, Kevin. 1990. *Reform without Liberalization: China's National People's Congress and the Politics of Instituitonal Change.* Cambridge, UK: Cambridge University Press.

———. 1994. "Agents and Remonstrators: Role Accumulation by Chinese People's Congress Deputies." *China Quarterly* 138: 359–380.

Ostwald, Kai, and Paul Schuler. 2015. "Myanmar's Landmark Election: Unresolved Questions." *ISEAS Perspectives*, no. 68: 1–7.

Paler, Laura. 2005. "China's Legislation Law and the Making of a More Orderly and Representative Legislative System." *China Quarterly* 182: 305–318.

Pan, Jennifer, and Yiqing Xu. 2017. "China's Ideological Spectrum." *Journal of Politics* 80, no. 1: 254–273.

Peisakhin, Leonid, and Arturas Rozenas. 2018. "Electoral Effects of Biased Media: Russian Television in Ukraine." *American Journal of Political Science* 62, no. 3: 535–550.

Pepinsky, Thomas. 2014. "The Institutional Turn in Comparative Authoritarianism." *British Journal of Political Science* 44, no. 3: 631–653.

Pham, Duy Nghia. 2016. "From Marx to Market: The Debates on the Economic System in Vietnam's Revised Constitution." *Asian Journal of Comparative Law* 11: 263–285.

Pincus, Jonathan. 2009. "Vietnam: Sustaining Growth in Difficult Times." *ASEAN Economic Bulletin* 26, no. 1: 11–24.

Pincus, Jonathan, and Vu Thanh Thu Anh. 2008. "Vietnam Feel the Heat." *Far Easter Economic Review* 28, no. 34: 171.

Pop-Eleches, Grigore, and Graeme Robertson. 2015. "Information, Elections, and Political Change." *Comparative Politics* 47, no. 4: 459–495.

Porter, Gareth. 1993. *Vietnam: The Politics of Bureaucratic Socialism.* Ithaca, NY: Cornell University Press.

Proksch, Sven-Oliver, and Jonathan Slapin. 2012. "Institutional Foundations of Legislative Speech." *American Journal of Political Science* 52, no. 3: 520–537.

———. 2015. *The Politics of Parliamentary Debate.* New York: Cambridge University Press.

Przeworski, Adam. 2009. "Constraints and Choices: Electoral Participation in a Comparative Perspective." *Comparative Political Studies* 42, no. 1: 4–30.

Reuter, Ora John, and Graeme Robertson. 2015. "Legislatures, Cooptation, and Social Protest in Contemporary Authoritarian Regimes." *Journal of Politics* 77, no. 1: 235–248.

Riedel, James, and William Turley. 1999. "The Politics and Economics of Transition to an Open Market Economic in Vietnam." Organisation for Economic Co-operation and Development.

Ripberger, Joseph. 2011. "Capturing Curiousity: Using Internet Search Trends to Measure Public Attentiveness." *Policy Studies Journal* 39, no. 2: 239–259.

Rivera, Mauricio. 2016. "Authoritarian Institutions and State Repression: The Divergent Effects of Legislatures and Opposition Parties on Personal Integrity Rights." *Journal of Conflict Resolution* 61, no. 2: 1–25.

Rodan, Garry. 2018. *Participation without Democracy: Containing Conflict in Southeast Asia*. Ithaca, NY: Cornell University Press.

Roeder, Philip. 1995. *Red Sunset*. Princeton, NJ: Princeton University Press.

Rose, Carol. 1998. "The 'New' Law and Development Movement in the Post-Cold War Era: A Vietnam Case Study." *Law & Society Review* 32, no. 1: 93–140.

Rozenas, Arturas. 2016. "Office Insecurity and Electoral Manipulation." *Journal of Politics* 78, no. 1: 232–248.

Rundlett, Ashlea, and Milan Svolik. 2016. "Deliver the Vote! Micromotives and Macrobehavior in Electoral Fraud." *American Political Science Review* 110, no. 1: 180–197.

Salomon, Mathieu. 2007. "Power and Representation in the Vietnamese National Assembly: The Scope and Limits of Political Doi Moi." In *Vietnam's New Order*, edited by Stephanie Balme and Mark Sidel, 198–216. New York: Palgrave Macmillan.

Schedler, Andreas. 2002. "Elections without Competition: The Menu of Manipulation." *Journal of Democracy* 13, no. 2: 36–50.

Schedler, Andreas, and Bert Hoffman. 2016. "Communicating Authoritarian Cohesion." *Democratization* 23, no. 1: 93–117.

Schoenhals, Michael. 1985. "Elite Information in China." *Problems of Communism* 34: 65–71.

Schuler, Paul. 2018. "Position Taking or Position Ducking? A Theory of Public Debate in Single-Party Legislatures." *Comparative Political Studies* OnlineFirst.

Schuler, Paul, Dimitar Gueorguiev, and Francisco Cantu. 2013. "Risk and Reward: The Differential Impact of Authoritarian Elections on Regime Decay and Breakdown." Social Science Research Network Working Paper.

Schuler, Paul, and Edmund Malesky. 2015. "Authoritarian Legislatures." In *Oxford Handbook of Legislatures*, edited by Martin, Shane, Thomas Saalfeld, and Kaare Strom, 676–695. Oxford: Oxford University Press.

Schuler, Paul, and Kai Ostwald. 2016. "Delayed Transition: The End of Consensus Leadership in Vietnam?" *ISEAS Perspective*, no. 2 (January).

Schuler, Paul, and Mai Truong. 2019. "Leadership Reshuffle and the Future of Vietnam's Collective Leadership." *ISEAS Perspective,* no. 9 (February).

Schuler, Paul, and Chad Westerland. 2018. "Reconsidering the Rubber Stamp Thesis: A Consolidation Theory of Expropriations and Legislatures in Party-Based Autocracies." Paper presented at the Annual Meeting of the American Political Science Association, August 30–September 2, Boston.

Schulhofer-Wohl, Sam, and Miguel Garrido. 2013. "Do Newspapers Matter? Short-Run and Long-Run Evidence from the Closure of the Cincinatti Post." *Journal of Media Economics* 26, no. 2: 60–81.

Scott, James. 1990. *Domination and the Arts of Resistance.* New Haven, CT: Yale University Press.

———. 2010. *The Art of Not Being Governed: An Anarchist History of Upland Southeast Asia.* New Haven, CT: Yale University Press.

Shi, Tianjian. 1999. "Voting and Nonvoting in China: Voting Behavior in Plebiscitary and Limited-Choice Elections." *Journal of Politics* 61, no. 4: 1115–1139.

Shineman, Victoria Anne. 2016. "If You Mobilize Them, They Will Become Informed: Experimental Evidence That Information Acquisition Is Endgenous to Costs and Incentives to Participate." *British Journal of Political Science* 48: 189–211.

Shirk, Susan, ed. 1993. *The Political Logic of Economic Reform in China.* Berkeley: University of California Press.

———. 2011. *Changing Media: Changing China.* Oxford: Oxford University Press.

Simonivits, Gabor. 2012. "Competition and Turnout Revisited." *Electoral Studies* 31, no. 2: 364–371.

Simpser, Alberto. 2013. *Why Governments and Parties Manipulate Elections: Theory, Practice, and Implications.* Cambridge, MA: Cambridge University Press.

Slater, Dan. 2003. "Iron Cage in an Iron Fist: Authoritarian Institutions and the Personalization of Power in Malaysia." *Comparative Politics* 36, no. 1: 81–101.

Slater, Dan, and Joseph Wong. 2013. "The Strength to Concede: Ruling Parties and Democratization in Developmental Asia." *Perspectives on Politics* 11, no. 3: 717–733.

Smith, Benjamin. 2005. "Life of the Party: The Origins of Regime Breakdown and Persistence under Single-Party Rule." *World Politics* 57, no. 3: 421–451.

Smyth, Regina, William Bianco, and Kwan Nok Chan. 2019. "Legislative Rules in Electoral Authoritarian Regimes: The Case of Hong Kong's Legislative Council." *Journal of Politics* 81, no. 3: 892–905.

Snyder, James, and David Stromberg. 2010. "Political Coverage and Accountability." *Journal of Political Accountability* 118, no. 2: 355–408.

Sondheimer, Rachel Milstein, and Donald Green. 2010. "Using Experiments to Test the Effects of Education on Voter Turnout ." *American Journal of Political Science* 54, no. 1: 174–189.

Soroka, Stuart. 2002. *Agenda-Setting Dynamics in Canada*. Vancouver: University of British Columbia Press.

Stern, Lewis. 1985. "The Overseas Chinese in the Socialist Republic of Vietnam, 1979–82." *Asian Survey* 25, no. 5: 521–536.

Stromseth, Jonathan, Edmund Malesky, and Dimitar Gueorguiev. 2017. *The China Governance Puzzle: Enabling Transparency and Participation in a Single-Party State*. New York: Cambridge University Press.

Svolik, Milan. 2012. *The Politics of Authoritarian Rule*. New York: Cambridge University Press.

Tang, Wenfang. 2016. *Populist Authoritarianism: Chinese Political Culture and Regime Sustainability*. Oxford: Oxford University Press.

Tanner, Murray Scot. 1999. *The Politics of Lawmaking in Post-Mao China*. Oxford: Clarendon Press.

Teets, Jessica. 2013. "Let Many Civil Societies Bloom: The Rise of Consultative Authoritarianism in China." *China Quarterly* 213: 19–33.

Thai, Quang Trung. 1985. *Collective Leadership and Factionalism: An Essay on Ho Chi Minh's Legacy*. Singapore: ISEAS.

Thayer, Carlyle. 1991. "Political Developments in Vietnam: From the Sixth to Seventh National Party Congress." In *Vietnam 1991: An Update*. Canberra: Australian National University.

———. 1992. *Political Developments in Vietnam: From the Sixth to the Seventh National Party Congress*. Canberra: Australian National University Discussion Paper Series.

———. 2009a. "Political Legitimacy of Vietnam's One-Party State: Challenges and Responses." *Journal of Current Southeast Asian Affairs* 4: 47–70.

———. 2009b. "The Trial of Lê Công Định: New Challenges to the Legitimacy of VIetnam's Party-State." *Journal of Vietnamese Studies* 5, no. 2: 196–207.

———. 2015. "Background Briefing: Vietnam's 12th Party Congress; What to Expect and Why it's Important." Thayer Consultancy.

Truex, Rory. 2014. "The Returns to Office in a Rubber Stamp Parliament." *American Political Science Review* 108, no. 2: 235–251.

———. 2016. *Making Autocracy Work: Representation and Information in China*. New York: Cambridge University Press.

———. 2017. "Consultative Authoritarianism and Its Limits." *Comparative Political Studies* 50, no. 3: 329–361.

———. 2018. "Authoritarian Gridlock? Understanding Delay in the Chinese Legislative System." *Comparative Political Studies* OnlineFirst.

Tsai, Lily. 2007. *Accountability without Democracy: Solidary Groups and Public Goods Provision in China*. Cambridge, UK: Cambridge University Press.

Tsang, Steve. 2009. "Consultative Leninism: China's New Political Framework ." *Journal of Contemporary China* 18, no. 62: 865–880.

Tsebelis, George. 2002. *Veto Players: How Political Institutions Work*. Princeton, NJ: Princeton University Press.

Tucker, Joshua. 2007. "Enough! Electoral Fraud, Collective Action Problems, and Post-Communist Colored Revolutions." *Perspectives on Politics* 5, no. 3: 535–551.

Turley, William. 1980. *Vietnamese Communism in Comparative Perspective*. Boulder, CO: Westview Press.

———. 1993. "Party, State, and People: Political Structure and Economic Prospects." In *Reinventing Vietnamese Socialism: Doi Moi in Comparative Perspective*, edited by William Turley, 257–276. Boulder, CO: Westview Press.

Unger, E. S. 1988. "The Struggle Over the Chinese Community in Vietnam, 1946–1986." *Pacific Affairs* 60, no. 4: 596–614.

United Nations Development Programme (UNDP). 2017. *PAPI 2016: The Viet Nam Provincial Governance and Public Administration Performance Index*. Hanoi: UNDP.

Văn Phòng Quốc hội. 2007. *Lịch sử Văn phòng Quốc hội*. Hanoi: Nhà Xuấn bản Chính trị.

Varulkar, H., and Orif Winter. 2007. "Criticism of the Upcoming Syrian Parliamentary Elections in the Official Syrian Press and Among the Syrian Opposition." Middle East Media Research Institute Working Paper, Inquiry and Analysis Series no. 345.

Vasavakul, Thaveeporn. 2019. *Vietnam: A Pathway from State Socialism*. New York: Cambridge University Press.

Vliegenthart, Rens, and Stefaan Walgrave. 2011. "Content Matters: The Dynamics of Parliamentary Questioning in Belgium and Denmark." *Comparative Political Studies* 44, no. 8: 1–29.

Vo, Van Ai. 1990. "Reform Runs Aground in Vietnam." *Journal of Democracy* 1, no. 3: 81–92.

Vu, Mao. 2004. "Chất vấn và trả lời chất vấn phát thanh truyền hình trực tiếp— quãng đường mười năm." Personal communication to author.

Vu, Quang Viet. 2009. "Vietnam's Economic Crisis: Policy Follies and the Role of State-Owned Conglomerates." *Southeast Asian Affairs*, 389–417. https://www.jstor.org/stable/27913394.

Vuving, Alexander. 2010. "Vietnam: A Tale of Four Players." *Southeast Asian Affairs*, 366–391. https://www.jstor.org/stable/41418575.

———. 2013. "Vietnam in 2012: A Rent-Seeking State on the Verge of a Crisis." *Southeast Asian Affairs*, 323–347. https://www.jstor.org/stable/23471152.

———. 2019. "Vietnam in 2018: A Rent-Seeking State on Correction Course." *Southeast Asian Affairs*, 374–393.

Walgrave, Stefaan, Stuart Soroka, and Michiel Nuytemans. 2008. "The Mass Media's Political Agenda Setting Power: A Longitudinal Analysis of Media, Parliament, and Government in Belgium (1993 to 2000)." *Comparative Political Studies* 41, no. 6: 814–836.

Wang, Zhengxu, and Long Sun. 2017. "Social Class and Voter Turnout in China: Local Congress Elections and Citizen-Regime Relations." *Political Research Quarterly* 70, no. 2: 243–256.

Wang, Zhongyuan. 2017. "Playing by the Rules: How Local Authorities Engineer Victory." *Journal of Contemporary China* 26, no. 108: 870–885.

Warshaw, Christopher. 2012. "The Political Economy of Expropriation and Privatization in the Oil Sector." In *Oil and Governance: State-Owned Enterprises and the World Energy Supply*, edited by David Victor, David Hults, and Mark Thurber, 35–61. New York: Cambridge University Press.

Wedeen, Lisa. 2015. *Ambiguities of Domination: Politics, Rhetoric, and Symbols in Contemporary Syria*. Chicago: University of Chicago Press.

Wehner, Joachim. 2009. "Institutional Constraints on Profligate Politicians: The Conditional Effect of Partisan Fragmentation on Budget Deficits." *Comparative Political Studies* 43, no. 2: 208–229.

White, Stephen, and Daniel Nelson. 1982. *Communist Legislatures in Comparative Perspective*. Albany: State University of New York Press.

Wilkerson, John, and Andreu Casas. 2017. "Large-Scale Data Computerized Text Analysis in Political Science: Opportunities and Challenges." *Annual Review of Political Science* 20: 529–544.

Wilson, Matthew Charles, and Joseph Wright. 2015. "Autocratic Legislatures and Expropriation Risk." *British Journal of Political Science* FirstView: 1–17.

Wintrobe, Ronald. 1998. *The Political Economy of Dictatorship*. New York: Cambridge University Press.

Wolfinger, Raymond, and Steven Rosenstone. 1980. *Who Votes?* New Haven, CT: Yale University Press.

Wolters, O. W. 1983. *History, Culture, and Region in Southeast Asian Perspectives*. Singapore: Institute of Southeast Asian Studies.

Womack, Brantly. 1997. "Vietnam in 1996: Reform Immobilism." *Asian Survey* 37, no. 1: 79–87.

Woo, Ae sil, and Courtenay Conrad. 2019. "The Differential Effects of 'Democratic' Institutions on Dissent in Dictatorships." *Journal of Politics* 81, no. 2: 456–470.

Woodside, Alexander. 1979. "Nationalism and Poverty in the Breakdown of Sino-Vietnamese Relations." *Pacific Affairs* 52, no. 3: 381–409.

Wright, Joseph. 2008. "Do Authoritarian Institutions Constrain? How Legislatures Affect Economic Growth and Investment." *American Journal of Political Science* 52, no. 2: 322–343.

Xie, Guihua, and Yangyang Zhang. 2017. "Seeking out the Party: A Study of the Communist Party of China's Membership Recruitment among Chinese College Students." *Chinese Journal of Sociology* 3, no. 1: 98–134.

Zaller, John, and Stanley Feldman. 1992. "A Simple Theory of the Survey Response: Answering Questions versus Revealing Preferences." *American Journal of Political Science* 36, no. 3: 579–616.

Ziegenhain, Patrick. 2008. *The Indonesian Parliament and Democratization*. Singapore: ISEAS Publishing.

Index

Page numbers followed by the letter *f* indicate a figure.
Page numbers followed by the letter *t* indicate a table.

A, Nguyen Quang, 56, 58
Access to Information Law, 139
An, Bui Thi, 163
Anh, Duong Quoc, 76
Anti-Corruption Law, 139
Asian Barometer Survey, 39
authoritarian electoral and legislative institutions, uniqueness of, 32–35
authoritarian representative institutions, existing explanations for, 18; co-optation, 18–19; information acquisition, 20–22; power sharing, 19–20, 39; rationalization and bureaucratic bargaining, 22–23; rent distribution, 20; signaling, 23–25
authoritarianism, 3; "authoritarian deliberation," 28; broader understanding of, 8–9; "fragmented authoritarianism," 7, 20
authority, delegation of, 7
autocracy, within multiparty elections, 2

Ba'ath Party, 196
Bac Kan province, 50
Bach, Tran Xuan, 109
Ba Ria-Vung Tau province, 136
Binh, Pham Thanh, 167
Budget and Planning Committee, 75

build-operate-transfer (BOT) road construction schemes, 85

Cambodia, 90, 93
Can, Cu Huy, 159
candidates: candidate meetings, 57t; model of candidate election voting preference, 133; sacrificial lamb candidates, 133
Central Committee Resolution 4, 120
Central Economic Commission, 169
Central Election Commission, 49–50, 52, 59–61, 63–64, 216n4
Central Inspection Commission, 169
Central Organization Committee, 119, 121, 169
Central Propaganda Committee, 119, 121
Cheibub, Gandhi, Vreeland (CGV) measure, 194
China, 7, 10, 33, 38, 62, 66, 89, 110, 117; the "China model," 5, 10, 28; growth in, 10; inactivity of the legislature in, 220n5; legislatures of, 2, 197; reliance of on consultation mechanisms, 3; retaliatory attack of on Vietnam, 91; rule of law concept in, 214n34; and the "signature incident," 101, 199–200; single-party settings in, 126; tensions with Vietnam, 95

Chinese Communist Party (CCP), 27–28
citizen information theory, 23, 31, 66, 73, 87, 91, 127, 139–40; and the ability to distinguish between the party and the government, 204n8; argument for, 110, 111, 116, 137; channels of, 97; VNA debate as an example of, 169
citizens: citizen preferences, 27; citizen preference theory, 21–22, 23. *See also* citizen information theory
Club of Former Resistance Fighters (CFRF), 95, 96
Cold War, the, 2
Congress of People's Deputies (Soviet Union), 10
"consultative Leninism," 28
Council for Mutual Economic Assistance (CMEA), 93
Council of State, 102
Criminal Code, 103

Danlambao blog, 82
Dao, Le Quang, 108–9, 114
democracy/democracies, 43–45, 124, 147
democratization, 189–90; do single-party elections and legislatures matter for democratization?, 198–200
Deng Xiaoping, 109
Dieu, Phan Dinh, 55, 143
Dinh, Le Cong, 57, 157–60, 158*f*
Dinh, Nguyen Khac, 83
dissidents, 57, 61; repression of, 144, 152, 154, 157, 217n21
Dong, Pham Van, 110
"Downsian closeness hypothesis," 45
Duan, Le, 110
Duc, Huy, 108–9, 204n13
Dung, Nguyen Sy, 53, 55, 61, 62, 116–17, 157
Dung, Nguyen Tan, 119, 155, 159, 165, 166–67, 168, 169, 201; failure to win the general secretary position, 200

Eastern Bloc countries, 1, 2, 6, 10, 94
Egypt, 30, 61
Election Law (1959), 99, 212n12
Election Law (1960), 213n27
Election Law (1980), 206n4, 206n9

Election Law (1997), 207n21
Election Law (1992), 206n4
Election Law (2015), 11, 50, 51, 59, 65; Article 10 of, 60–61; Article 67 of, 65–66
election management, empirical implications for, 40–43; implications for delegate behavior, 47; implications for legislative institutionalization, 45–47; implications for public opinion, 47–48; observable implications of the signaling argument for elections, 43
electioneering: impact of on district competitiveness, 134*t*; identification of, 131–33
elections, 22, 25, 33*t*, 34–35; authoritarian elections, 26–27; do single-party elections matter for democratization, 198–200; election campaigns, 64–66; electoral fraud, 42; heavily manipulated elections, 30–31; hybrid elections, 191–93; impact of candidate quality on election results, 64*t*; importance of, 203–4n7; in Mexico, 26, 27, 65; mobilizing elections, 142. *See also* election management, empirical implications for; People's Council elections; Vietnam National Assembly (VNA), elections of
electoral district strength, 132–33
Eritrea, 1
exclusive economic zone (EEZ), 154–55

factionalism, 7
Far Eastern Economic Review, 112
Fatherland Front, 65
foreign aid, 88–89, 92, 96, 211n1

Gibbs sampling, 147
Google, 216n7
Gorbachev, Mikhail, 8
Great Britain, 92
Greene, Kenneth, 65

Hai, Dao Minh, 158
Hai, Dao Van, 158
Haiyang Shiyou Oil Rig 981 (HYSY 981) incident, 154–55
Hanoi, 50, 80

He Yafei, 10
Ho Chi Minh City, 50, 80, 94, 96, 109
Ho Chi Minh City People's Council, 57
Human Rights Watch, 159
Hung, Bui Manh, 219n38
Hung, Nguyen Sinh, 59, 163, 164
Hung, Pham, 112
Hussein, Saddam, 196–97, 199

information, 41, 42; cadre control information theory, 22; cadre quality information, 31; impact of knowledge, turnout, and competitiveness on electoral information, 125–26; importance of the source of information, 34; information acquisition, 20–22; information generation, 4–5; informational deficiencies, 5; informational models, 23; intimidating and distorting of, 23; misleading information, 24; regime strength information theory, 21; on voter preferences, 31. *See also* citizen information theory
Institutional Revolutionary Party (PRI), 26
institutions: legislative, 32–35; state-sanctioned, 32; visibility of, 32
Iran, 7
Iraq, 196–97
issue sensitivity, 161

Japan, 92

Kerkvliet, Benedict J. Tria, 217n21
Khai, Phan Van, 118, 121, 165–66
Khanh, Nguyen Thi Quoc, 78, 163–64
Khanh Hoa province, 81
Khmer Rouge, 91
Khoa, Dang Van, 57
Khoi, Ma, 58
Kien, Nguyen Duc, 76
Kien Giang province, 81
Kiet, Vo Van, 100, 110, 112, 118, 120–21, 201; competition of with Do Muoi, 205n6; and the Vinashin crisis, 165
Khrushchev, Nikita, 33

Land Law, final debate concerning, 164–65
Lao Dong, 100, 119

latent dirichlet allocation (LDA) model, 147–48, 149–50, 216n5
Law on Foreign Investment, 103
Law on National Assembly Oversight Activities, 84
Law on the Organization of the Vietnam National Assembly, 11, 72, 99, 102, 104, 113–14, 210n31, 210–11n40
Law on the Promulgation of Legal Documents, 79
Legislative Committee, 75
legislative reform, contextual factors concerning (Vietnam), 90–91, 97t; economic reforms and *doi moi*, 91–92, 101; foreign aid, 93–94; natural resources, 92–93; societal demands, 94–96
legislatures, 33t, 34–35, 203n6; association of single-party legislatures with economic growth and political stability, 7–8; authoritarian, 192–93; conditions favoring a binding, informative legislature, 88–90, 90t; functions of, 17; hybrid legislatures 191–93; and information generation, 4–5; and informational deficiencies, 5; informational utility of, 5; and nonelectoral incentives, 4; primary purpose of in single-party regimes to signal authoritarian dominance and legitimacy, 5–6; provincial legislatures, 205n4; role of single-party legislatures, 2–3, 5; salutary effects of, 193, 197, 220n1; and top-down incentives, 4. *See also* legislatures, as multitask institutions
legislatures, as multitask institutions, 26–28; and the tradeoff between domination and participation, 28–31
Lenin, Vladimir, 112
liberalization, 21, 37, 109, 117; partial liberalization, 198–99; political liberalization, 200, 201, 200–202. *See also* Vietnam National Assembly (VNA), political liberalization in
Linh, Nguyen Van, 100, 102, 111–13, 121
Luong, Luu Binh, 220n6
Luu, Uong Chu, 83, 162

Mai, Au Thi, 66
Manh, Nong Duc, 108
manipulation, of elections and electoral laws, 61–64
Mao, Vu, 54, 109, 118
Maritime Law, 103
mediation analysis, 185–87, 186*t*, 187*f*; and preference falsification, 187–88
Mexico, elections in, 26
micro-level institutions, 17
Minh, Pham Binh, 156
Ministry of Industry, 158
Ministry of Justice, 79
Ministry of Police, 158, 168
Minstry of Public Security, 157, 158
Miodowicz, Alfred, 37
mobilization, 42–43, 44; alternative mobilization view, 138; of elections, 142; mobilization theory, 129, 136–37, 138
monarchies, the Stuart monarchy in England, 19
Mubarak, Hosni, 24, 30, 61
Muoi, Do, 6, 100, 112, 121, 205n6
Muslim Brotherhood, 61
Myagkov, Mikhail, 22

National Assembly (Cuba), 98
National People's Congress (NPC), 20, 27–28, 33, 35, 197, 200, 205n8
Netherlands, the, 92
Ngan, Nguyen Thi Kim, 164
Nghe An, 50
Nhan Dan (People's daily), 56, 100, 109
Nyerere, Julius, 6

Obama, Barack, 58
Office of the Government, 79
ordinary least squares (OLS) analysis, 56, 64, 132, 152–53

party officials, district-level, 62
People's Committee, 60
People's Council, 60; People's Council elections, 60
Phieu, Le Kha, 110, 118–19
Phuc, Vo Van, 162
pluralism, 52, 99, 113
Poland, 10, 37

policy co-optation model, 29–30
Pol Pot, 91
preference falsification, 21
principal-agent relationships, 41–42
propaganda, in Nazi Germany and China, 25
provincial party secretariat, multiple central committee members of, 207–8n28

Quan, Hoang Binh, 156
Quang, Nguyen Minh, 114, 163
Quang Ninh province, 81
Quoc, Duong Trung, 53, 78, 83, 143, 164, 200, 219n28

regime age, 204n9
regime strength, 24, 27; regime strength signaling theory, 24; and the signaling trap, 35–38
regimes, hybrid, 2, 9, 15, 134, 190; as opposed to single-party systems, 191–93
regimes/legislatures, single-party, 35, 189–90, 191–93, 204n10; and the allowing for debate, 38–40; better outcomes for, 193–94, 195*f*, 196–98; 196*f*; do single-party legislatures matter for democratization?, 198–200; as less sure of their strength than multi-party regimes, 36–37; and the signaling trap, 35–38
regimes, multi-party, 36–37
regimes, security threats to, 89–90
regimes, theoretical arguments concerning: Argument 1—a regime will limit its ability to inform itself, 31–32; Argument 2—single-party regimes prioritize the signaling function for legislatures and elections, 35; Argument 3—single-party non-response to the need for more information or improved performance by allowing competition, 38
rent: rent-based co-optation, 30, 205n5; rent distribution, 20, 26, 29, 203–4n7
Reuter, Ora John, 38–39
Riedel, James, 94
Russia, 38; regional legislatures in, 19

Sang, Truong Tan, 159
security threats, 89–90

selectorate theory, 89
Shakin, Dimitri, 22
signaling, 23–25; extreme signaling, 28–30; fundamental problem of, 6–7; and the signaling trap, 35–38. *See also* signaling theory; signaling value, of the VNA
signaling theory, 9, 204n2; observable implications of the signaling theory, 127–28, 128t; strength signaling theory, 24
signaling value, of the VNA, 170–71; theory and hypotheses concerning, 171–74. *See also* signaling value, of the VNA, data and research design concerning
signaling value, of the VNA, data and research design concerning, 174–76, 175t, 175–76t; amount of balance between groups in the survey, 177t; control variables concerning, 176; dependent and mediating variables concerning, 177, 178f, 179, 179f, 180f; downstream variables, 183–85, 183t, 184f, 185f; results of, 181–83, 181f, 182f, 182t, 183f. *See also* mediation analysis
Son, Nguyen Minh, 76
South China Sea, 144, 149, 154–57, 155f
Soviet Communist Party, 8
Soviet Union, 8, 37, 93; endurance of as a single-party regime, 9–10; collapse of, 9, 10, 211n6
Special Economic Zone Law (SEZ [2018]), 68, 80–82, 83–84; timeline of the passage of, 81t
Spratly Islands, 92, 155
Stalin, Joseph, 33
state-owned enterprises (SOEs), 151, 160; management of, 144
Suharto, 199
Syria, legislature of during the "Damascus Spring," 1–2

Tanzania, 6
Thailand, 130, 215n3
Thanh, Ngo Ba, 101, 113
Thanh Hoa, 50
Tho, Nguyen Huu, 98
Thuyen, Nguyen Ba, 164–65

Thuyet, Nguyen Minh, 76, 117, 124, 160, 165; television speech of, 1, 2, 3, 200
Ti, Huynh Van, 59
Tiananmen Square "Signature Incident," 101, 199–200
Tien Lang incident, 161, 161f, 164
Tiep, Huynh Van, 164
Trans-Pacific Partnership, 139
Triet, Nguyen Minh, 159
Trong, Nguyen Phu, 119, 162, 168
Tuan, Tran Quoc, 49
Tuoi Tre, 100, 109

United Nations Convention of Law of the Seas (UNCLOS), 154, 155, 210n35

Van, Le Thanh, 83
Van Giang, 161, 161f, 163
vetting, 53–54; central versus local nominees, 53–54; Gate 1—first negotiation, setting the structure, 54–55; Gate 2—second negotiation, introducing the delegates, 55; Gates 3 and 4—meeting with constituents and coworkers, 55–58; Gate 5—determining the final ballot, 58
Viet, Vu Quang, 167
Vietnam, 7, 33, 39–40; Champa and Angkor kingdoms of, 94; Chinese investors in, 82; economy of (1985), 92; electoral system of, 49–50; financial difficulties of, 95; growth in, 10; invasion of Cambodia, 90; minorities in, 211–12n7; political and economic reforms in, 110–11; political liberalization in, 200–202; probit model of voter turnout in Vietnam's 2016 election, 136t; proxy voting in, 135; restrictions placed on the ethnic Chinese population in Saigon, 212n8; rule of law concept in, 214n34; single-party settings in, 126; tensions with China, 95. *See also* Vietnam, explanations of reforms in; Vietnam, legislatures of
Vietnam, explanations of reforms in, 111; reform to personnel, 111–17; sequence of reforms, 120–22; and the televising of query sessions, 117–19; and the vote of confidence measure, 119–20

Vietnam, legislatures of, 1, 2, 197; and
  agenda control, 145; legislative debate
  in, 144–45; legislative reform and economic growth, 3–4; and party-state
  divisions, 145–47, 146; reform to legislative institutions in, 117; vetting of
  candidates for, 4
Vietnam Communist Party (VCP), 1, 3, 38,
  200–201; Central Election Committee
  of, 50, 63, 104, 145–47, 158, 162, 163;
  Organization Committee of, 86; Party
  Committee of, 86; Politburo of, 62, 63,
  98, 118, 156, 168, 169
Vietnam Historians Association, 53
Vietnam National Assembly (VNA), 1, 2,
  3, 10–12, 38, 59, 66, 200–201; block voting system of, 129; candidates per seat
  in, 52*f*; case of, 9–10, 12; composition
  of, 71*t*; days in VNA sessions and laws
  passed per session, 107*f*; decisions passed
  per year (1975–2016), 106*f*; divisions
  of draft laws in, 100–101; elections of,
  62, 189–90; innovations of, 143; liberalization of, 15–16, 87, 106, 200–202;
  malapportionment in, 51*f*; percentage
  of delegates in, 105*f*; plenary session of
  (2017), 82–83; reinterpretation of the
  institutionalization of, 122–23; relationship between candidates per seat and
  non-party members, 115*f*; and the representation of citizen interests, 4; role of
  in governance, 10–12; structure of, 69*t*,
  87; well-known self-nominated candidates for, 53–54, 59*t*. *See also* Vietnam
  National Assembly (VNA), case studies
  of hot button issues faced by; Vietnam
  National Assembly (VNA), evolution
  of; Vietnam National Assembly (VNA),
  legislative organization in; Vietnam National Assembly (VNA), legislative and
  oversight processes of; Vietnam National
  Assembly (VNA), timeline of legislative
  reforms in
Vietnam National Assembly (VNA), case
  studies of hot button issues faced by,
  153–54; arrests of Cu Huy Ha Vu and
  Le Cong Dinh, 157–60, 158*f*; land use

rights, 161–65; oversight of Vinashin,
  165–69, 166*f*; the South China Sea,
  154–57, 155*f*
Vietnam National Assembly (VNA), evolution of, 87–88; conditions favorable
  to, 88–90
Vietnam National Assembly (VNA), legislative organization in, 68; and permanent
  committees, 75–77; powers and selection of the VNASC, 68, 70–72, 69*t*, 70*t*,
  71*t*, 72*t*; and the selection of full-time
  delegates, 72–75, 74*t*
Vietnam National Assembly (VNA),
  legislative and oversight processes of,
  77, 84–85, 143–44; lawmaking and the
  legislative calendar, 77–78; party control
  mechanisms of, 85–86; and the possibility of input, 80–84; and the process
  of a bill becoming a law, 79. *See also*
  Vietnam National Assembly (VNA),
  legislative and oversight processes of,
  testing the theory of
Vietnam National Assembly (VNA), legislative and oversight processes of, testing
  the theory of, 147–48, 161*f*; and data
  combination, 149–50, 150*f*; empirical
  testing, 150–53; and measuring public
  attention, 148–49; and the need for a
  "tokenizer," 148
Vietnam National Assembly (VNA), timeline of legislative reforms in, 97–98; days
  per session of, 103*f*; existing explanations
  for, 109–11; initial reforms, 101–7; later
  reforms, 107–9; and "old thinking" in
  the VNA, 98–101; reforms to legislative
  institutions, 117
Vietnam National Assembly (VNA) Economic Committee, 76, 167, 168–69
Vietnam National Assembly Standing
  Committee (VNASC), 49, 51, 54, 59,
  61, 66, 67–68, 74, 75–76; agenda-setting power of, 82–83; composition of,
  72*t*; control exercised by, 98; debates
  organized by, 82; decisions passed per
  year (1975–2016), 106*f*; dominance of,
  122–23; number of directives issued by,
  105–6; and oversight responsibilities;

84–85; power of over the Election
Board, 99; power of over the legislative
calendar, 78, 86; proposal of for debate
schedules, 77–78
Vietnam Provincial Governance and Pub-
lic Administrative Performance Index
(PAPI), 13, 56, 135, 137
Vietnamese Constitution (1946), 99
Vietnamese Constitution (1959), 99
Vietnamese Constitution (1980), 99
Vietnamese Constitution (1992), 99, 113,
212–13n26
Vietnamese Constitution (2002), 99
Vietnamese Constitution (2013), 59, 60,
78, 99
Vinashin crisis, 165–69, 166*f*
Vinh, Nguyen Trong, 159
VNA Economic Committee, 169
Vo, Dang Hung, 58

voting: and FL ratios, 130, 131*f*, 132, 132*f*,
133–34, 134*t*, 135–36, 137; proxy voting,
135; and SF ratios, 129, 130*f*, 131*f*, 132*f*,
strategic voting, 128–34, 215n2; voter
knowledge, 137–39, 140*f*, 141*f*; voter
turnout, 134–37
voters/voter preferences, 31, 125–26; voter
behavior, 43–45
Vu, Cu Huy Ha, 57, 157–60, 158*f*
Vu Hong Thanh, 211n41
Vuon, Doan Van, 161, 162, 163, 164

Walesa, Lech, 37
Wan Li, 200
World Trade Organization (WTO), 46

Xi Jinping, 3, 156

Yiechi, Jang, 155

Also published in the
Shorenstein Asia-Pacific Research Center Series

Fateful Decisions: Choices that will Shape China's Future
Edited by Thomas Fingar and Jean C. Oi (2020)

Dynasties and Democracy: The Inherited Incumbency Advantage in Japan
Daniel M. Smith (2018)

Manipulating Globalization: The Influence of Bureaucrats on Business in China
Ling Chen (2018)

Poisonous Pandas: Chinese Cigarette Manufacturing in Critical Historical Perspectives
Edited by Matthew Kohrman, Gan Quan, Liu Wennan, and Robert N. Proctor (2017)

Uneasy Partnerships: China's Engagement with Japan, the Koreas, and Russia in the Era of Reform
Edited by Thomas Fingar (2017)

Divergent Memories: Opinion Leaders and the Sino-Japanese War
Gi-Wook Shin and Daniel Sneider (2016)

Contested Embrace: Transborder Membership Politics in Twentieth-Century Korea
Jaeeun Kim (2016)

The New Great Game: China and South and Central Asia in the Era of Reform
Edited by Thomas Fingar (2016)

The Colonial Origins of Ethnic Violence in India
Ajay Verghese (2016)

Rebranding Islam: Piety, Prosperity, and a Self-Help Guru
James Bourk Hoesterey (2015)

Global Talent: Skilled Labor as Social Capital in Korea
Gi-Wook Shin and Joon Nak Choi (2015)

Failed Democratization in Prewar Japan:
Breakdown of a Hybrid Regime
Harukata Takenaka (2014)

New Challenges for Maturing Democracies in Korea and Taiwan
Edited by Larry Diamond and Gi-Wook Shin (2014)

Spending Without Taxation: FILP and the Politics of Public Finance in Japan
Gene Park (2011)

The Institutional Imperative: The Politics of Equitable Development in Southeast Asia
Erik Martinez Kuhonta (2011)

One Alliance, Two Lenses: U.S.-Korea Relations in a New Era
Gi-Wook Shin (2010)

Collective Resistance in China: Why Popular Protests Succeed or Fail
Yongshun Cai (2010)

The Chinese Cultural Revolution as History
Edited by Joseph W. Esherick, Paul G. Pickowicz, and Andrew G. Walder (2006)

The authorized representative in the EU for product safety and compliance is:
Mare Nostrum Group
B.V Doelen 72
4831 GR Breda
The Netherlands

www.ingramcontent.com/pod-product-compliance
Lightning Source LLC
Chambersburg PA
CBHW030355270326
41926CB00009B/1113

9 781503 614741